Advocacy, Counselling and Mediation in Casework

Edited by Yvonne Joan Craig

Foreword by Daphne Statham

Jessica Kingsley Publishers
London and Philadelphia

First published in the United Kingdom in 1998 by
Jessica Kingsley Publishers Ltd
116 Pentonville Road
London N1 9JB, England
and
325 Chestnut Street, Philadelphia
PA 19106, U S A

Copyright © 1998 Jessica Kingsley Publishers

Library of Congress Cataloging in Publication Data
A CIP catalogue record for this book is available from the
Library of Congress

British Library Cataloguing in Publication Data
Advocacy, counselling and mediation in casework: processes
of empowerment 1. Social case work 2. Social service -
Citizen participation I. Craig, Yvonne
361.3'2

ISBN 1 85302 562 3

Printed and Bound in Great Britain by
Athenaeum Press, Gateshead, Tyne and Wear

Contents

Acknowledgements

We would like to express our appreciation to all those people who have helped and supported us in the production of this book. Our foremost thanks are for families, friends and colleagues who have encouraged our work and writing, and also for the organizations and associations to which we belong and from which we have received advice and assistance.

We are also grateful to the public libraries we have consulted, as well as professional ones including the Centre for Policy on Ageing, the National Institute for Social Work and the Royal College of Nursing, and academic ones such as the British Library of Political and Economic Science, the University of London Library and other university libraries.

We are indebted to the staff of the publishers, and Charles Catton in particular, for their technical expertise in transforming our manuscripts into a book which we hope will be a landmark in the literature, as it is the first to be written on this subject.

Our deepest gratitude is reserved for all those service users and providers with whom and for whom we work. To them we dedicate this book.

Finally, as editor, I wish to express my personal appreciation of the great value of our authors' contributions, and their patient co-operation with the publishers' requirements and editorial requests. I am responsible for any mistakes involved in the book's publication, and for the opinions expressed in the Introduction and Conclusion , although I believe them to be widely held among advocates, counsellors, mediators and caseworkers.

Yvonne Joan Craig

Foreword

This collection of papers is written by practitioners in the fields of advocacy, mediation and counselling. The contributors have all been part of developing new approaches to tackling current social and relationship problems. In effect they are part of the process of re-inventing practice and so restructuring the theories on which it is based. Taken as a whole the book demonstrates that far from the demise of practice, it has been quietly transforming itself during the last twenty years. Its relevance has been re-created for a multiracial and multicultural society which has undergone massive social, economic and demographic changes.

Practice went through hard times during the 1970s and 1980s. In the mid 1970s, the fault was expert solutions which failed to take into account race, gender, disability and sexuality, as well as social class perspectives together with over-promising what could be delivered. In the 1980s, social work, and to a lesser extent social care, was blamed for creating a dependency culture and not supporting individual and family responsibility. Like all stereotypes there is an element of truth in them, but they are far from the whole picture.

During these twenty years practice was far from static; workers from different professional backgrounds were working together to take on board new issues and to develop approaches which took into account discrimination and exclusion. The emphasis was on recognizing both differences and commonalities between people, their expertise and experience and finding ways to increase their participation so that they had greater control over decisions which affected their lives and those of their communities. These moves went far beyond direct practice and include the sort of provision available and the policies which framed it.

The descriptions of practice in this book clearly identify the skills and expertise needed to promote partnerships and empowerment whether with or between individuals, families or communities. The analysis of the contributors is confirmed by current research on practice, and the experience of peo-

social care. Skills in negotiation, mediation, counselling, conflict resolution, in working with people in ways which use their experience and expertise and promote independent living and social inclusive relationships, are all central to the new forms of practice.

The papers show that practice can be responsive to black and minority ethnic communities and that with proper attention it can be made culturally and internationally relevant. Throughout there is explicit attention to the outcomes as experienced by the people who use these services. It is appropriate then that the final chapter is about a user-led project which is working on outcomes defined by users themselves. I am also very proud that the National Institute for Social Work (NISW) is playing a part in this project.

Although much has changed, there is also much we need to hold on to and not 'mislay' in the whirlwind of change which is part of our everyday lives. The worker's ability to develop relationships is still a major resource. Similarly, the need to pay careful attention to the process, the how as well as what is done, remains important. These are skilled activities which take time. They can easily be undervalued in these days when what is valued is often only what can be counted. The essential underpinning of good practice can become invisible in this culture. It is all our responsibilities to ensure that our practice develops and that good practice is both visible and is valued. The pride as well as the expertise of the practitioners shines through this book and provides a sound foundation for the future.

Professor Daphne Statham CBE
Director of the National Institute for Social Work

Introduction

Yvonne Joan Craig

This network approach suggests that there is a pattern of potentially changeable boundaries between different occupational groups and theoretical ideas. (Payne 1996, p.14)

The nature of the work undertaken by different health professionals and inter-professional boundaries are constantly shifting. Sharing of skills is a more sensible subject for discussion than transfer of tasks. The views of users of health services on inter-professional substitution need to be considered. (Hopkins, Solomon and Abelson 1996, pp.364–371)

The professional social worker as collaborator will, together with the client, select interventive roles – 'conferee', broker, negotiator, advocate, counselor, caseworker, case manager, group leader, organizer, assessor, administrator or policy formulator – that are dictated by the problem at hand, rather than in an a priori fashion, reflective of the methodological proclivities or ideological preferences of the practitioner. (Simon 1997, pp.8–9)

Advocacy, counselling and mediation are common social processes enabling us to fulfil common personal needs and empowering us in our struggle for common human rights.

They also provide professional pathways in the variety of human services which use common core practices of casework as part of a continuum including care management and community development. Thus in our current concern for interdisciplinary collaborative care (Hornby 1993; Loxley 1997), based on user-involved and user-led services (Croft and Beresford 1993; Wilson 1995), it is timely to note the extent to which our formal knowledge, skills and values are grounded in our natural individual abilities and collective capacities.

Most people can represent their own views, needs or interests, or those of their friends, as in *advocacy*. Parents can provide supportive listening and help with their children's emotional problems, as in *counselling*. Many of us enable others to negotiate constructive outcomes to quarrels and conflict, as in *mediation*. When we need special help with complex problems, we seek professional aid from agencies which will share their experience and expertise with us.

This book aims to help us explore the processes and skills of advocacy, counselling and mediation which we may, or may not yet be, using in our individual relationships and work, looking at casework from the widest perspective of helping people who wish for happy and healthy lives in the current cultural and social context.

Bill Jordan was one of the first British radical social workers to write about the skills necessary in 'counselling, advocacy and negotiation', pointing out that 'in day-to-day social work people will need someone to mediate between themselves and the formal agencies...' (1987, p.144). Since then, others such as Gale Wood and Ruth Middleman (1989), and Martin Davies, in his *The Essential Social Worker*, have stressed the need for using all these skills in 'pastoral pluralism' (1994, p.206). Health service workers similarly interchange their roles, or specialize in them, as Allison Murdach says when describing mediating skills in healthcare decision making (1995, p.189).

Advocates, counsellors and mediators share core communication competences which have been cross-fertilizing, but differentiation has often been unclear. Janet Fook says that 'the role of advocate is one who acts for, mediates or intercedes for another' (1993, p.101), thus blurring boundaries, while Judith Brierley's *Counselling and Social Work* (1995) shows the close interface of all these skills.

So this book hopes to clarify confusions by showing how advocacy, counselling and mediation are practised in different areas, while avoiding what Paulo Friere has called 'supercertitude' (1996, p.115) about definitions of our continually expanding general experience and casework knowledge, where we still have much to learn.

The British Association of Social Workers (BASW) describes casework as the enhancement of human well-being, the relief and prevention of hardship, and working with individuals, families and groups. This is a shared concern in healthcare, advocacy, counselling and mediation, as is the egalitarian focus on working with service users as collaborating citizens . References to 'cases' in this book denote situational focus, not personal reductionism.

However, Daphne Statham, Director of the National Institute for Social Work (NISW), points to the 'continuous and interacting change and diversity' of fragmented systems of personal and social care (1996, p.1), which is also reflected in agencies which specialize in advocacy, counselling and mediation. The authors of *Health and Social Care Management* not only reinforce this idea of changing systems, but suggest that the existing order may have to be destabilized to promote improvements and that resulting conflicts will need handling with multiple skills and boundary crossing (Whiteley, Ellis and Broomfield 1996).

Advocates may be trained as lawyers, or as community and special group activists; counsellors may be accredited and supervised members of organizations such as the British Association for Counselling (BAC), or work in voluntary befriending services; and mediators may have ongoing professional training with evaluated practice in family mediation and industrial conciliation, or work as volunteers in community conflict resolution centres. Legal advocates may become professional mediators. Counsellors may develop into advocates for vulnerable populations or into mediators between quarrelling couples. Mediators may find that deep emotional conflicts necessitate counselling skills.

From complex perspectives of situations at home, at work or in health concerns, people may find themselves using all of these processes in one day, as when parents advocate for their children against a school, counsel them about drugs, and then mediate between them in a squabble about TV watching. Caseworkers may advocate for a service user's access to resources, counsel them about their anxiety problems and mediate if there is family conflict.

A further complication is that advocacy, counselling and mediation are not unitary processes, but are different types, practised in diverse settings and in various ways, some of which will be illustrated in this book. Their naming is also problematic, depending on individual and social usage. For instance, unless authors specify differently, counselling and psychotherapy are here used interchangeably, while mediation is often called conciliation, alternative dispute resolution, conflict management or negotiation (although many trainers restrict this term to two-party bargaining).

Advocacy has general and particular meanings, although it is often linked to promoting user-centred or user-led services and developing partnerships between professionals, patients and others. Some caseworkers call themselves professional advocates for welfare rights, although the financial aspects of welfare work concerning claimants and benefits are not discussed here in detail, despite the fact that these are critical issues troubling many service users and workers, whether involved in advocacy, counselling or mediation.

The aims, themes and values of the book

This book is the first to be written on this subject. It aims to be of special value to caseworkers and service users of the multidisciplinary caregiving services of the statutory, voluntary and independent sectors, as well as to individuals and groups specializing in advocacy, counselling and mediation, and interested members of the general public. It has extensive references to support casework teaching and training, although authors provide these variously, together with case illustrations which are either typical or anonymous.

There is a shared awareness that language can be influenced by ideologically driven 'received ideas' (Rojek, Peacock and Collins 1988), leading to the critique that casework is a socially constructed activity (Payne 1991) determined by political and socioeconomic pressures which can lead to unhealthy societies (Wilkinson 1996). However, the authors are robust writers, respected for their resistance to imposed social judgements about controversial issues (Gambrill and Pruger 1992), realizing that they, as well as service users, need empowerment to maintain integrity and independence. Caseworkers have also pioneered controversial discussions (Bailey and Brake 1975), and this book will continue these.

Empowerment is an underlying theme of this book, as it is in health, social and community care (Braye and Preston-Shoot 1995; Jack 1995), and although the empowerment industry may be viewed cynically, this 'ritual word' (Local Government Management Board 1992), like those of love, justice and peace, can be seen as central to our human progressive vocabulary. It is critically connected to concepts of unequal power (Foucault 1980) and powerlessness which empowerment is concerned to redress. However, we recognize the disempowering contradictions of 'us' empowering 'them'.

Empowerment is also a key professional value (Pinderhughes 1983; Stevenson and Parsloe 1993), and Barbara Simon (1997) shows its dominance throughout caregiving history. It increasingly focuses on support for user-led services and participation (Beresford and Harding 1993; Lindon and Morris 1995), another theme of this book.

This idea of partnership between service users and workers (Williamson 1993) is based on the belief that there are ethical imperatives for democratic involvement in systems of social intervention and management in order to build social capital (Wann 1995). Also, there are pragmatic advantages to all involved concerning constructive co-operation, rather than competition, in policies, planning and strategies.

This is facilitated by good active networking between organizations, projects, community groups and interested individuals. This book is a model of interdisciplinary collaboration, arguing for the more difficult co-ordination of services which joint working groups encourage (Clarke, Hunter and Wistow 1997), especially in health education for young adults (Bloxham 1997). However, sustaining interprofessional collaboration is difficult (Vanclay 1996) and can lead to collusion, while Sam Porter (1997) warns us that widening interdisciplinary networks can lead to the unintended consequence of increasing professional power over people (Foucault 1973; Illich 1977).

Nevertheless, there has emerged a consensual view about a partnership model of local social justice (McCormick and Harvey 1997), with co-operation between professionals and the public in working for the common good (Jordan 1989). This is an allied theme raised in the book.

A further general theme is that of valuing volunteers as well as paid workers, who should all aim for professionalism, by enriching mutual understanding and respect, and by recognizing and identifying differences in roles and responsibilities.

Although our authors discuss their own ideas and values, the book is based on a socially inclusive approach which respects the rights and responsibilities of each unique individual; problematizes situations rather than special populations; balances affirmation with careful critique; advocates non-discriminatory, non-stereotypical, non-demeaning and de-stigmatizing practices; follows equal opportunity guidelines, and recommends egalitarian, anti-oppressive ways of working.

However, it is recognized that, as Daphne Statham says, there are 'conflicts and contradictions in policies, values and practice' (1996, p.2), and it is significant that in her earlier *Radical Social Work* (1978) she reminds us that social workers reflect similar uncertainties to those of the general population when confronting inequities of resources, as do all multidisciplinary caseworkers.

There is also a corporate concern that advocacy, counselling and mediation are not used to subvert social attention from the deficits and inadequacies of the infrastructure, but increase pressure on central and local government to maintain, increase and extend economic resources to the most vulnerable and marginalized members and groups in society. Social marginality and poverty contribute to many of the problems with which caseworkers deal and which require collective challenge if inclusive citizenship is to become a reality (Lister 1996).

Nevertheless, the welcome diversity of our authors ensures that many different opinions will be expressed. There is a variety of views about critical theory (Habermas 1976), structuralism and post-structuralism (Mullaley 1993; Wood and Middleman 1989), as well as in ideas about modernism and post-modernism (Giddens 1990), but unless these affect their chapters, these and other theories will not be discussed. Caseworkers wishing to consider these subjects further are referred to the *British Journal of Guidance and Counselling* (Lynch 1997), the *British Journal of Social Work* (Blaug 1995; Dominelli 1996), the *Journal of Social Policy* (Hillyard and Watson 1996) and *Social Work and Social Sciences Review* (Parton 1994). It is also relevant to note that the July 1996 editorial of *International Social Work* advises readers to be open to pluralistic learning from theories, rather than allowing specific ones to inhibit this.

Many references in this Introduction come from the social work domain, because casework was widely developed there following its origins in British Victorian charities and the work of Eileen Younghusband (1967) and the NISW (not to mention that of American pioneers, Jane Addams (1910), Mary Richmond (1917), Charlotte Towle (1945) and Helen Perlman (1957)). However, it is stressed that the book is highly relevant to the casework practised in other equally important areas, some of which are described by authors who work in them, while the health services provide an increasingly varied literature, references to which have already been given.

All contributors to this book are committed to principles of social justice in the interests of individual integrity and fulfilment, and realize that we have much to learn from each other in furthering these, as we know little about the full extent of our human potential for growth and development.

The structure of the book

The first part of the book has three chapters introducing advocacy, counselling and mediation, written by authors who have extensive experience and knowledge of these areas.

The second part focuses on the social use of advocacy, counselling and mediation in practical casework, with chapters comparing and contrasting the processes and skills applied in widely different areas of care. These have been written by authors who are greatly respected for their practitioner wisdom and skills.

The book closes with a brief conclusion that discusses advocacy, counselling and mediation in the context of 'private troubles and public issues' (Mills 1959), and how far these processes can contribute to developing user-involved services and social citizenship (Rees 1995).

Editorial hopes

The opinions expressed in this Introduction and the Conclusion are mine alone, although it is hoped that the book's contributors and readers share in its principles, although they may interpret these variously and critically.

The unfinished discussion which this book begins raises 'therapeutic uncertainty' (Pozatek 1994), but it is hoped that locally produced knowledge by service users and workers to which we contribute can help towards reversing power imbalances which disempower and deskill people. I hope that the book will be of value on many counts, especially in the salutary, if uncomfortable, task of opening our minds to new ideas, shaking over-established convictions and empowering us all in constructive collaborative networking which will increase our access and effectiveness to those who are most in need of care and help.

We also pay tribute to the personal commitment, knowledge and skills of all those caseworkers who work publicly and privately with and for other people who ask for their help, and have to cope with managing the contradictions (Darvill 1997) of heavy public demands on health and social services. The book is also a homage to our mentors; those who endure, overcome or transform suffering with dignity and determination, and who inspire us to face the future with hope and trust (Friere 1996; Fukuyama 1995) and a determination to work for social justice.

The contents and authors of the book

Part I introduces advocacy, counselling and mediation in three chapters, which are followed by those in Part II that are linked in threes, each group featuring authors working principally with these different processes, but in similar age or subject areas. Most contributors are authors of publications, which are either listed in the references of their chapters or in their profiles at the end of the book.

Vera Ivers, experienced caseworker and consultant in the statutory and voluntary sectors of community, health and social services, writes the first chapter of Part 1 on advocacy, its aims and different varieties, including describing project developments and cases.

Tim Bond, former Chair of the BAC, contributes the second chapter, focusing on the organization's high ethical values and good practices. These can provide a standard for other agencies in seeking to be reliably professional, while welcoming members, voluntary or paid workers, at differing career stages.

Marian Liebmann, former Director of Mediation UK, discusses the definitions, organizational contexts, social usefulness, principles and empowerment values of mediation. Her chapter describes issues of independence, voluntarism and professionalization, standards and accreditation, and the possible misuse of mediation.

Christine Piper of Brunel University introduces Part 2 with a chapter on legal advocacy for children, focusing on issues arising from the separation of parents and the different professional roles involved. Christine is concerned that children are heard and represented so as to maximize their rights, and has contributed to major academic work on the subject.

Ann Heyno, an extensively experienced student counsellor and trainer, describes the stresses and crises of further education in Chapter 5, which shows young and older adults with inner conflicts and externally competitive and depressive situations, succeeding, and sometimes failing, in life and career challenges.

Val Carpenter, British pioneer and practitioner in the theory and training of prejudice reduction work, writes Chapter 6 on bullying in schools and other contexts, from the perspective of conflict management and theory, of which she has extensive knowledge and skills.

Colin Barnes, disabled Director of Leeds University Disability Research Unit, in Chapter 7 examines competing theories of disability, the advocacy needs of disabled people, and the importance of user-led organizations controlled and run by disabled people. Colin has an international reputation for his work.

Gillian Walton, Director of London Marriage Guidance, writes the next chapter on couples counselling, giving detailed case histories in which her psychotherapeutic knowledge and skills show the inner conflict, interpersonal dynamics and social contexts of troubled relationships.

Yvonne Joan Craig, founder member of Mediation UK and the Elder Mediation Project, describes the value of mediation in Chapter 9 about families facing separation and divorce, and with older adults who are vulnerable to elder abuse, institutional mistreatment and community disputes.

David Brandon has pioneered mental health advocacy for many years, and has written and edited many publications. David's chapter describes the stigmatization of people with mental health problems and the struggle of a patient for her rights against heavy odds, arguing for service user self determination with social support.

Graz Kowszun, accredited BAC counsellor, trainer and supervisor, and registered psychotherapist, specializes in working with people involved with substance abuse. Her chapter clarifies popular misperceptions, and describes skills which can assist and support drug users and their caregivers.

Jean Wynne, senior probation officer, has pioneered practitioner and theoretical work involving British probation services in victim-offender mediation and reparation, of which she has extensive international knowledge. Jean's chapter describes these initiatives and related criminal justice policies.

Stephanie Ellis, Community Health Council Chair in a poor multicultural area, and Patients' Association Secretary, writes Chapter 13 on the need for health advocacy and education to empower patients in choices, complaints and contributions to policy making in user-led services.

Bill Kirkpatrick, psychiatric nurse, chaplain and author, has pioneered befriending and day centre work for people with HIV and AIDS, and in Chapter 14 shares stories about his advocacy, counselling and mediation work with them and their loved ones as they face crises, death and bereavement.

Yvonne Joan Craig and Masana De Souza describe healthcare mediation in Chapter 15, illustrating its use with health authority and family doctor complaints, which Masana pioneered, and its value in institutional conflicts and medical ethics decision making.

Stephen Palmer, director of the Centre for Stress Management, in Chapter 16, describes the role of counselling in what may be arguably the fastest-growing area of relief for human distress, as social and occupational pressures and crises overburden people in their personal and working lives.

Masana De Souza and Yvonne Joan Craig discuss cross-cultural mediation work in Chapter 17, which describes the Newham Conflict and Change Project which Masana leads, and mediation's general importance in empowering diverse communities in anti-discriminatory conflict management.

Sue Balloch, Peter Beresford, Clare Evans, Tessa Harding, Martin Heidensohn and Michael Turner write the final chapter about user-centred, user-involved and user-led services, and the importance of user participation and empowerment, in the context of the Shaping Our Lives Project at NISW, but of fundamental relevance to this book.

References

Addams, J. (1910) *Twenty Years at Hill House.* London: Macmillan.

Bailey, R. and Brake, M. (eds) (1975) *Radical Social Work.* London: Edward Arnold.

Beresford, P. and Harding, T. (1993) *A Call to Change.* London: National Institute for Social Work (NISW).

Blaug, R. (1995) 'Distortions of the face-to-face'. *British Journal of Social Work 25,* 423–439.

Bloxham, S. (1997) 'The contribution of interagency collaboration to the promotion of young people's health.' *Health Education Research 12,* 1, 91–101.

Braye, S. and Preston-Shoot, M. (1995) *Empowering Practice in Social Care.* Milton Keynes: Open University Press.

Brierley, J. (1995) *Counselling and Social Work.* Milton Keynes: Open University Press.

Clarke, M., Hunter, D. and Wistow, G. (1997) 'Local government and the NHS – the new agenda joint working and improved working relationships.' *Journal of Public Health Medicine 19,* 1, 3–5.

Croft, S. and Beresford, P. (1993) *Getting Involved.* London: Open Services Project.

Darvill, G. (ed) (1997) *Managing Contradictions and Avoidance.* London: NISW.

Davies, M. (1994) *The Essential Social Worker.* London: Heinemann Educational Books.

Dominelli, L. (1996) 'Deprofessionalizing social work.' *British Journal of Social Work 26,* 2, 153–175.

Fook, J. (1993) *Radical Casework.* London: Allen and Unwin.

Foucault, M. (1973) *The Birth of a Clinic.* London: Tavistock.

Foucault, M. (1980) *Power/Knowledge.* New York: Pantheon Books.

Friere, P. (1996) *The Pedagogy of Hope.* New York: Continuum.

Fukuyama, F. (1995) *Trust.* London: Hamish Hamilton.

Gambrill, E. and Pruger, R. (eds) (1992) *Controversial Issues in Social Work.* Needham Heights MA: Allyn and Bacon.

Giddens, A. (1990) *The Consequences of Modernity.* Cambridge: Polity Press.

Habermas, J. (1976) *Legitimation Crisis.* Cambridge: Polity Press.

Hillyard, P. and Watson, S. (1996) 'Post-modernism and social policy.' *Journal of Social Policy 25,* 3, 321–346.

Hopkins, A., Solomon, J. and Abelson, J. (1996) 'Shifting boundaries in professional care.' *Journal of the Royal Society of Medicine 89,* 7, 364–371.

Hornby, S. (1993) *Collaborative Care.* Oxford: Blackwell Scientific Publications.

Illich, I. (1977) *Limits to Medicine – Medical Nemesis the Expropriation of Health.* Harmondsworth: Penguin.

International Social Work, 1996, July, p.1.

Jack, R. (ed) (1995) *Empowerment in Community Care.* London: Chapman and Hall.

Jordan, B. (1987) 'Counselling, advocacy and negotiation.' *British Journal of Social Work 17,* 2, 135–146.

Jordan, B. (1989) *The Common Good – Morality and Self-Interest.* Oxford: Blackwell.

Lindon, V. and Morris, J. (1995) *Service User Involvement.* London: Joseph Rowntree Foundation.

Lister, R. (1996) 'Poverty.' *Community Care Research Matters,* April/October, 10–12.

Local Government Management Board (1992) *Citizens and Local Democracy.* London: LGMB.

Loxley, A. (1997) *Collaboration in Health and Welfare.* London: Jessica Kingsley Publishers.

Lynch, G. (1997) 'Therapeutic theory and social context.' *British Journal of Guidance and Counselling 25*, 1, 5–15.

McCormick, J. and Harvey, A. (eds) (1997) *Local Routes to Social Justice.* London: Institute of Public Policy Research.

Mills, C. (1959) *The Sociological Imagination.* New York: Oxford University Press.

Mullaley, R. (1993) *Structural Social Work.* Toronto: McClelland and Stewart.

Murdach, A. (1995) 'Decision-making situations in health care.' *Health and Social Work 20*, 3, 187–191.

Parton, N. (1994) 'The nature of social work under conditions of (p)modernism.' *Social Work and Social Science Review 5*, 2, 93–112.

Payne, M. (1991) *Modern Social Work Theory.* Basingstoke: Macmillan.

Payne, M. (1996) *What is Professional Social Work?* London: Venture Press.

Perlman, H. (1957) *Social Casework.* Washington, DC: National Association of Social Workers.

Pinderhughes, E. (1983) 'Empowerment for our clients and ourselves.' *Social Casework 64*, 6, 331–338.

Porter, S. (1997) 'The patient and power: sociological perspectives on the consequences of holistic care.' *Health and Social Care in the Community 5*, 1, 17–20.

Pozatek, E. (1994) 'The problem of certainty.' *Social Work 39*, 4, 396–403.

Rees, A. (1995) 'The promise of social citizenship.' *Policy and Politics 23*, 4, 313–325.

Richmond, M. (1917) *Social Diagnosis.* New York: Russell Sage Foundation.

Rojek, C., Peacock, G. and Collins, S. (1988) *Social Work and Received Ideas.* London: Routledge.

Simon, B. (1997) *The Empowerment Tradition in American Social Work.* New York: Columbia University Press.

Statham, D. (1978) *Radical Social Work.* London: Routledge and Kegan Paul.

Statham, D. (1996) *The Future of Social and Personal Care.* London: NISW.

Stevenson, O. and Parsloe, P. (1993) *Community Care and Empowerment.* York: Joseph Rowntree Foundation.

Towle, C. (1945) *Common Human Needs.* Silver Springs, MD: National Association of Social Workers.

Vanclay, L. (1996) *Sustaining Collaboration between General Practitioners and Social Workers.* London: CAIPE, the UK Centre for the Advancement of Interprofessional Education.

Wann, M. (1995) *Building Social Capital.* London: Institute of Public Policy Research.

Whiteley, S., Ellis, R. and Broomfield, S. (1996) *Health and Social Care Management.* London: Arnold.

Wilkinson, R. (1996) *Unhealthy Societies – the Afflictions of Inequality.* London: Routledge.

Williamson, V. (1993) *Users First.* Brighton: University of Brighton.

Wilson, G. (1995) *Community Care – Asking the Users.* London: Chapman and Hall.

Wood, G. and Middleman, R. (1989) *The Structural Approach to Direct Practice in Social Work.* New York: Columbia University Press.

Younghusband, E. (ed) (1967) *Social Work and Social Values.* London: Allen and Unwin.

Useful addresses

British Association for Counselling (BAC)

1 Regent Place
Rugby
Warwickshire CV21 2PJ
Tel: 01788 550899 Minicom 01788 572838
Fax: 01788 562189

Mediation UK

Alexander House
Telephone Avenue
Bristol BS1 4BS
Tel: 0117 904 6661
Fax: 0117 904 3331

National Institute for Social Work

5 Tavistock Place
London WC1H 9SN
Tel: 0171 387 9681
Fax: 0171 387 7968

PART I

The Social Construction of Advocacy, Counselling and Mediation

CHAPTER 1

Advocacy

Vera Ivers

Over the past two or three decades the case for advocacy has been made by all manner of organizations from the United Nations to the smallest voluntary group. In particular, personal one-to-one advocacy and group advocacy as practised by campaigning organizations have received a degree of attention.

In introducing the subject of advocacy this chapter will explore the development and practical application of citizen advocacy and consider some other forms of advocacy which have influenced this development. It also explores advocacy as a tool which can be used by caseworkers for the benefit of service users, either by calling on a citizen advocate or by acting as advocates as part of the caseworker or care broker role.

Citizen Advocacy

This type of advocacy has enjoyed a degree of acclaim and was first developed in North America in the 1960s. A community worker, Wolf Wolfensberger, was drawn to the cause of children suffering from cerebral palsy and their parents. The parents realized that their children were more likely to receive good health and social care when they, the parents, were able to advocate and negotiate on their behalf. The obvious long-term worry was about the children's future when their parents died or could no longer look out for their interests. Wolfensberger developed the idea of introducing concerned citizens who would commit themselves to a child and undertake to act *in loco parentis* in this context, doing so purely in a voluntary and humane activity (Wolfensberger 1977).

A colleague of Wolfensberger who has been influential in helping the citizen advocacy movement to spread describes it thus:

> A valued citizen who is unpaid and independent of human service
> social workers creates a relationship with a person who is at risk of

social exclusion and chooses one of several of many ways to understand, respond to and represent that person's interests as if theory were the advocate's own thus bringing their partners' gifts into the circle of ordinary life. (O'Brien 1987, p.3)

During the 1970s the movement spread to this country and writers here have taken note of the changing role of social workers acting as care brokers and suggest that professional advocacy will become even more common and organized than in the past (Beresford and Croft 1993). This chapter argues that advocacy whether practised by a volunteer citizen advocate or a professional caseworker must be based to some extent upon similar underlying principles.

In describing this very personal and intimate type of advocacy it is worth mentioning other forms of advocacy with which it shares some objectives.

Legal Advocacy

The most common is obviously legal advocacy, which has been practised since the days of the early Roman scholars whose works remain required reading for students of law. One writer described legal advocacy in a way which makes absolute sense for the advocacy practised by volunteers or caseworkers: Macmillan says that it is the advocate's business to present to the court all that the client would have said for himself if he had possessed the requisite skill and knowledge (Macmillan 1937).

However, it is unlikely that a barrister would identify with the Age Concern England definition of citizen advocacy as being a process of empowerment (Greengross 1987).

Collective advocacy

Another common form of advocacy which has everything to do with empowerment is sometimes referred to as 'group advocacy', and by Wolfensberger (1977) as 'class advocacy'.

Many organizations at national, local and international level fall within this category and may seek to serve a wide variety of groups. For example, trade unions will campaign and represent workers' rights while an organization such as MIND campaigns for those with particular disabling conditions.

Self advocacy

In the UK there is a growing movement termed 'self advocacy' which is promoted among people who suffer some form of mental health condition. It encourages people who have traditionally not been consulted, even on the most personal aspects of their lives, to obtain the necessary skills and confidence to demand that their voices be heard.

From my own practical experiences, the ability to develop these self-advocacy skills is often a by-product of other forms of advocacy even where the emphasis is not on self development. It will be interesting to see whether the extension of professional advocacy will promote or reverse this trend. It is certainly the case that most citizen advocacy schemes emphasize the need to promote self advocacy wherever possible, with the obvious underlying message that advocates should not encourage dependency among their partners.

Peer advocacy

Another popular type of advocacy which should be mentioned is that referred to earlier and suggested by Beresford and Croft (1993). It is also the basis upon which the Beth Johnson Foundation built an advocacy scheme in the 1980s (Ivers 1994). Peer advocacy developed in that instance primarily because older people needed advocates and other older people wished to become advocates. There are a number of other examples of peer advocacy, all of which identify a group within which one person can advocate for another who is regarded as a member of their peer group.

The need for advocacy

Practising caseworkers are able to draw on a number of tools and techniques which may help to ensure that service users gain the maximum benefit from their intervention. Many professionals regard the advocacy role as a proper and relevant part of their professional life. It is common for social workers to challenge other agencies, such as a health authority, the Benefits Agency or a housing department. They may also find themselves advocating for a user within their own agency. Nurses have always felt that they are the patient's advocate when challenging doctors, especially where medical decisions have not taken account of a patient's lifestyle and personal needs or wishes.

There is a school of thought which questions the ability of professional service providers to provide effective advocacy. A number of writers have emphasized the need for absolute independence and refer to the many constraints within which professionals commonly work. They point to the need to follow agency procedures, to satisfy a manager that this is good use of their time and to remain credible with colleagues.

If the advocacy task involves challenging an employer or a colleague, it might be extremely difficult for them to pursue the cause with absolute loyalty to their partner. Even where the task involves challenging another professional agency, there may well be formal or informal reciprocal arrangements which hinder the advocacy role (Ivers 1994; Sang and O'Brien 1984).

However, the expanding social work role as care broker has caused some writers to think again and to suggest that the volunteer citizen advocacy role suffers from a fundamental weakness which has to do with the variety of skills and roles which it attempts to embrace (Bateman 1995). This writer firmly supports the idea that professionals can learn advocacy skills and suggests that it is an appropriate role for doctors, social workers, nurses, advice workers, members of the clergy, and housing and education officials.

Most professional organizations have been slow to define the advocacy role for their members, apart from the legal profession of course. The other exception is nursing, where the United Kingdom Code of Professional Conduct and the International Council of Nurses clearly expect nurses to act as advocates for their patients. This role was confirmed during interviews with nurses who point out their traditional role of advocate where patients might need to challenge the medical profession or community service providers (Ivers 1994). However, Bateman (1995) explains the difficulties faced by nurses when they attempt to challenge the power of a high status doctor.

In an evaluative study of a citizen advocacy scheme, it appeared that even if paid staff were aware that elderly people in their care had needs outside of those being provided, they might not have been able to establish what those needs were or to spend the necessary time in pursuing solutions (Ivers 1994).

The advocacy role

The complex role of an advocate is remarked upon by Wolfensberger (1977), who divided it into two fairly distinct elements. One is being able to help their partner gain access to services and benefits, and the other is to become a warm, caring and supporting friend. If this dual role is accepted then professional advocates might well find themselves in some difficulties. The second element could extend the professional role into something unwieldy which might interfere with their commitment to other service users and to contractual requirements.

Certainly there may be a need for someone to provide emotional support for a person who is feeling devalued and marginalized (Ivers 1994). Although she admits the sample contacted in this research was not typical of all old people needing services, it was typical of those needing an advocate in order to access those services. During the period of one month, during which 20 people were interviewed, only six contacts had occurred which did not feature a paid health or social worker. Consequently, when the elderly person was introduced to a citizen advocate whose sole purpose was to offer help and support, there was a risk that she or he would become emotionally dependent on their advocate.

Another major difference between volunteer and professional advocacy concerns the whole area of recompense. Professional advocates are working within a contractual framework and receive proper remuneration. However, there are differing opinions about recompense for volunteer advocates, with some projects taking the line that advocates are giving something of themselves to a fellow citizen out of concern or love. This body of opinion maintains that to offer anything in return would be to devalue the gift.

Others point to the tradition of recruiting volunteers from middle-class backgrounds, while Dunning (1995) argues that advocates be recruited from a wide variety of backgrounds. The question of social class and historical experiences could be a major factor in the situation where a service user is not receiving the help that he or she most wishes or prefers. The difficulty in conveying their message to one or more powerful and articulate professionals may have prevented him or her from entering into an effective dialogue in order to access the services.

Dunning (1995) advocates volunteers being placed with partners from similar backgrounds. However, the experiences of advocacy projects both in the UK and in North America show that the more confident, articulate advocate, who most often comes from a middle-class background, is the more successful in obtaining services for her or his partner. If indeed it is more acceptable to recruit volunteers from different backgrounds, the question of recompense becomes important. The decision to pay or not to pay out-of-pocket expenses at least, may very well affect the success of a recruiting strategy which aims to reach people who may be living on very low incomes and where the cost of a bus journey is one expense too many.

To add another dimension to this debate, there is another development which is gaining ground. For some people suffering from the most advanced dementia and communication difficulties, a paid advocate who is independent of service providers is sometimes employed. This service is more commonly known in children's services but there are examples of hospitals where patients are to be moved due to some closure or reorganization which have adopted such strategies.

Whether expenses are paid to volunteers or not is one more consideration for professional service providers who will be seen as being there precisely because they are doing their job, while the volunteer advocate is seen as a concerned, helpful citizen demonstrating care for fellow human beings.

Clearly some professionals feel comfortable with the notion of involving a third person in the relationship with a service user. This is not so for all professionals, however, and there is evidence that unless the staff in a social or health facility welcome advocacy it will not be possible to offer it (Sang and O'Brien 1984).

Having described the effort needed to enable this three-way relationship to work, there are a number of examples where it proves to be most effective. In the Beth Johnson Foundation evaluation there are recorded comments from professionals who have expressed satisfaction that a service user moves from being deeply unhappy with the service provided to exhibiting contentment, because an advocate has been able to negotiate a response which better serves their expressed needs and preferences.

A code of practice

To enable advocates to work within the partnership and with service users, most advocacy projects will require advocates to sign up to a code of practice before undertaking the work. A model ten-point code has been suggested to secure the rights of people represented by advocates. This recognizes the role of any known relatives and people providing services, while maintaining the independent status of advocates (Dunning 1995).

For advocacy to be effective, or even useful, the relationships between the advocacy partnership and the professionals must be open and honest. Sang and O'Brien (1984) describe work with professionals in London in the 1970s by maintaining that advocacy is not a possibility in this country except at the behest of the authorities. An annual report from a citizen advocacy scheme in east Yorkshire offers evidence that a positive relationship had developed. It included comments from a service manager who saw advocacy as one of the keystones to enabling people to aspire to and achieve equal opportunities within the local community. He maintained that such an excellent service must be continued and expanded because the statutory services are more and more dependent on our volunteer colleagues for quality.

Advocacy at work

Much of the work of an advocacy partnership takes place within one-to-one contact: advocate and partner, advocate and service provider. However, it may be even more important for a service user to have access to an advocate where case conferences, reviews or other meetings are involved. The prospect of facing a line-up of doctors, nurses and social workers can feel threatening for even the most confident of people. For some who already feel disempowered and overwhelmed it may prove to be impossible to take a meaningful part in the process.

In such circumstances advocates can accompany their partners and put their views to the meeting. This can be a difficult task, especially where a compromise is being negotiated. Advocates are bound to keep checking and encouraging their partners to consider the options under discussion and to make some choices.

This process can delay the meeting, and even postpone it, so that the professionals involved need to exercise a degree of patience. Perhaps in itself this constitutes a learning process which may benefit future service users. For the partner it is often illuminating to discover that the professional team is human and able to compromise. It can also assist in developing confidence in dealing with figures of authority in future situations.

Since the implementation of the National Health Service and Community Care Act 1990 two other situations have arisen where an advocate can play a vital part. One is the emphasis placed upon consulting with carers when provision of services is required. Earlier we saw how many older people requiring advocacy are without significant family or friends; however, even where there is a family the needs and wishes of the user may be different.

An example of this occurred with an elderly woman hospitalized following a fracture. She received visits from her three daughters, and as the time for discharge drew near it emerged that each daughter wanted something different for her mother. The first daughter wanted her to take up residence in a residential home in a part of the city near to the daughter's home. The second daughter also felt that her mother should enter a residential home but knew of an ideal place near to her own family home. The third daughter was disgusted by her sisters' wish to 'put Mum away' and offered to take her mother into her own home. Mrs M asked her advocate to help her resist all of these pressures, for she only wanted to go back to her own house.

The professionals involved felt that Mrs M would have difficulty living alone but had no view on which would be the best option. A meeting of all the players took place at the hospital and the advocate attended with Mrs M. It was possible to represent her wishes to her family and the professionals although the advice was still that Mrs M would be at some risk if she lived alone.

After a lengthy discussion during which Mrs M became tearful, the daughters began to see their mother's side of the story. With her advocate's help she continued to maintain that she wished to go home and try to manage by herself. With everyone's agreement a trial period was negotiated where Mrs M would be supported by a package of community care services and would be visited regularly by each daughter on a rota basis. The advocate continued to visit Mrs M at home to ensure that she was happy with the arrangement and to support her should she be subjected to more pressure. Mrs M was able to continue in her own home for another two years, when she became ill again. At that time she felt ready to enter a nursing home and was able to negotiate with her daughters about which one she would find acceptable.

Apart from the fact that Mrs M enjoyed her two extra years of 'normal' life, this exercise helped her very caring daughters to respect the fact that their mother was still able to take personal responsibility and make sound judgements for herself. The advocate remained loyal to Mrs M, although she found herself acting to some extent as a mediator between the daughters.

The mediation role can sometimes interpose itself upon the advocacy role and this project learned from this situation. For the future they were more aware of possible conflicting roles and were ready to involve a professional as mediator or, in some circumstances, to call upon an independent mediator.

Advocacy as part of assessment

The second development directly attributable to the National Health Service and Community Care Act 1990 is the need to base individual care packages on multi-agency assessments. Most agencies go to great lengths to get the user or a carer to agree to the decisions arrived at and to obtain their signature on the document agreeing the plan. It was not unusual in the early days of this process to receive a referral from health or social workers who were assessing someone suffering from confusion or dementia. They would ask if an advocate could provide the signature.

Most projects will set great store in providing training for their volunteers which will include the development of listening skills and will seek to develop attitudes which allow the advocate to remain loyal to their partner and to avoid becoming judgmental or directive. There is no pretence to train volunteers as qualified counsellors, but the basis on which therapeutic counsellors build relationships is relevant. Advocates can learn that their partners may be suffering from more than the initial referral suggests. Underlying problems may be complex and of long standing, and may or may not be dealt with within the new relationship. If not, then the advocate needs to know about other specialist agencies and can refer on if the partner agrees. Listening at several levels is a valuable skill which can often encourage partners to share feelings more easily.

Where partners are not able to comprehend fully the situation they are in because of confusion or dementia, there is a greater responsibility upon the advocates, who may have to spend a great deal of time in establishing the relationship and attempting to understand their partners' wishes, needs and preferences. An example of this occurred when an advocate was introduced to a man who had very disturbed short-term memory. His residential home was about to close and residents were to be accommodated elsewhere. Mr A was not able to make any articulate contribution to the decision-making process but accepted an advocate. He did not always recognize the advocate, but when he did he was happy to go out for walks and especially to take a turn around the garden. The advocate noticed how happy this activity made his partner. He was happy to be among plants and could quite often remember their names. The advocate established that Mr A had been a keen gardener and had always had a large garden of his own where he spent most of his time. The advocate was able to attend the meeting where his partner's future was to be decided and pleaded for a placement with a garden to which he would have access.

Without the help of an advocate Mr A would probably have been allotted a place in a home where there was no garden but where staff were happier about security. They had interpreted his interest in the garden as confused wandering with consequent risk.

Conclusion

The above examples of advocacy in action might suggest that the process is all one way, with advocates as providers and partners as recipients. It has already been noted that advocates need to take the initiative in developing the relationship with a partner and must be articulate and confident in their dealings with professionals.

However, as in all human situations, there are frequently other outcomes, and we have already noted the notion of reciprocity. The gift relationship, as described by Titmuss (1970) and Wenger (1981), draws attention to the gain to each individual where human relationships are formed and advocates and partners frequently become long-term friends, appreciating each others gifts. We have already noted that professionals have expressed a greater satisfaction from knowing that service users are happy with the service provided as a result of being able to take part in the planning process.

This chapter has endeavoured to introduce advocacy as part of a range of techniques available to help users and workers within service agencies. In particular it has described the way in which quality of life, as perceived by the service user, can be improved by means of a service which falls outside traditional provision. Through advocacy, counselling and mediation it might be possible to address the concerns expressed by Ignatieff (1990), who maintains that old people are sometimes enabled only to survive, when they ought to be helped to live to their full potential and to flourish.

References

Bateman, N. (1995) *Advocacy Skills.* Aldershot: Arena.

Beresford, P. and Croft, S. (1993) *Citizen Involvement: A Practical Guide for Change.* London: Macmillan.

Dunning, A. (1995) *Citizen Advocacy with Older People: A Code of Good Practice.* London: The Centre for Policy on Ageing.

Greengross, S. (1987) *Political Action and Advocacy.* Copenhagen: Danish Medical Bulletin Special Supplement Series 5.

Ignatieff, M. (1990) *The Needs of Strangers.* London: Hogarth Press.

Ivers, V. (1994) *Citizen Advocacy in Action: Working with Older People.* Stoke-on-Trent: The Beth Johnson Foundation.

Macmillan, B. (1937) *Law and Other Things.* Cambridge: Cambridge University Press.

O'Brien, J. (1987) *Learning from Citizen Advocacy Programs.* Atlanta GA: Advocacy Office Georgia.

Sang, J. and O'Brien, J. (1984) *Advocacy: The UK and American Experience.* London: The King's Fund Centre.

Titmuss, R. (1970) *The Gift Relationship: From Human Blood to Social Policy.* London: Allen and Unwin.

Wenger, G. (1981) 'Ageing in rural communities: family contact and community integration.' *Ageing and Society 2,* 2, 211–229.

Wolfensberger, W. (1977) *A Multicomponent Advocacy and Protection Scheme.* Toronto: The Canadian Association for the Mentally Retarded.

Further Reading

Gathercole, C. (1988) *Citizens First.* Clitheroe: Citizens First North West.

Useful addresses

Beth Johnson Foundation
Parkfield House
Princes Road
Hartshill
Stoke-on-Trent ST4 7JL
Tel: 01782 844036

CHAPTER 2

Counselling[1]

Tim Bond

Ten years ago David Charles Edwards, the then Chief Executive of the British Association for Counselling (BAC), convened a working party to study the interface of counselling and mediation. Since then BAC has itself become an important advocate for the counselling movement, and many of its members belong to advocacy groups. Some BAC members also work as mediators. In addition, caseworkers in the multidisciplinary health and welfare services seek training from, or referrals to, counselling, advocacy or mediation. So it is timely to review BAC's distinctive contributions to some of the concerns which these social agencies also share.

The success of counselling in establishing itself in the United States and Britain is quite remarkable and it is spreading world-wide. It is all the more remarkable because it is a trend which is independent from any change in technology. Unlike the cultural changes associated with the development of computers and microchips, the counselling movement is founded on ideas, attitudes and feelings about what it means to be human and how to assist people with the challenges of being human. Counselling crosses the boundaries of several pre-existing categories of human activity, including religion/philosophy on matters of meaning, and also health and well-being over issues of recovery from trauma.

There are unresolvable questions about the extent to which counselling is susceptible to scientific analysis, which is probably the most prestigious current intellectual methodology, and whether it is confined to Anglo-American 'Westernized' culture or has a wider application. In spite of these potential inherent disadvantages or vulnerabilities, the counselling movement has

---

1   This chapter is a revised version of the author's address to the 1996 annual conference of the British Association for Counselling as its retiring Chair.

prospered, especially over the last thirty years, in Britain. One of BAC's Vice Presidents, Hans Hoxter, was influential in the 1960s in bringing ideas about counselling training from the United States to British universities in the 1960s. From modest beginnings, techniques derived from counselling have permeated the voluntary, commercial and statutory sectors of our society. The numbers of people involved are awesome if Department of Employment estimates from 1993 are correct. They estimated that over 2.5 million people use counselling (in the widest sense of this term, which includes what are sometimes referred to as 'counselling skills') as a major component of their jobs. It has been estimated that over 290,000 people provide counselling in the voluntary sector, with more than 8000 people earning a living from counselling (Julie Janes Associates 1992). Even when allowance is made for the estimated nature of these figures, the counselling movement is a substantial size, with considerable potential for social good and harm. The numbers of people involved and the volume of economic activity suggest that we are sometimes quite appropriately referred to as an industry. The totality of counselling-related activity has outgrown many other industries.

BAC is at the centre of this burgeoning movement. With over 13,500 individual members and 802 organizational members, it is the largest counselling organization in Britain and the largest outside the United States. BAC is a learned society, dedicated to the advancement of counselling rather than a direct service provider, and is well positioned to be the forum in which service providers and others can join together in setting the ethical standards for counselling.

Again, the achievements have been impressive. By working in a consultative style which encouraged debate within the association, and by pooling the available knowledge, quite sophisticated codes and guidelines have been developed for counselling, supervision, training and the use of counselling skills which are used well beyond the membership of the association. An impressive range of accreditation and recognition schemes have also been developed to help the public and others to be more discerning in their choice of services. An effective complaints procedure has been established to protect service users from exploitation. BAC has been at the centre of a government initiative to define competences and new ways of training in counselling. A national register has been launched in association with the Confederation of Scottish Counselling Agencies and a range of major providers of counselling. This list of achievements is impressive and it is not exhaustive. BAC has a well-founded claim to be at the heart of ethical standard setting for counselling in Britain. In celebrating BAC's successes I do not want to suggest that any of these achievements are incapable of further improvement. This association has a good record of constantly reviewing its work and learning from experience. Codes and procedures are regularly revised.

All this is very laudable. BAC is entitled to be proud of its achievements, and as such represents a useful model for the newer social organizations involved in mediation and advocacy, which seek to follow similar ethical principles in ensuring that they offer user-centred services based on respect for client self determination and worker competence. Mediation and advocacy face similar dilemmas to counselling with regard to issues of professionalism and voluntarism, respect for cultural diversity and the need for complaints procedures. However, the process of formalizing the infrastructure of counselling has been challenging and one of the greatest challenges has been retaining the values which inspired the origins of counselling in circumstances which are considerably changed by its growth and success. Advocacy and mediation are also facing these challenges and will do so to a greater extent in the future. I hope that some reflections on the experience of BAC will be of interest to those concerned with the national representation of mediation and advocacy.

Important values within counselling

Britain is a culturally and ethnically diverse society. This constitutes a considerable challenge to the provision of counselling, which is an activity which requires the counsellor, regardless of therapeutic orientation, to make an imaginative leap into the inner world of the service user. Too great a social distance in terms of power and status or culture is probably inimicable to the provision of counselling. Service users are reluctant to approach or trust counsellors if the social divide is too great between them. Counsellors cannot always see their way through cultural assumptions to understand the world as the service user sees it, or to do so considerably protracts the counselling to overcome cultural obstacles which may not be central to the user's concerns. Counselling is of necessity an egalitarian activity in which the values of integrity and equality have taken on a particular significance in both the organizational ethos of BAC and in its approach to standard setting and professionalization.

The commitment to social inclusivity rather than exclusivity was expressed most tangibly in the original commitment to maintain open membership of BAC in order to include as wide a range of the counselling movement as possible. If the counselling movement is likened to a metaphorical comet – an idea first suggested by Ray Woolfe in discussion – it becomes apparent that there is considerable diversity within the movement in terms of competence, commitment and orientation towards counselling. The nose cone consists of the paid professional counsellors with wide ranging or generic competence who have the resources and commitment to drive counselling on and provide a sense of direction. The body of the comet consists of a much larger number of counsellors working in voluntary (or non-profit) organizations who are high on commitment but less well resourced. They are often providing specialized counselling to specific user groups and are therefore less homogeneous as a group than the nose cone. The tail, which is extended and diffuse, consists of many more people than the cone and body combined, and represents all those who adopt elements of counselling values, theory and practice and adapt them to enhance their performance in some other role, that is, the people who use counselling skills. BAC deliberately seeks to include all these elements of the metaphorical counselling comet within its membership as well as those who are predominantly trainers, supervisors or managers of counsellors. In this respect, BAC is different from any other organization in representing 'listening cures' in Britain.

However, the commitment to the values of inclusivity and equality has often come into conflict with other values associated with BAC's commitment to advance standards in counselling concerning ethical and competent practice. I have written elsewhere about the debates about sex, suicide and secrecy which were so influential in the refinement of BAC's ethical codes during the 1980s (Bond 1991). The development of codes raised the spectre of exclusivity by requiring adherence to them as a condition of membership and quickly afterwards the issue of how to respond to members who breached the codes by unethical practice. The development of complaints procedures which could lead to the expulsion of members was the first, and perhaps least controversial, step in compromising inclusivity in the interests of the integrity and responsibility of counselling. The codes offered protection of the egalitarian ethos of the association and established a basis for treating all members equally within the complaints procedures. This contrasted with the challenge posed by the development of accreditation.

Alongside the commitment to inclusivity existed a suspicion of, and sometimes a strong antipathy to, elitism and hierarchy within the association. Just as the development of a complaints procedure challenged too uncritical an understanding of non-judgemental inclusivity, the development of accreditation could be considered to violate a value of equality between members. Commenting on the early years of the BAC scheme, David Charles Edwards wrote that

> Counsellors…are generally not enamoured with authoritarian models of society, and some feel uncomfortable with the unavoidable judgemental component of accreditation. There has also been, within

BAC, a reluctance to afford respect to particular experienced members and the concept of a distinguished British counsellor almost seems a contradiction in terms. (Charles Edwards, Dryden and Woolfe 1989, p.405)

I have chosen accreditation to illustrate the dilemmas of introducing a strategy designed to promote standards which nonetheless encounters a considerable struggle with the values of the association. It is arguable that accreditation was designed to meet other values of equal importance to the dynamics of our association, those of integrity and responsibility. Any association which is at the centre of a burgeoning growth of services to the public and which proclaims itself as setting ethical standards for its members, needs to consider issues of responsibility for protecting the public from malpractice and incompetence. Although any accreditation scheme is an imperfect way of achieving these goals, it does set standards of training, supervision and experience to which all practitioners can aspire in order to be identified as 'mature professional practitioners'. For the public and would-be employers of counsellors, it provides a useful indication of the status of a counsellor in the opinion of other members of this association. For counsellors, it has created forces which drive up standards.

As with the development of the complaints procedure, not to have developed an accreditation scheme would have undermined the integrity of the organization in its claims to be committed to the advancement of counselling – a commitment which changes with social context. It is not that commitments to inclusivity and equality have been extinguished as important values but that they exist in conjunction with other values, and in particular to ensuring that the accreditation schemes that have developed remain as inclusive, non-elitist, non-hierarchical as possible – especially when you compare them with schemes of comparable professions. Our sister organizations such as the British Psychological Society and the United Kingdom Council for Psychotherapy demand graduate entry, and for the former the degree must be in psychology. The British Confederation of Psychotherapy is pitched at a comparable level of entry.

In contrast, the accreditation developed by BAC does not require a prescribed educational level or training. At the moment, the requirements are defined in terms of volume and coherence of training and a prescribed minimum of supervised experience with evidence of the counsellor's theoretical insight and practice by the presentation of written case studies. This method of defining training has the advantage of being open to considerable diversity between counsellors training to work in many different contexts. The

disadvantage is that the criteria are merely indirect indicators of the competence that they are intended to indicate.

The diversity of personal experience and variations in natural aptitude of
counsellors means that defining training in terms of duration is an imprecise
indication of the level of achievement at the end of that training. A more accurate measure would be to assess actual performance in terms of 'competences' which are achieved (regardless of how they are acquired), which is
one of the reasons why BAC has been so heavily involved in the development
of National Vocational Qualifications (NVQs) for counselling. The philosophy which underpins NVQs is to provide an alternative to the obstacles of
time and finance of prescribed training routes, characteristic of many professions, and thus making entrance to a profession more accessible. The emphasis on achievement rather than educational input is an egalitarian principle
which has an innate appeal to counsellors, although whether the reality of
NVQs lives up to these hopes has yet to be tested in practice.

The use of accreditation as an important criterion for registration on the
newly developed United Kingdom Register for Counsellors has intensified
attention on the extent to which an organization's public commitment to
protecting standards of competence can be divisive within the membership
and whether the values of equality and inclusivity must inevitably exist in
tension with a commitment to competent practice. Important arguments
have been advanced against registration and, by implication, accreditation
(Mowbray 1995) from the perspective of the human potential movement. I
recognize their concerns but consider that to exclude counselling from the
usual mechanisms which publicly signal a commitment to sound standards of
practice and public safety is a much more serious difficulty. I shall return to
this when I consider counselling as a profession. In my view, the creation of a
system of registration committed to equality of opportunity in achieving its
requirements, and one which includes counselling provided by voluntary organizations as well as the independent private practitioner, does much to
mitigate the undermining of an ethos of equality and inclusivity.

Earlier I used the metaphor of a comet to describe the broad range of the
counselling movement represented by BAC. Much of what I have discussed
so far is of much more interest to the 'nose cone' and 'body' of the comet than
to the more numerous and diverse range of people who use counselling skills.
From a counselling perspective, it is counselling skills that are the common
heritage, the shared base between counselling, advocacy and mediation. I define 'counselling skills' as skills in relating and communicating which are historically associated with counselling and used in ways consistent with the
values of counselling but not necessarily within a formal counselling rela-

tionship. It is the historical association and value base which distinguishes them from general communication skills.

Some traditions within counselling view the different elements of the comet hierarchically, with either counselling psychology or psychotherapy as the pinnacle. I consider that this view is mistaken because it underestimates the level of sophistication and competence in counselling skills that some people achieve and many others would benefit from achieving. The level of counselling skills used by a competent mediator working with people whose distress is amplifying their mutual hostility can be considerable. Similarly, an advocate may need considerable counselling skills in order to elicit the wishes of someone disempowered and alienated from the social system in which they live. From this perspective, a skilled therapist is no more or less than a highly competent practitioner of counselling skills within a context readily visible to counsellors.

The levels of skill used by a competent mediator or advocate are no less merely because they are less readily apparent to members of BAC. If there is a hierarchy of competence in counselling skills, it is not exclusive to counsellors and is not necessarily reflected by a distinction between counselling and users of counselling skills. It seems much more important to focus on the values which inform counselling skills. The egalitarian values which are at the heart of counselling skills may be expressed as impartiality, integrity and respect for the service user's capacity for self determination. These are values which counsellors, mediators and advocates all share. We may express them differently within our respective organizations and sometimes harbour secret fantasies (usually based on ignorance) that our organization or role expresses them more wholeheartedly than the others (Bond and Russell 1993), but these are our core values which we strive to live up to in our respective roles. It seems to me that we have so much more to unite us than divide us, especially as a distinctive cohort within the caring profession who are committed to an egalitarian approach to service delivery rather than importing attitudes of superiority and social distance which are characteristic of some of the more traditional professions.

Professionalism: protection of the public good or self-protectionism?

There have been many obvious reasons why the concept of professionalization has been controversial in BAC. Counselling has always had a radical tradition which has found expression with regard to mental illness, sexuality, child care, the happiness versus health debate, and so on. The first known user of the term 'counselling' in a therapeutic sense was Frank Parsons, a one-man Fabian Society working in highly capitalist Boston at the turn of this century. Carl Rogers (1961) adopted the term 'counselor' from him because as a non-medic Rogers was prevented from calling himself a psychotherapist and because he wanted to emphasize a shift in the therapeutic power relationship away from the therapist/counsellor to the service user. The seeds of radical traditions in counselling have their origins right at the beginning of our movement.

There have also been pragmatic issues. Most counselling is provided on a voluntary basis and is unpaid or only paid at nominal rates. If you define a profession by its quest for financial gain, then counselling is evidently not a profession. However, I consider that this approach to professions is too rooted in a tradition of academic cynicism about professions from the 1960s which is probably less justified in the 1990s. Professions are much more closely scrutinized by academics and the media and are expected to be accountable to service users in ways which were unthinkable in the 1960s. In this respect the gulf between paid and unpaid service providers has closed in a public expectation that both will operate at professional standards. Those in the voluntary sector that achieve these standards are often rewarded by public funding and are subject to systems of accountability as rigorous as those applying to paid service providers.

I do not want to suggest that there is an absence of self interest in joining together into a professional organization. It is a question of compatibility between creating ethical standards which effectively protect the public and enhance their rights being held in creative tension with enlightened self interest of the profession. In this respect, all professions are changing.

Traditional professions were exclusive in that members had to have completed one of a limited set of courses and obtained qualifications of sufficient academic or financial difficulty to restrict the numbers of new entrants. They maintained strict admission procedures, claims to a distinctive body of knowledge, and the protection of economic and social status, creating an elite which holds statutory powers to regulate itself and prohibits outsiders using the professional title. The existence of professions of this kind has been viewed positively by some as contributing to social stability; an essential link between government and the people and a way of maximizing the credibility and competence of the profession. Others have concentrated on the negative aspects of these arrangements which can create a powerful elite more concerned to protect their income and professional autonomy than to provide an effective service, which becomes increasingly distanced from the people they claim to serve.

However, professionals are not exempt from social change. International competitive pressures, the needs of organizations and changes in patterns of employment have and will continue to expand the range of professions (Watkins, Drury and Preddy 1992). In pre-industrial society the traditional professions were lawyers, clergy and doctors; this expanded with industrialization to include engineers, chemists and accountants. More recently, new professions have become established in welfare (teachers and social workers), in enterprise (business and management specialists) and in information technology. The development of counselling, mediation and advocacy continues a well-established trend. The proliferation of professions has diminished the status of being a professional, blurred the boundaries between professions and created competition between them. Government has also intervened to erode restrictive practices. The combined effects of these trends has resulted in new professions becoming more egalitarian than some of the older professions by their openness to new members; more flexible in their knowledge base, which has to be constantly updated; and more accountable to service users and the public. These changes in the nature of modern professions may mean that what constitutes a profession is much more fluid and we have the potential of defining the kind of profession that we want to become.

I consider it much less problematic to urge the professionalization of counselling today than I would have done even a few years ago. The case for doing so is compelling. We need a collective authority to establish and develop ethical standards for our work. We each need that status to negotiate with government and other professional bodies to secure our values and ethical standards. Otherwise our egalitarian values could so easily be lost to others who are much more eager to be authoritarian and exclusive. We need to question critically our suspicion of power in society and to use the power that our success has earned for us, creatively and ethically, to advance our collective values and ethical standards. The arguments for a modern style of professionalism seem equally applicable to mediation and advocacy.

Conclusion

There is a price for success. The price is change, letting go of the familiar and embracing the new. Values have to be re-expressed if they are to remain credible. I am convinced that none of the changes that face us require the extinction of values that have been important to us, just the imagination and conviction to find new ways of expressing them and resolving potential conflicts between them. This is not easy when change is so rapid. The successful growth of counselling in volume and status has been so rapid that we are trying to make changes on a scale which more established professions have taken many hundreds of years to achieve. We are not alone in facing this challenge and can learn from others who share our fundamental values.

References

Bond, T. (1991) 'Suicide and sex in the development of ethics for counsellors.' *Changes, The International Journal of Psychology and Psychotherapy 9*, 4, 284–293.

Bond, T. and Russell, J. (1993) *A Report on Ethical Standards and Equality of Opportunity in Advice, Guidance and Counselling.* Report commissioned by the Advice, Guidance and Counselling Lead Body (now Advice, Guidance, Counselling and Psychotherapy Lead Body). London: Department of Employment.

Charles Edwards, D., Dryden, W. and Woolfe, R. (1989) 'Professional issues in counselling.' In W. Dryden, D. Charles Edwards and R. Woolfe (eds) *Handbook of Counselling in Britain.* London: Routledge.

Julie Janes Associates (1992) *Advice, Guidance and Counselling Lead Body Occupational Mapping.* Report Commissioned by the Advice, Guidance and Counselling Lead Body (now Advice, Guidance, Counselling and Psychotherapy Lead Body). London: Department of Employment.

Mowbray, R. (1995) *The Case Against Psychotherapy Registration – A Conservation Issue for the Human Potential Movement.* London: Transmarginal Press.

Rogers, C. (1961) *On Becoming a Person.* London: Constable.

Watkins, J., Drury, L. and Preddy, D. (1992) *From Evolution to Revolution: The Pressures on Professional Life in the 1990s.* Bristol: University of Bristol.

Further Reading

BAC (1984) *Code of Ethics and Practice for Counsellors.* Rugby: BAC.

Bond, T. (1996) 'Competition or collaboration within the talking therapies.' In I. James and S. Palmer (eds) *Professional Therapeutic Titles: Myths and Realities.* Leicester: The British Psychological Society, Division of Counselling Psychology Occasional Papers, pp.31–33.

Dryden, W. (1996) 'A rose by any other name: a personal view on the differences among professional titles.' In I. James and S. Palmer (eds) *Professional Therapeutic Titles: Myths and Realities.* Leicester: The British Psychological Society, Division of Counselling Psychology Occasional Papers, pp.29–30.

Frankland, A. (1996) 'Exploring accreditation.' In S. Palmer, S. Dainow, and P. Milner (eds) *Counselling: The BAC Counselling Reader.* London: Sage.

CHAPTER 3

Mediation

Marian Liebmann

Introduction

Interest in mediation as a method of conflict resolution has grown immensely during the last few years. Mediation has been hailed as a new phenomenon which, like many other innovative practices, has come from the United States. It has also drawn on Australian experience, and on much older 'traditional' ways of resolving conflict, still practised in Asia and Africa, and by Aboriginal, Maori and Native American peoples.

In recent centuries we have developed an 'adversarial' system of handling conflict: if two people or groups do not agree, we assume that the best way forward is to fight it out or to get someone else to decide who is right. However, war is destructive and legal solutions costly – we need to develop new approaches.

Many disputes arise over something quite small and even sometimes accidental. This may be interpreted as a deliberate slight or provocation, whereupon the other party decides to retaliate. If the original party does not even realize that he or she has caused offence, then he or she will see this act as unprovoked aggression. Soon the dispute escalates on a tit-for-tat basis, and may draw in other members of the families or friendship circles. Both parties by now have probably lost sight of the original problem and only see each other as the problem in a personal vendetta. A court case, even if successful, will do nothing to improve relationships between the parties.

Many people feel the amount of conflict in their lives has increased and put forward various reasons, such as lifestyle clashes, a more mixed population, less tolerance, overcrowding, general stress, poverty, louder noise-making equipment and more vulnerable, unsupported people in the community. Each of these would need its own research project to come to a firm conclusion, but meanwhile they fuel the growing interest in the possibilities of mediation.

What is mediation?

It may be helpful to include some definitions (Mediation UK 1995), as there is sometimes confusion over different terms:

- *Negotiation* is a general term for the process of disputants working out an agreement between themselves.

- *Mediation* is a process by which an impartial third party helps two (or more) disputants to work out how to resolve a conflict. The disputants, not the mediators, decide the terms of any agreement reached. Mediation usually focuses on future rather than past behaviour.

- *Arbitration* is a process in which an impartial third party makes a final, usually binding, decision. The discussion and decision, whilst structured, may not be as regulated by formal procedures and rules of evidence as is a courtroom procedure.

- *Litigation* is the process of settling a dispute in court according to legal statutes, with advocates presenting evidence on behalf of the parties. Litigation is an adversarial process, in which a judge (or jury) adjudicates in favour of one party after hearing both sides.

In general, these processes range from the least intervention (negotiation) to the most intervention (litigation).

The mediation process

Mediation is a staged process, providing a structure to help disputants to move through a natural process, from telling their story and view of events to eventual building of an agreement between them. There are many different ways of running the process, according to context and purpose (so that, for instance, the process in commercial mediation differs somewhat from that used in community mediation), but they all have in common a structured, staged process.

The process given here is a seven-stage one, developed for the Mediation UK *Training Manual in Community Mediation Skills* (1995), but is also applicable to many other situations.

1. *Initial contact with the first party.* The mediator (or mediators – see comments on co-mediation below) listens to the first party's story and assesses whether mediation is the best way forward. At this stage, it may become clear that counselling or advocacy is more suitable and the service user needs to be referred on to appropriate resources. If mediation is appropriate, the mediator will check

whether it is all right to contact the second party and, if so, what information may be passed on to him or her.

2. *Initial contact with the second party.* The mediator then contacts the second party and listens to his or her story, trying hard to set on one side any prejudices established by the first party's view. Engaging the second party is usually more difficult than with the first party, because he or she may not feel there is anything wrong, or may feel that the first party is bringing an unjustifiable complaint against him or her. Many cases stop at this stage because the second party does not want to take part. It is part of the mediator's training to handle this stage most constructively.

3. *Preparing to work on the dispute.* At this stage the mediator is working with both parties separately to clarify issues and options. If face-to-face mediation is the best way forward, then both parties may need some preparation to ensure that they know what to expect and so that both come with a positive attitude towards resolving the dispute. Discussion may be needed concerning who should attend. A suitable neutral venue needs to be organized.

4. *Setting the scene: hearing the issues.* At a face-to-face mediation session, the mediator welcomes the parties, seats them comfortably so that they can see, but are not directly facing, each other, outlines the process and makes clear the ground rules for the session (such as no interruptions, no name calling, respect, time limits, breaks, etc). The mediator then invites each party in turn to outline the situation from his or her point of view, without interruption. The mediator feeds back a summary of what they have heard, and may ask for clarification on any points which are not clear.

5. *Exploring the issues.* At this stage the discussion widens and can become quite heated. It will draw on the mediator's skills in ensuring it does not get out of hand. Mediators also try to spot when a focus on the past begins to repeat itself, and try to move the parties on to look at the future and what they can do to resolve the conflict. This may involve reframing accusations into statements of how they are affected – for example, reframing one party's statement, 'You've got to get rid of your dog' to, 'So you find the dog barking very disturbing?' Another key concept of mediation is helping people to look at their interests (what they want) rather

than their positions; for example, instead of 'That dog has got to go' (position), suggest 'I need some peace and quiet' (interest).

6. *Building agreements.* By this time it should be clear what the issues are and what each party wants or needs. This stage concentrates on practical ways of achieving this in as even-handed a way as possible. The mediator encourages the parties to look at all the options before selecting the most promising. If there are several issues, it may be best to start with the one that seems most easily resolvable, provided that it is one seen as important by both sides. Where a written agreement is appropriate, this needs to be clear and concrete, with a timetable for action. The agreement is signed by both parties, and often the mediator too.

7. *Closure and follow-up.* The mediator rounds off the session, thanks the parties for their hard work and ensures that any loose ends are tied up. If the parties are uncertain that the agreement will be kept, the mediator may arrange a follow-up session or arrange to telephone both parties after a specified time.

These stages normally run chronologically, although there may be considerable overlap between them. Cases may terminate anywhere along the way, either because one party decides not to proceed or because an agreement has been reached by other means, for example by the parties meeting privately without the mediator. The mediation process would also be set aside if other interventions, such as counselling or advocacy, seemed more appropriate. On occasions an outcome of mediation can be that one party seeks counselling, for example for bereavement, if the mediation results in a realization that this is a factor exacerbating the conflict.

Shuttle mediation

Not all mediations result in a face-to-face meeting with both parties. Sometimes people are too frightened to meet or there is a risk of aggressive behaviour. In these cases, 'shuttle' mediation can take people through most of the process, with the mediator moving between the parties without the parties meeting. Although the greatest benefit can come from people meeting each other and seeing each other as human beings, it is still possible to achieve workable agreements using indirect mediation. Sometimes the resulting lessening of tension from an agreement achieved this way enables people to meet more constructively at a later stage.

Co-mediating

Mediators can work alone or in pairs. While there are obviously resource implications, co-mediating has many benefits:

- two heads are better than one in difficult conflict situations
- one mediator can take an observer role while the other is controlling the process, and may notice important things
- it is possible to match disputants' backgrounds, where this is seen to be important
- mediators can model co-operative working
- mediators can learn from each other
- it provides a good structure for training new mediators.

Benefits of mediation

Some of these are implicit from the description of the process, but it is worthwhile listing the benefits of mediation collectively:

- mediation encourages parties to focus on the problem between them rather than on each other as 'the enemy'
- the process gives both parties an opportunity to tell their version of events fully and to hear the other party's story
- people are more likely to change their actions if they hear how their behaviour is affecting the other person
- people are more likely to keep to a solution they have been involved in than one imposed from outside
- people can reach agreements appropriate to their particular situation
- mediation is confidential
- although mediation looks at the past, it focuses on the future – important because many disputes involve people with a continuing relationship.

Limitations of mediation

It is important to know when mediation is appropriate and when it is not (Acland 1995; Liebmann 1994).

Mediation can help when:

- the law is not clear

- both parties want to keep on good terms with each other
- it is in both parties' interests to sort things out
- both parties are tired of the dispute
- there is good will on both sides.

Mediation is not appropriate if:

- either party is unwilling
- it is not really in one party's interest to settle
- the power imbalance means that one party will agree to anything
- there are threats or fear of violence
- the dispute needs a public judgement.

Where there is a large power imbalance, advocacy is more appropriate to re-dress the balance.

Conflict resolution principles

Implicit in mediation work are a set of ideas and values which emphasise such concepts as (Cornelius and Faire 1989; Liebmann 1994, 1996):

- listening to others, for feelings as well as facts
- co-operation with others, valuing their contributions
- looking for common ground rather than differences
- affirmation of self and others as a necessary basis for resolving conflict
- speaking for oneself rather than accusing others
- separating the problem from the people
- trying to understand other people's points of view
- using a creative problem-solving approach to work on conflicts
- looking at what people want for the future rather than allocating blame for the past
- looking at all the options before selecting one to try
- looking for a 'win/win' solution, where everyone's interests are satisfied, rather than the adversarial 'win/lose' approach where one person wins and the other loses.

Mediation in different contexts

This section gives brief historical outlines of the way mediation operates in different contexts (Liebmann forthcoming). More detail is given in later chapters.

Industrial mediation

The Advisory, Conciliation and Arbitration Service (ACAS) was set up as a result of the Trade Union and Labour Relations Act 1974. It is best known for resolving high profile industrial disputes, but also works 'behind the scenes', preventing disputes from escalating, promoting good industrial relations and dealing with individual cases of employee and employer (ACAS 1996). Although ACAS is a statutory body, it has guaranteed independence from government. ACAS conciliators are usually full-time employees.

Family mediation

The Finer Committee (1974) first recommended family courts with conciliation services attached to them, but the government did not respond. In 1978 the first independent Family Conciliation Service was set up, and 20 local services came together in 1981 to form the National Family Conciliation Council, which became known as National Family Mediation in 1992 (Fisher 1993). There are now 70 family mediation services offering mediation concerning arrangements for children when parents separate or divorce. Seventeen services now also offer 'all-issues mediation', including property and finance issues. Most family mediators are qualified professionals who have also trained as mediators and are usually paid per session.

There is a separate organization, Family Mediation Scotland, which covers Scotland. The Family Mediators Association, founded in 1988, offers the help of two mediators who work together as a team – one is an experienced family solicitor, the other a qualified professional with experience in marital and family work, both with mediation training.

In 1996 these three bodies jointly founded the UK College of Family Mediators, to promote family mediation, establish recognized standards of training and make available details of registered mediators.

The Family Law Act 1996 was the second piece of legislation in the UK providing for mediation. For the first time, legal aid could be claimed for mediation in the same way as for legal representation (National Family Mediation 1996). Mediation will be available from the three family mediation organizations and the increasing number of solicitors who have trained in family mediation.

Victim/offender mediation

The main interest in victim/offender mediation started in the early 1980s, as a result of visits from US and Canadian mediation professionals. In 1984 there were 23 such initiatives in the UK (Marshall 1984), and these came together in that year to form the Forum for Initiatives in Reparation and Mediation (FIRM), a registered charity. In 1991 FIRM changed its name to Mediation UK, to describe itself more simply and to reflect its purpose more clearly.

Victim/offender mediation can help victims and offenders to reach a greater understanding, and sometimes to arrange appropriate reparation. It can be offered at any stage of criminal proceedings, pre-court, at court, or post-sentence; and for any crime involving a personal victim; and for any victims and offenders, provided both are willing. The recent emphasis on helping victims and current government concern with reparation have also stimulated new interest in this whole area.

There is also great interest in a related development known as Family Group Conferencing, Community Conferencing or Victim/Offender Conferencing. In the model closest to victim/offender mediation, an independent co-ordinator convenes a 'conference' of all those involved in the crime: the offender(s) and families; the victim(s) and families; other people important in their lives; others in the community affected by the crime. As in mediation, all the stories are heard, and then the whole group puts forward ideas for repairing the damage done by the crime, and for future avoidance of crime.

Community/neighbour mediation

The first community mediation service started in 1983 in London, and by 1985 there were seven such services (Marshall and Walpole 1985). The large increase in neighbour disputes has led housing and environmental health services to fund mediation services in recent years, so that community mediation is probably the fastest-growing kind of mediation in the UK at the moment, with the greatest number of services (97 in 1997).

Community mediation services mediate between neighbours in conflict and others in the community. A mediation may be between two next-door neighbours or involve a whole street concerned with vandalism and rowdy behaviour. About 60 per cent of neighbour disputes are about noise problems, while other frequent causes of conflict are dogs, other pets, children's behaviour, verbal abuse, harassment, car parking, rubbish, damage and boundary problems.

Most community mediation services are affiliated to Mediation UK. A typical local service is an independent registered charity with a paid co-ordinator and trained volunteer mediators from all walks of life, selected for their listening skills and non-judgemental attitudes.

Schools conflict resolution and mediation

The first schools conflict resolution project started in 1981 as a result of a local Quaker initiative. Several other Quaker groups followed this example, and Quaker Peace & Service provided support through twice-yearly meetings for all those (not just Quakers) interested in conflict resolution in schools. They also helped to form the European Network in Conflict Resolution in Education in 1990.

For the first few years, most of the schools work concentrated on teaching children, mostly in primary schools, about conflict resolution, using a variety of games and exercises. Several independent projects provide training, and several schools have incorporated conflict resolution practices into their framework. More recently this work has developed to include schools-based peer mediation, in which children are trained to mediate in playground disputes. Peer mediation has also moved into secondary schools, and a National Network of Peer Mediators started in 1997. There are currently 22 schools projects (mostly affiliated to Mediation UK), working in a much larger number of schools.

Mediation UK

Mediation UK is now the umbrella organization for almost all the community, victim/offender and schools mediation services, and helps bring new mediation initiatives in these fields into being. It is the only national mediation organization which also has a membership scheme for anyone wishing to join and receive its quarterly mailings.

Commercial mediation

The first scheme for commercial mediation, the Centre for Dispute Resolution (CEDR), was launched in November 1990 (CEDR 1996). CEDR handles cases where two (or more) firms are in dispute and would otherwise go to court. Mediation can save substantial money and time, especially if several parties are involved. The same principles apply as for other kinds of mediation. CEDR carries out its own training and accredits its own mediators. Other organizations offering commercial mediation and training include the

Alternative Dispute Resolution Net, the Academy of Experts and the National Mediation Centre.

Medical mediation

Many Family Health Service Authorities have been offering informal conciliation/mediation services for several years to patients making complaints about their doctors. Since 1996, all health authorities have been asked to ensure that conciliation services are available to both parties to a complaint (National Health Service Executive 1996).

Environmental mediation

Environmental mediation has been used for many years in North America to help resolve disputes concerning environmental and planning issues. It has been pioneered in the UK by a few individual practitioners and by Environmental Resolve (part of the Environment Council), which started in 1992 to provide consensus-building consultancy and training, and has developed a network of mediators and facilitators. Environmental mediation usually involves many 'stakeholders' and can be slow – but the decisions are owned by all. A further aim is to use the process to *prevent* conflict and make better decisions in the first place (Baines and Ingram 1995).

Elder mediation

The Elder Mediation Project has pioneered resolving conflicts involving older people in institutions, families and the community.

Organizational and workplace mediation

Many organizational consultants have seen conflict resolution as part of their general remit in helping organizations to move forward, especially as unresolved conflict often plays a part in these organizations becoming 'stuck'. Often they now undertake mediation skills training to enhance their ability to resolve conflict; meanwhile mediators have been widening their scope to include organizations and workplaces. Two recent specialist services are: (1) the National Council for Voluntary Organisations Voluntary Sector Dispute Resolution Service, started in 1995; and (2) the Association of Chief Executives of National Voluntary Organisations and CEDR (see above) service for disputes involving chief executives and their organizations, started in 1996.

Issues in mediation

Several issues and dilemmas have surfaced in recent years, as mediation becomes more established.

Independence

Mediators must be impartial and have nothing to gain or lose from the outcome of a mediation. To achieve this, many mediation services are independent voluntary organizations, usually registered charities. Some mediation services are funded and managed by a statutory organization, for example a local authority housing department or probation service, and some people fear this may compromise the independence of the mediation service. Many such services try to ensure independence by having a multi-agency committee to advise on the running of the service.

Equal opportunities and multicultural mediation

Most mediation services have developed, or are developing, an equal opportunities policy to cover all procedures, including recruiting paid staff and volunteer mediators, publicity and awareness raising of the service, training and mediation. Mediation services try to recruit mediators to represent as wide a cross-section of the local community as possible. Mediators are trained to mediate in cross-cultural situations, when cultural factors may lead to misunderstandings.

Empowerment and service delivery

From the early days, there have been two strands of thinking which have informed the mediation movement, especially in community mediation. The first is the 'grass roots' aim of providing self-help schemes for people to sort out their own problems. This emphasizes informality, volunteer help, education of all in managing conflict, benefits to the community as a whole and community-based independent management of mediation services.

The second strand is more 'agency-led', a response by local authorities and other statutory organizations to the ineffectiveness and expense of legal solutions to disputes. Moreover, if they fund a local mediation service, they want it to be effective in their terms. This philosophy emphasizes clear procedures, formality, measurable outcomes and, if it is more efficient, paid mediators.

Standards and professionalization

As mediation becomes established and funded, those paying the bill want to know whether they are getting value for money and a good standard of service. Mediation UK has introduced accreditation for mediation services as a way of ensuring high standards. The government has set up a lead body to develop National Vocational Qualifications for mediators. Many in the mediation world welcome these developments, as they ensure and value a high standard of mediation for clients. However, some are worried about the danger of professionalization and the demise of the voluntary ethos of mediation.

Mediation, counselling and advocacy

By this stage, many of the similarities and differences between mediation, counselling and advocacy will be obvious. Nevertheless, it is worth summarizing them here.

The main similarities between mediation, counselling and advocacy are the uses of the same stock of basic skills: listening, paraphrasing, summarizing, problem solving, looking at options, and so on. Some skills, such as reframing, are used perhaps more in mediation than in the other two processes. All three processes have a valuable role to play in helping to resolve conflict, depending on the situation.

The main differences between mediation and the other two processes are that mediation focuses on two (or more) parties in conflict equally, whereas advocacy and counselling generally focus on one of the parties; and that mediation is impartial with respect to both parties, whereas advocacy and counselling are concerned with one party's needs, except in couples, family and group counselling and advocacy.

Mediation, counselling and advocacy are not rival, competing processes; rather they are complementary in that they apply to different situations. They may also be available in a single service, as in the Family Law Consortium of Solicitors, Mediators and Counsellors. A hypothetical example may help to clarify how community mediation services observe boundaries.

Suppose a local community mediation service answers a telephone call from someone asking for help with a neighbour problem. After a long conversation, it becomes clear that the problem has only seemed bad since the recent death of a close relative, and that this event is still a source of great distress. The intake worker suggests bereavement counselling and gives the caller the local telephone number. It seems important to sort this out first and then see if there is still a neighbour problem.

The next caller complains about severe racial abuse, and asks what mediation would involve. The intake worker listens and wonders whether this is a mediation case. He or she refers the caller to an advocacy service supporting victims of racial abuse, to get advice and support. Possibly mediation might be suitable at a later stage, with support, but first something needs to be done to empower the weaker party.

The last call of the afternoon is from someone who has fallen out with his or her neighbour over a noisy party held by teenage sons. As they used to have a good relationship, this is very upsetting. There is no extra problem indicating counselling, there seems to be no great imbalance of power, and advocacy for one side could polarize things even further. After some discussion, this seems a suitable case for mediation and the intake worker promises to allocate two mediators the next day.

Conclusion

Mediation, along with advocacy and counselling, is a useful process of empowerment. It has a special contribution to make in the resolution of conflict, in enabling people to participate in the solution and learn from the process. Care must be taken to be clear when mediation, advocacy or counselling are appropriate, so that the most constructive use is made of all the processes.

References

ACAS (1996) 20 Years of Improving Industrial Relations. London: ACAS.

Acland, A. (1995) Resolving Disputes Without Going to Court. London: Century.

Baines, J. and Ingram, H. (1995) Beyond Compromise: Building Consensus in Environmental Planning and Decision Making. London: The Environment Council.

CEDR (1996) Resolutions 15, November. London: Centre for Dispute Resolution.

Cornelius, C. and Faire, S. (1989) Everyone Can Win. Sydney: Simon and Schuster.

Finer Report (1974) Report of the Committee on One-Parent Families. London: HMSO.

Fisher, T. (1993) The History of Family Mediation Services. London: National Family Mediation.

Liebmann, M. (1994) Neighbours' Quarrels. London: Channel Four Television.

Liebmann, M. (1996) Arts Approaches to Conflict. London: Jessica Kingsley Publishers.

Liebmann, M. (forthcoming) Mediation in Context. London: Jessica Kingsley Publishers.

Marshall, T. (1984) Reparation, Conciliation and Mediation. Home Office Research and Planning Unit, Paper 27. London: HMSO.

Marshall, T. and Walpole, M. (1985) *Bringing People Together: Mediation and Reparation Projects in Great Britain.* Home Office Research and Planning Unit, Paper 33. London: HMSO.

Mediation UK (1995) *Training Manual in Community Mediation Skills.* Bristol: Mediation UK.

National Family Mediation (1996) *The Family Law Bill: The Importance for Mediators.* London: National Family Mediation.

National Health Service Executive (1996) *Complaints Guidance Pack for General Medical/Dental Practitioners.* London: NHS Executive.

Useful addresses

Academy of Experts

2 South Square
Gray's Inn
London WC1R 5HP
Contact: Michael Cohen
Tel: 0171 637 0333

Cost-efficient dispute resolution is one of the organization's principal aims and it aims to ensure there are trained and experienced neutrals available for the community. It trains and accredits neutrals in the various mediation and dispute resolution fields, and deals with personal, consumer and commercial disputes in addition to providing specialist services for organizations. Members are qualified and come from a wide range of disciplines.

ADR Group

Equity and Law Building
36–38 Baldwin Street
Bristol BS1 1NR
Contact: Randoll Meadows
Tel: 0117 925 2090
Fax: 0117 929 4429

Operates a national mediation programme in commercial and family disputes, with mediators in 24 locations around the country. Also provides central case administration services and runs a number of industry-specific schemes. Provides training and accreditation for mediators.

Advisory, Conciliation and Arbitration Service (ACAS)

27 Wilton Street
London SW1X 7AZ
Contact: Tony Shepherd
Tel: 0171 210 3636
Fax: 0171 210 3919

Collective conciliation provides a means whereby employers and trade unions can be helped to reach mutually acceptable settlements of their disputes by a neutral and independent third party, ACAS. Its essential characteristics are that its use is voluntary and that agreements reached in conciliation are the responsibility of the disputing parties.

Centre for Dispute Resolution

7 St Katherine's Way
London E1 9LB
Contact: Bill Marsh
Tel: 0171 481 4441
Fax: 0171 481 4442

Aims are the promotion of alternative dispute resolution (ADR); the training of mediators; and the provision of mediation and ADR services for businesses, the public sector and civil litigation.

Elder Mediation Project (EMP)

27 Ridgmount Gardens
London WC1E 7AS
Contact: Yvonne Craig
Tel: 0171 580 9706

EMP is based on empowering older persons and all those working with and for them in Mediation UK member organizations, statutory and voluntary organizations, to resolve by mediation the family, community and residential care conflicts that arise in later life. Free multicultural consultancy/training is offered to those wishing to start their own local EMPs. EMP also works with disability groups.

ENCORE (European Network for Conflict Resolution in Education)

Education Advisory Programme
Friends House
Euston Road
London NW1 2BJ
Contact: Marigold Bentley
Tel: 0171 387 3601
Fax: 0171 388 1977

Aims to: encourage and support the development of conflict resolution and mediation skills in schools and colleges throughout Europe; to provide information about available resources and develop new resources; to encourage education authorities, governments and international agencies to support this work and to implement the recommendations contained in the Council of Europe report, *Violence and Conflict Resolution in Schools*; and to maintain links with similar networks in Europe and other continents.

Environmental Resolve (an undertaking of the Environment Council)

The Environment Council
21 Elizabeth Street
London SW1W 9RP
Contact: Hally Ingram
Tel: 0171 824 8411

Environmental Resolve promotes the use of consensus building in preventing and resolving environmental disputes. Using independent facilitators people involved in an environmental problem can find common ground, leading to mutually satisfactory solutions which can save time, money and the environment.

Family Law Consortium of Solicitors, Mediators and Counsellors

2 Henrietta Street
London WC2E 8PS
Tel: 0171 420 5000

Family Mediators Scotland (FMS)

127 Rose Street
South Lane
Edinburgh EH2 4BB
Contact: Elizabeth Foster
Tel: 0131 220 1610
Fax: 0131 220 6895

FMS supports affiliated services throughout Scotland to meet the needs of children in separating and divorcing families. FMS promotes, develops and supports family mediation by co-ordinating and developing services; maintaining high standards of practice; educating the public and professionals; and disseminating and fostering relevant research.

Family Mediators Association (FMA)

PO Box 2028
Hove BN3 3HU
Contact: Ruth Hindley
Tel: 01273 747750

Mediators trained by FMA offer mediation on all issues in separation and divorce, such as arrangements for children and financial and property issues. Two mediators meet jointly with couples at any stage of separation or divorce. A lawyer mediator experienced in divorce and family work co-mediates with an experienced family mediator. Widely available in England and Wales.

Mediation UK

Alexander House
Telephone Avenue
Bristol BS1 4BS
Contact: Tony Billinghurst
Tel: 0117 904 6661
Fax: 0117 904 3331

Mediation UK is a network of projects, organizations and individuals interested in mediation and other alternative forms of conflict resolution. It is a registered charity supported by grants, donations, membership fees and sales from publications. Mediation UK is the only umbrella organization for all initiatives and individuals interested in conflict resolution in the UK. It also has specialist networks for community, victim/offender and schools mediation.

National Family Mediation

9 Tavistock Place
London WC1H 9SN
Contact: Thelma Fisher
Tel: 0171 383 5993
Fax: 0171 383 5994

Formed in 1981, National Family Mediation has played a vital role in stimulating and supporting the rapid expansion of local divorce mediation services. It is an independent organization funded solely by subscriptions and charitable trusts. It provides mediation in disputes over children when their parents are divorcing or separating.

Quaker Peace & Service (QPS)

Friends House
Euston Road
London NW1 2BJ
Contact: Marigold Bentley
Tel: 0171 387 3601
Fax: 0171 388 1977

QPS, the international department of the Religious Society of Friends in Britain, is active at an international and local level in peace making and conflict resolution. QPS has supported many Quaker-based mediation schemes around Britain and actively supports conflict resolution in schools through the Education Advisory Programme.

Speak Out: The National Network of Peer Mediators

c/o 68 St George's Road
Bolton BL1 2DD
Contact: Jo Bird
Tel/Fax: 01204 430418

Speak Out is the national network of peer mediators. It aims to exchange ideas and skills between peer mediators and to arrange meetings and conferences for and by peer mediators. It is run by young people with the active support of adults.

UK College of Family Mediators

24–32 Stephenson Way
London NW1 2HX
Contact: Liz Walsh
Tel: 0171 391 9162

The three most long-standing family mediation organizations in the UK, the Family Mediators Association, Family Mediation Scotland and National Family Mediation, have jointly established this professional body to build on past practice and develop standards in family mediation. It sets standards and makes available details of registered mediators qualified to provide family mediation.

Voluntary Sector Dispute Resolution Service

NCVO
Regents Wharf
8 All Saints Street
London N1 9RL
Contact: Andrew Woodgate
Tel: 0171 713 6161
Fax: 0171 713 6300

Organizational mediation for disputes within voluntary organizations. These may be between trustees, between trustees and staff, among staff or between branches or groups of members. The service is open to all voluntary organizations in England, and anyone involved can make the initial contact. NCVO may be able to meet some of the costs for smaller organizations.

PART II

The Social Uses of Advocacy, Counselling and Mediation

CHAPTER 4

Child Advocacy

Christine Piper

Introduction

Advocacy – that of the child's wishes and feelings, views and interests – has become a growth industry, witnessed by the formation of child advocacy organizations, the development of professional guidelines and by judicial pronouncements. This has led to difficulties for practitioners in relation to developing appropriate professional procedures and techniques, setting role boundaries and determining the limitations of advocacy itself. To understand the nature of these difficulties created for professionals we need to locate the development of child advocacy in a double consensus that emerged during the 1980s among those professionally concerned with children and their families. There were two themes in the consensus: children should be allowed a greater say in what happens to them and parents should, together, retain responsibility for making decisions about their children. These two ideas have been given priority by family lawyers, family court welfare officers, the judiciary, mediators, counsellors, psychologists and social workers, and yet they are self-evidently not always compatible and the focus on parental responsibility may well operate to the detriment of the aim of hearing the child.

This has led to two quite different developments. First, in those circumstances where parents do not, or cannot, make decisions about the upbringing of their children (or where the children themselves wish, and are legally able, to contest the parental decision) those decisions are made in professionally dominated arenas where the child is at a disadvantage. In these circumstances it is accepted that the child must have an adult advocate for his or her views and interests. The questions this raises are then the following: who can advocate most effectively for the child and how does the advocate ascertain what to say on behalf of the child? A focus on those advocacy-centred questions, however, makes invisible other questions: has the advocate responsibility for the psychological health of the child and when and how should counselling be available?

The second development is in regard to what might be termed 'indirect advocacy' of the child's wishes. The focus on parental responsibility has led to professional guidelines and statutory duties which enjoin professionals to encourage and empower parents to listen to the child's wishes and to incorporate those wishes in family decision-making. Indirect advocacy may well, therefore, shade into mediation processes.

The questions these developments raise are further complicated by the fact that there is no unitary theoretical framework underpinning the development of advocacy initiatives: two quite different strands fed into the pressure for giving the child a voice. On the one hand there emerged rights-based arguments for greater self-determination by children and, on the other, welfare-based concerns that children are damaged by being marginalized from decision making. These different motivations are still present and lead to the fundamental question of whether the advocate should seek out and articulate the child's views and wishes or the child's interests and welfare.

This chapter therefore examines advocacy in its different meanings and looks at the ways in which the resulting conflicts of aim and role confusions are being resolved in practice. Because this is a vast subject area and because child advocacy takes place within a legal framework there will be a focus on those professionals operating within the courts – solicitors, judges, guardians *ad litem* (GALs) and court welfare officers – in relation to private and public law proceedings as well as to mediators and solicitors trying to avoid the use of courts.

The Children Act 1989 also provides rights for the child to be heard in administrative proceedings relating to local authority duties and powers. This chapter, therefore, also looks briefly at the role of social workers in ascertaining the child's wishes and reports research findings in relation to the 'Independent Person' and the complaints procedure under section 26 of the Act.

The chapter concludes that advocacy not only has ill-defined links with counselling and mediation services, but also itself incorporates aspects of mediation and counselling. These fusions may be theoretically untenable (King and Piper 1995) and, in practice, do not always help the child.

Advocacy for the child of separating parents

Given that child advocacy in relation to parental divorce and separation is a recent development, and that much more has been written about advocacy in relation to public law, this may seem a strange place to start. However, more children experience parental separation than become the focus of care and adoption applications. This is also a very public issue: during debates prior to the passage of the divorce law sections of the Family Law Act 1996 much play was made of the potential harm to the child 'caused' by divorce. The resulting amendments impose duties on professionals to ascertain and take account of the child's wishes and interests within the new legal framework for divorce.

There are therefore pressing practice issues to be resolved before the Act is implemented, in addition to those caused by implementation of the Children Act 1989. To see whether developments in divorce-related advocacy are appropriate and adequate, this section will look first at the relevant legal duties which provide the framework (and also funding) for professional practice and then look at what is known about actual practice. Some of the difficulties discussed will also be relevant to the subsequent discussion on child advocacy within public law proceedings.

The Children Act 1989 and the Family Law Act 1996

Most of the new duties in the Family Law Act 1996 encourage indirect advocacy for the child. The compulsory information meeting for all seeking a divorce must provide information to the parent(s) about 'the importance to be attached to the welfare, wishes and feelings of children' (section 8), and the Lord Chancellor may make rules which impose a similar duty on a legal representative of a spouse (section 12). Mediators funded by the Legal Aid Board must likewise have in place 'arrangements designed to ensure that the parties are encouraged to consider – the wishes and feelings of each child,' and such mediators must also consider whether the child should attend mediation to express those wishes (section 27). Section 11 places a new duty on the divorce court to 'have particular regard' to, *inter alia*, 'the wishes and feelings of the child' when deciding whether to exercise its powers under the Children Act 1989.

Some of these duties already operate in relation to professionals involved with divorcing parents. The checklist in section 1 of the Children Act 1989 includes a requirement that, when considering applications for contested section 8 applications (and also for care and supervision orders), the court should take into account the wishes and feelings of the child. In addition the transaction criteria for divorce solicitors franchised by the Legal Aid Board include a requirement that, when there may be a dispute about residence or contact, they should ascertain the child's wishes (Piper 1997).

Similarly the *National Standards for Probation Service Family Court Welfare Work* state that, in the course of compiling welfare reports, 'All children should be seen by the court welfare officer unless there are strong grounds for not doing so.... Wherever their age and maturity permit it children should be offered the opportunity to express their wishes and feelings' (Home Office 1994, para. 4.17). The welfare report would normally be the means by which the court sought to obtain the views of the child because prominent judges have explicitly discouraged the judiciary from talking to children themselves (Lord Justice Balcombe 1994; Mrs Justice Booth 1993).

There is also the question of direct advocacy of the child's wishes under these two major pieces of legislation. The Children Act 1989 allows children to make section 8 applications (with leave of the High Court) for residence and contact orders, and children can be made parties to proceedings. The Lord Chancellor may also make regulations under section 64 of the Family Law Act 1996 to provide for the separate representation of children in divorce proceedings.

Who currently conveys the child's wishes?
THE SOLICITOR FOR THE PARENT

There is relatively little research on who finds out what the child wants and whether such information is taken into account by the decision makers. What evidence there is suggests that most children of divorcing parents currently have no independent advocate of their wishes and are rarely in a position to advocate for themselves.

In one small research project most of the solicitors interviewed – whether or not subject to the Legal Aid Board checklist – did not directly ascertain the child's wishes (Piper 1997). Most recorded what the parent who was their client told them, but did not use such information as they believed it was inherently unreliable. The following scenario is based on what one solicitor told me in the course of that research:

> Mrs Bond had an initial interview with her local family law solicitor, Miss Andrews, in connection with her proposed divorce. Miss Andrews realized that another appointment was necessary to discuss in more detail the residence and contact arrangements for the two children. She told Mrs Bond not to bring the children with her. However, when Mrs Bond arrived for the appointment she was accompanied by her nine-year-old son Billy, who was not at school because he had stomach ache. Mrs Bond would not let Billy stay on his own in the waiting area. When Miss Andrews starting gaining information about the potential residence dispute, Mrs Bond said, 'Go on, tell her Billy, tell her you want to live with me.'

As Miss Andrews always discouraged participation of children as being too stressful for them, she said to Billy, 'It's OK, I know you're not feeling very well today. I don't expect you to have to tell us anything. You can doze while I talk to your Mum.' She therefore gained information from Mrs Bond about the practical problems that would arise if Billy lived with Mr Bond and then asked Mrs Bond to go away and think about possible contact arrangements if Billy lived with her.

Was the solicitor's response to the situation created by Billy's Mum appropriate? Miss Andrews, like many of the solicitors interviewed, reassured herself that if the case resulted in an application to court then the court welfare officer would find out 'properly' (Piper 1997).

THE COURT WELFARE OFFICER

It is not clear whether solicitors have a false sense of security in this matter: James and Hay (1993) found that many court welfare officers did not interview the child alone. In more recent research the majority of court welfare officers did see children in most cases and, if seen, children were usually seen separately from their parents (Hester, Pearson and Radford 1997, pp.30–31). Nevertheless, this leaves the welfare officer with unenviable decisions, as made clear in an article by two court welfare officers (Cantwell and Scott 1995). They describe one of their own cases to reveal the problems involved in giving attention to the wishes of the child. Below is a summary of that case study using fictitious names:

> Mr and Mrs East separated when their son Mark was four. Mrs East began a lesbian relationship and agreed Mark should live with his Dad, who now lives with his parents. However, these grandparents successfully hindered regular contact between Mark and his Mum, despite Mark's parents agreeing contact arrangements twice at court. The situation was brought to a head on a recent contact visit when Mark – now aged eight – told his Mum he did not want to go out with her for the day again. Mrs East applied to the court and a welfare report was ordered. Both parents told the court welfare officers that they would be happy to go along with what Mark wanted, though Mrs East wanted the officer to see Mark on his own to find out what Mark really wanted.

What should a court welfare officer do, if he wants to take seriously the court's duty to have regard to the child's wishes, when faced with a case like this? In the event Cantwell and Scott refused to interview the child and, instead, talked to Mark about his family generally for an hour in front of his parents. At the end of that time, when they saw Mrs East alone, she said, 'I have to let go, haven't I?' She then explained to Mark why she would not be visiting him and Mr East offered to maintain indirect contact. Cantwell and Scott believed that the situation had thereby been defused and that there was hope of change in the future. 'Implicitly accepting that neither the court nor the child could be expected to fulfil the current vacuum of parental responsibility, the mother grasped the nettle' (1995, p.351).

This is a brave and imaginative approach which I hope proves to have been right. Yet the story leaves me anxious. The child's wish for the end of an intolerable contact situation was granted but he 'lost' his mother – until he is old enough to cope with adult hostility and/or until his grandparents die – because his mother realized that only she had the opportunity and strength to break the cycle of conflict. Is that what Mark wanted or needed?

THE MEDIATOR

So far only a small minority of mediated cases have involved the attendance of children at any stage, and mediators are divided on the issue (National Family Mediation (NFM) 1994, pp.12–15; Simpson 1991, pp.390–394). There has recently been a rapid development of ideas and practices to provide ways in which children can be 'consulted', either directly or indirectly (Best 1995; NFM 1994, p.20). This will be important if mediation does become the normal method of dispute resolution in divorce.

Mediators use a variety of techniques (for example, the empty chair) to focus parents on the child's welfare and to enable parents themselves to hear what their children are saying. Children are also given information directly (written or verbal) and via role play and so on, which reduces the child's marginalization. There are, however, some problems with these positive developments. As Richards (1994) points out, mediation cannot, and should not, address directly the child's emotional needs, but the boundaries of mediation and counselling need further thought. Second, techniques to encourage parents to concentrate on the children's needs can be perceived more oppressively by the care-taking parent. This can lead to inappropriate agreement to particular arrangements or to resentment which hinders implementation of arrangements (Piper 1993).

THE ADVOCATE FOR THE CHILD AS PARTY

Theoretically a child can apply for a section 8 order but decided cases have considerably reduced the circumstances in which the court might grant leave to do so (Monro and Forrester 1995, p.164). Furthermore, the solicitor asked to make an application for leave would first need to be satisfied that the child had sufficient understanding to instruct him or her. This difficult decision is one which might depend on the solicitor's attitudes to children's rights and protection, as well as knowledge of child development. Indeed, Sawyer (1997) argues, on the basis of her research, that the personal values of the solicitor influence the assessment of the child's competence and, therefore, access to an advocate.

The problem might be the lack of authoritative guidance. Several published documents give professional guidance (e.g. the Solicitors' Family Law Association's (SFLA's) *Guide to Good Practice for Solicitors Acting for Children* 1996) but the messages are not always identical and are not binding. (Guidance may be attached to the forthcoming Annual Report of the Children Act Committee.) They are, however, documents which attest to the commitment of many solicitors to representing children properly and appropriately. The SFLA Guide, for example, stresses that solicitors taking on a child client must be prepared to deal with the whole case personally.

This 'special treatment' does of course raise the question of the extent to which child and adult clients should be treated alike (Leeco 1996, p.312). Should they be given the advantage of readier access to counselling? Should they have the disadvantage of having 'to jump through hoops many of our adult clients would never manage' (Ray 1993, p.16)?

Children can also be joined as parties to existing proceedings which could result from the separation or divorce of parents. In these circumstances the Official Solicitor (whose Office dates from 1876) is usually appointed. He has a unique amalgam of roles, acting as solicitor and GAL, but this latter role takes precedence: he does not have to act on his 'client's' instructions if he believes his client's best interests lie elsewhere. The court can now allow a child to be represented solely by a solicitor but in the recent case of *Re S (a minor) (Independent Representation)* [1993] 2 FLR 437 did not do so. Should the court be so reluctant to allow a child to be separately represented?

The limitations of child advocacy in divorce

The above research studies show that professionals involved in the legal process of divorce have valid concerns about the wisdom of asking children what they want in the post-separation situation. Solicitors, welfare officers, judges and mediators all refer to the possible detriment to children who 'speak out' and harm fragile family relationships and to the 'burden' placed on a child who perceives expressing a view as equating to choosing between parents.

There is also the influence of the cross-disciplinary consensus that the parent should decide. The child's right or need to express a view is trumped by a welfare card which equates the exercise of parental responsibility for decision making with the best interest of the child.

It may be, therefore, that the child's negative feelings of marginalization from decision making have to be responded to differently. Parents can be enjoined ever more frequently to take such wishes into account but there are two problems here: it is insulting to those parents who do hear what their children say and it ignores the fact that – as all parents know – children tend to assume parents have not listened to them! Placing a similar requirement on parents as that in the Children (Scotland) Act 1995 (section 6(1)) might not therefore be helpful. Three suggestions to respond to this dilemma are worth considering.

COMMUNICATION

It may be better to abandon advocacy on behalf of the child and substitute communication to the child by a professional able to explain in appropriate and authoritative language why a decision has been made. As we have seen, this is already being developed by mediators, and a circular to court welfare officers suggests this also be done in particular cases decided by the court (Association of Family Court Welfare Officers 1995).

MORE DIRECT ADVOCACY

If the abandonment of advocacy is not acceptable then 'real' advocacy needs to be substituted. Currently no one group of professionals is taking responsibility for advocacy, with the result that most children are falling through the net.

There are three possible solutions. First, as one solicitor I interviewed explained, 'children should be separately represented [by a solicitor] if their views are relevant'. Second, as another solicitor commented, 'The only way you can get round it is by having someone like a guardian *ad litem* acting for children in divorce proceedings'; in other words, a social work-trained officer should be appointed to represent the child's interests. The third solution was rejected by the Scottish Law Commission (1992) on grounds of cost: that there should be a court report in every case with a clear duty on the court welfare officer to ascertain and record the child's views.

COUNSELLING

Those working within the legal system have made creditable efforts to incorporate knowledge and skills from the 'psy-sciences' in their professional practice and mediators are developing new skills to consult children. Perhaps, however, in relation to private law, this may not be helping children. What is needed are clearer boundaries, each profession working to its own strengths. Therefore, it might be better to place the duties in relation to the emotional and psychological needs of children of divorce elsewhere, that is, outside the legal system (Douglas, Murch and Perry 1996). Perhaps some form of counselling-based service would give the child, not an advocate with power to influence decisions made, but at least empowerment to adjust satisfactorily to a new situation. The organization Independent Representation for Children in Need has pointed to the lack of any clearly identified service to which children can turn, and has piloted a child-centred service (Timms 1997, p.44).

Advocacy in relation to state intervention

It is also timely to focus on advocacy relating to applications for care and supervision orders because there are currently three main concerns: that financial constraints may reduce the child's access to a solicitor; that the GAL may not be sufficiently independent; and that the solicitor and GAL may not be sufficiently clear about their different roles.

The GAL and the solicitor

Theoretically there is less role confusion in relation to advocacy in public law proceedings: the GAL ascertains and puts forward the child's interests; the solicitor – a member of the Law Society's Children's Panel – represents to the court the child's views and, providing the interests identified by the GAL do not conflict with the ascertained views of the child, the child's interests as well. In other words, the solicitor would be advocating the GAL's views of the child's welfare *unless* the child's views conflict *and* the solicitor believes the child has sufficient understanding to instruct him or her directly. That latter decision is again the solicitor's decision.

This situation is therefore fraught with difficulties for all concerned. Direct advocacy for the child is undermined in two ways. First is the current belief in some quarters that a child does not need a solicitor as well as a guardian. Second, research shows that not all solicitors try to find out whether the child's views conflict with those of the guardian. One research study found that two-thirds of the child clients had not been seen by the solicitor, though the researcher, himself a guardian, found that some of these children, when interviewed, competently expressed views contrary to those of the guardian (Clark 1996, p.114).

The Association of Lawyers for Children (ALC) has argued that the *National Standards* for GALs (Department of Health/Welsh Office 1995) should have included firm guidance that the GAL must stress to the solicitor the need for him or her to see the child *as a client* wherever possible (ALC 1996). If the GAL and solicitor are not clear about their different roles 'the important balance is distorted, and the opportunity to achieve the best possible outcomes for children is lost' (Timms 1997, p.41).

The GAL and the local authority

The GAL service, instituted by the Children Act 1975 (and implemented in 1984), provides the court under section 41 of the Children Act 1989 with advocacy for the child's welfare. In relation to care proceedings the GAL must report whether the local authority's care plan is in the child's best interests. However, because GALs are appointed by a panel managed by the local authority, it is argued that 'However strenuously guardians may assert their independence, the reality is they are not... There is a danger that guardians may begin to feel that it does not always pay to bite the hand that feeds them' (Monro 1997, p.3; Timms 1997; Walton 1997). This may lead to particular difficulties in advocating a child's needs when there are cost implications (Thorpe 1995, p.30).

Mediation

Because of the potential for harm caused by child protection court proceedings, there have been attempts to extend the use of mediation to such cases. In the pilot project set up by the Tavistock Clinic and NFM children are not present but are seen by a psychiatrist who represents their views. The number of referrals from GALs and caseworkers has, however, been small, though some programmes in the US claim more success in attracting 'clients' (Edwards and Baron 1995).

Adoption

As the typical adoptee is no longer a baby the views of the child have assumed some importance. Such views may have more import if the proposal in the draft Adoption Bill to substitute the paramountcy welfare test for the existing 'first consideration' test is enacted, and also if the current trend towards post-adoption contact continues. It is not possible within the confines of this chapter to pursue these issues, but suffice it to say that pleas are being made that the lessons of divorce and separation in regard to children's needs and suitable dispute resolution processes should also be applied to the treatment of children who are to be parted from parents by adoption (Ryburn 1997, p.35). Consequently, advocacy for children involved in adoption proceedings should be addressed in similar terms to those in the discussion in the second section of this chapter.

Advocacy for the child in care

Section 22 of the Children Act 1989 states that if decisions are made about a child (potentially) being 'looked after' by the local authority, the wishes and feelings of the child must be ascertained and given due consideration. When the case is periodically reviewed, the child's wishes should also be sought and the outcome notified to the child. Section 26 introduced a complaints procedure whereby the local authority must consider representations made to it by, *inter alia*, a child being looked after by the local authority, or a child 'in need':

> The value of this arena for advocacy has been questioned: One of the key areas of concern about current s 26 procedures is the lack of any independent element in the investigation and the consideration of the complaint, as well as the young person's lack of effective representation at quasi-judicial hearings. (Timms 1997, p.43)

The procedure is governed by the Social Services Inspectorate Standard 9 and places a heavy responsibility on the 'Independent Person' who is appointed if the complaint is about, or on behalf of, a child. The Standards state that the Independent Person does not operate as the child's advocate – the role is to provide an 'objective' view – yet the Voice for the Child in Care provides personnel for that role in some areas. The Independent Person is sometimes a former social worker, again raising the same fears about lack of independence as are raised about the GAL. Williams and Jordan (1997) have researched the procedure in six local authority areas. They note that information about the complaints procedure is not always adequate, that sufficient resources are often not available, and that caseworkers, managers and complainant children are not always properly supported.

The criteria for Standard 10 include that the social services department provides an advocacy service to assist children in the complaints procedure. Williams and Jordan found that generally this was not complied with (1997, p.133). The Advice, Advocacy and Information Service for Children and Young People is also concerned that advocates sometimes step outside their proper role: 'If advocates start to decide what is in the best interests of a young person they have little to distinguish themselves from other professionals' (Childright 1994, p.19).

Conclusions

Many of the criticisms of existing law and practice of child advocacy made by the Children's Legal Centre during the drafting and implementation of the Children Act 1989 in relation to private law proceedings (Wyld 1991) have been addressed but, unfortunately, some have not. One example referred to in this chapter is the issue of assessing the child's competence to instruct a solicitor. Another is the question of who is ultimately responsible for telling a child about his or her possibilities in relation to advocacy.

In relation to children in care or in need there are also both positive developments and disappointing lacunae. Here, too, the main need is for professionals to stop trying to do everything and refocus roles on to those tasks and skills for which they are best qualified. In that way, children as well as adults may understand better the limits and potential of the different processes of advocacy, mediation and counselling.

This chapter has offered no solutions. As Shear, a children's lawyer in California, has written: 'There simply is no dos-and-don'ts checklist that will address the myriad issues facing children's attorneys' (1996, p.256), nor, of course, their mediators, GALs and caseworkers. But awareness that there are problems is half the battle.

References

Association of Family Court Welfare Officers (1995) 'Explaining court decisions to children.' *Newsletter 2*, 4, 1–2.

ALC (1996) *Newsletter.* Association of Lawyers for Children.

ASC (1994) 'The role of the children's advocate.' *Childright 109*, 19.

Balcombe, Lord Justice (1994) 'The voice of the child.' *Family Mediation 4*, 1, 11–12.

Best, R. (1995) 'Direct consultation with children: a progress report on training modules.' *Family Mediation 5*, 3, 8.

Booth, Mrs Justice (1993) Closing address to the Lawyers for Children Conference on 24 September 1993. *Family Law 23*, 652.

Cantwell, B. and Scott, S. (1995) 'Children's wishes, children's burdens.' *Journal of Social Welfare and Family Law 17*, 3, 337–353.

Clark, D. (1996) 'The older child and care proceedings.' *Family Law 26*, 113–115.

Department of Health/Welsh Office (1995) *National Standards for the Guardian ad Litem and Reporting Officer Service.* London: Department of Health.

Douglas, G., Murch, M. and Perry, A. (1996) 'Supporting children when parents separate – a neglected family justice or mental health issue?' *Child and Family Law Quarterly 8*, 2, 121–135.

Edwards, L. and Baron, S. (1995) 'Alternatives to contested litigation in child abuse and neglect cases.' *Family and Conciliation Courts Review 33*, 3, 275–285.

Hester, M., Pearson, C. and Radford, L. (1997) *Domestic Violence: A National Survey of Court Welfare and Voluntary Sector Mediation Practice.* Bristol: Policy Press.

Home Office (1994) *National Standards for Probation Service Family Court Welfare Work.* London: Home Office.

James, A. and Hay, W. (1993) *Court Welfare in Action*. Hemel Hempstead: Harvester Wheatsheaf.

King, M. and Piper, C. (1995) (2nd edn) *How the Law Thinks About Children*. Aldershot: Arena.

Leeco, E. (1996) 'Independent legal representation for children in custody and access cases.' *Family and Conciliation Courts Review 34*, 2, s303–319.

Monro, P. (1993) 'Children's representation – time for a change.' *Family Law 3*.

Monro, P. and Forrester, L. (1995) (2nd edn) *The Guardian* ad Litem. Bristol: Family Law.

NFM (1994) *Giving Children a Voice in Mediation*. London: NFM.

Piper, C. (1997) 'Ascertaining the wishes and feelings of the child: a requirement honoured largely in the breach?' *Family Law* (forthcoming).

Ray, P. (1993) SFLA Code of Practice – acting in the interests of the family. Speech delivered to the First World Congress on Family Law and Children's Rights, July, Sydney, Australia.

Richards, M. (1994) 'Giving a voice or addressing needs?' *Family Mediation 4*, 3, 13.

Ryburn, M. (1997) 'Welfare and justice in post-adoption contact.' *Family Law* 28–37.

Sawyer, C. (1997) 'The mature child – how solicitors decide.' *Family Law* 19–21.

Shear, L. (1996) 'Children's lawyers in Californian family law courts.' *Family and Conciliation Courts Review 34*, 2, 251–302.

Simpson, B. (1991) 'The Children Act 1989 and the voice of the child in family conciliation.' *Family and Conciliation Courts Review 29*, 4, 385–397.

SFLA (1996) (3rd edn) *Guide to Good Practice for Solicitors Acting for Children*. London: SFLA.

Thorpe, D. (1995) 'Some implications of recent child protection research.' *Representing Children 8*, 3, 27–31.

Timms, J. (1997) 'The tension between welfare and justice.' *Family Law* 38–47.

Walton, P. (1997) 'The guardian ad litem's independence.' *Family Law* 106–108.

Wyld, N. (1992) 'Children's participation – myth or reality?' *Journal of Child Law* April/June, 83–86.

Further Reading

Collins, Judge P. (1994) 'The voice of the child.' *Family Law* 396–397.

Di Bias, T. (1996) 'Some programs for children.' *Family and Conciliation Courts Review 34*, 1, 112–129.

Hamilton, I. (1995) 'Representation of children in private law proceedings under the Children Act 1989.' *Representing Children 8*, 3, 32–37.

Kroll, B. (1996) *Chasing Rainbows*. Lyme Regis: Russell House Publishing.

Rodgers, M. (1997) 'Changing names – who really decides?' *Family Law* 49–50.

Useful addresses

Advice, Advocacy and Information Service for Children and Young People (formerly Advocacy Service for Children)

1 Sickle Street
Manchester M60 2AA
Tel: 0800 616101

Association of Lawyers for Children

PO Box 2029
Buckhurst Hill
Essex IG9 6EQ
Tel: 0181 505 3900

Children's Legal Centre

University of Exeter
Wivenhoe Park
Colchester CO4 3SQ
Tel: 01206 872466

Family Law Bar Association

Bar Council
3 Bedford Row
London WC1R 4DB
Tel: 0171 242 0082

Family Rights Group

The Print House
18 Ashwin Street
London E8 3DL
Tel: 0171 923 2628

Independent Representation for Children in Need

23a Hawthorne Drive
Heswell
Wirral L61 6UP
Tel: 0151 432 7852

Law Society

Children Panel
Panel Administrator
Ipsley Court
Bermington Close
Redditch B98 0TD
Tel: 0171 242 1222
(same number for Law Society shop)

Legal Aid Board

Franchise Development Group
85 Gray's Inn Road
London WC1X 8AA
Tel: 0171 813 1000

National Family Mediation

9 Tavistock Place
London WC1H 9SN
Tel: 0171 383 5993

Solicitors' Family Law Association

PO Box 302
Orpington
Kent BR6 8QX
Tel: 0689 850227

A Voice for the Child in Care (Southern Office)

Unit 4
Pride Court
80–82 White Lion Street
London N1 9PF
Tel: 0171 833 5792

CHAPTER 5

Student Counselling

The Wailing Wall or a Force for Change?

Ann Heyno

Student counsellors are often seen as the unacceptable face of education – a symbol of its perceived failure. Their presence reminds institutions that we are all human and that education sometimes expects its students to be super-human. While it is acceptable for students to have practical problems, such as accommodation, poverty or poor job prospects, emotional problems can still be equated with failure and inadequacy. To name a problem can be experienced as depressing and unmanageable. The people who do talk about their problems have been described as a 'wailing wall' and, by association, student counsellors can also be experienced as unacceptable, the part of the institution some managers would most like to lose. The hope is that if you get rid of the counsellors you also get rid of the sense of inadequacy.

This association with pain, problems and failure is also common to many other caseworkers, especially those in the pressurized, under-resourced health and social services, too often regarded as a container/dumping ground for the underprivileged, unhappy, unwanted members of society.

A good and potent counselling service, like other caregiving services, can act as an important container of institutional anxiety and a reassuring source of support and advice. Provided that it is flexible, it can be a positive agent of change.

Adhesive learning

The idea of 'adhesive learning' came to me when I presented a paper to a conference in Barcelona in 1994. As a student counsellor and trainer of student counsellors, I was becoming increasingly aware that external factors such as unemployment, student poverty, increased student numbers and cuts in education were having an effect on the way students approached learning. I suggested that the market economy was in danger of producing a generation of students with an adhesive identification to learning rather than a truly internalized one (Bick 1968; Meltzer 1986).

We live in a culture which equates success with material gain. Personal worth is often seen in terms of a person's capacity to earn. The effect this has had on undergraduates is to make them highly competitive. As a result there are more students with exam anxiety, high stress levels, difficulties in relation to learning and suicidal thoughts. Many of the students we see are either too anxious to learn or too preoccupied with studying to do anything else with their lives. Many of them are struggling to keep themselves together on very little money and many are working and studying at the same time. For some of these students, education seems to have become a commodity and many have become desperate to get a qualification at any price. What I would like to suggest is that those students who do see education as a commodity are in danger of not allowing themselves to learn in any real sense of the word. Instead they are resorting to a superficial collecting of information in the hope that if they gather together enough of it they will get a good degree. A love of learning is replaced by an adhesive relationship to learning, in which what is learnt is 'stuck on' rather than absorbed and thought about.

This can also be true for general caseworkers who pile up their paper qualifications to ensure promotion and employer satisfaction. Bill was a former business person in his 40s whose return to education was part of a personal struggle to be more himself and less geared towards making money. For most of the time he studied successfully. However, at exam time he suddenly reverted to a business mentality in which success was everything and thought was impossible. He tried to apply the technique he had used to make money to study for his exams but it did not work. In this state of heightened anxiety, he failed his exams and this threw him into a quite severe depression from which he is currently recovering.

A range of other problems in student counselling arise from psychosexual distress and disturbances.

Pelvic affiliation in a perspex society

Recently a reviewer in a Sunday paper wrote about the latest phrase used in America to describe a sexual partner: pelvic affiliate. Later a radio interviewer introduced a short interview about a new craze which dictates that everything has to be perspex. The trend started with see-through, rather than metal, cans of coke and now there is even a demand for see-through vacuum cleaners, the idea being that you can only be sure your house is really clean if you can see the dirt being sucked up into the bag.

What I would like to suggest is that our current preoccupation with being open about everything to do with sex and sexuality has affected the unconscious minds of young people in such a way that many of them find it difficult to make satisfying emotional relationships. In some cases they become depressed, disturbed or suicidal, partly because of their despair about the possibility of not being able to form any sort of relationship.

I would also suggest that in our perspex society, the constant exposure in the media to every detail of the sexual and marital lives of our public figures is both a projection of primitive anxieties and a reflection of them. It is also an influence on the unconscious minds of young people in the way I have described. I believe that it expresses real unconscious anxiety about the nature of relationships and about the fragmentation of our capacity to relate to each other in a mature and loving way. Like children at play, society is acting out its anxieties through our public obsession with the minutiae of the sex lives and broken marriages of our politicians and our Royals.

On the one hand we live in a society which is apparently totally open about everything to do with sex and sexuality and, on the other, we are silent about the pressures that young people and students are under. This gives rise to the myth, to which I think many young people subscribe, that everyone everywhere is sexually active all of the time, the infantile fantasy of perpetually copulating parents (Klein 1929).

James told me he was worried that people would think him strange because he could not bring himself to have casual, sexual relationships, that is, part-object, pelvic affiliation. It was some months since he had broken off a long-term, unsatisfactory relationship which he had clung to since school and he was enjoying the freedom of being on his own. He explained that in his circle of friends, everyone had one-night stands and he could not understand why he did not feel able to do the same. In his opinion he was the only person in the country, other than a few religious people, who were not actively engaged in regular sexual intercourse most of the time.

I also think that society's more inhibited and unacceptable feelings about sexuality are often conveniently projected on to homosexual relationships. Public images of homosexual relationships tend to focus on promiscuity, disease and fears about the corruption of youth. The emphasis is on pelvic affiliate, part-object associations rather than on loving, long-term relationships, as if heterosexuality did not involve similar features. My feeling is that some of our anxieties about the most feared aspects of our sexuality are split off and projected on to homosexuality.

The market mentality has led us to believe that we can have anything we want as long as we want it enough. Sex and as many sexual partners, or pelvic affiliates, as we want are part of the deal. Many young people and students today have known no other culture. The perspex society provides the illusion that everything can be talked about when actually this is not the case and many people may need counselling to resolve their conflicts about their complicated feelings in relation to their sexuality.

Terrorists inside their heads

I would now like to describe several cases in which the terrorists inside students' heads are acted out in the form of uncontrolled and uncontrollable behaviour so that very little teaching and learning takes place.

For example, a final year student reported being less depressed, more integrated into his course and better able to socialize than he had been before he came for counselling. However, the day after his first paper, the picture changed dramatically. Jack was now despondent and pessimistic. His mind had gone blank and he had barely answered all the questions. Despite talking about the reasons for this, the pattern persisted throughout his papers and it was only after the exams were over that the reasons for the apparently meaningless sabotage became clear. Underlying his self-destructiveness was a perverse form of self-preservation. Deep down he was terrified of adulthood and of sexual relationships. If he passed his exams, he would no longer have his work as an excuse for not socializing, meeting girls and proving himself as a man.

Jack was sabotaging his academic success to avoid emotional and social development. His internal terrorist was stronger than his more conscious desire to succeed as a student. His conflict was further complicated by a fantasy that if he remained at home in a state of arrested development, he could save his parents' marriage from inevitable failure.

Here there is a situation in which it may have been appropriate to suggest a referral for mediation to improve communication in family relationships.

Elizabeth, a student in her early 30s, was another case linked to family conflict. She was having great difficulty with the creative and practical aspects of her course. At the time, she was in a relationship with a final year student on the same course who she felt was constantly criticizing her work. Ever since school, she had wanted to develop the creative part of herself and coming on the course represented this to her. Ever since childhood her father had encouraged her in the science subjects. Even now, she felt her father disapproved of her new career. In fact, he had had a very interrupted career himself and was apparently quite envious of his daughter's talents.

When my student realized this, she noticed that every time she talked enthusiastically to her father about the course, he looked bored and disapproving. She also realized that she had chosen a partner exactly like her father. However, when she recognized that she had some choice about allowing other people's disapproval to interfere with her creativity, her work improved quite noticeably. In this case it may not have been helpful to suggest mediation because of the nature of the emotional problems involved.

External events in students lives can also affect their studies. Nick, a mature student, was referred for counselling because a long-standing relationship with a fellow student had broken up within weeks of the course ending. He was in a very distressed state, he could not eat, he could not sleep and he could not study. Although he was one of the best students in his year, he could not concentrate enough to revise for his exams. He was furious with himself but he could not pull himself together.

In counselling Nick was able to work out that his distress at the broken relationship, and his fury at having to go on seeing his former girlfriend around the building, were being directed towards the one thing he really wanted, which was to get his degree. Once he had worked through some of his hurt and anger, he was able to free himself enough to revise and go on to get the 'first' for which he had hoped.

Shanti, an overseas student, also unable to study, came for help shortly after hearing that her grandfather had died while she was studying for her second year exams. Her parents had kept the news from her because they were worried in case it affected her exam performance. In the event, their over-protectiveness proved to be counter-productive. The student was so distressed by learning the news too late to attend the funeral, that she spent a large part of her final year unable to come to terms with what had happened and quite unable to study.

The educational struggle

Outside factors which are not directly related to the learning process can also have a considerable effect on it. Situations such as homelessness, financial hardship, broken relationships and bereavement can often get in the way of effective learning. Other students are affected by the learning process itself. After all, learning can be quite a persecuting activity. To learn something new students have to admit to themselves and to others what they do not know. Some students find this very worrying. Because lecturers are in a position of greater knowledge and students are in a position of being judged and graded, this can create anxieties about dependency and closeness. Rather than admit their lack of knowledge, some students will cover up the gaps, fail to ask questions and try to outwit the lecturer in an attempt to avoid humilia-tion. Avoidance of closeness of teacher/learner relationships can have its ori-gins in family problems. Again, with younger students, family mediation may be considered, depending on the feelings and wishes of the student, to help negotiate boundaries and decision making in relationships.

In other cases, the difficulty may hinge on the inequality of the relation-ship with the tutor. Some students are so envious of their lecturer's knowl-edge and position that they find it extremely difficult to take anything in or to produce anything in the form of essays or exams for fear of being found to be less knowledgeable than the lecturer.

Jane is an example of a student in her 40s who had problems of this nature which came to the surface just as she was leaving. Earlier, she had worked as a secretary but had found the experience humiliating because she felt she was just as good as, but far less recognized, than the people for whom she worked. So, she left her job to take a place on a law degree, where she almost dropped out because she was so envious of her lecturers. She had imagined that once she got her degree she would take her place as a senior member of her profession. When she realized that she was still only on the first rung of her professional ladder, she became very depressed and felt let down by eve-ryone.

Additionally, the locations and rituals of institutional life, whether in col-leges or universities, voluntary or independent health or social services, can be very confusing and off-putting experiences. Ali, a Mauritian student, was so disorientated and depressed by the end of the first term that the college doctor considered hospitalization. When I saw him he was very unhappy in-deed. He said he could not make a decision, could not concentrate and con-stantly felt dizzy. He complained of a pain in his back and confided that he thought he might be going mad. After listening to him talk over a period of several weeks, it became obvious that what he was suffering from was cultural shock and extreme homesickness. He desperately missed his wife and family and found London a cold and unfriendly place. He hated the food and found eating in restaurants far too expensive. He wanted to return home but was anxious about doing so when so much had been invested in coming to Eng-land.

Ali was a mature, highly successful student who had been sponsored by his company to do a post-graduate course in London. If he went home, he would have to face failure and disappointment. If he stayed, he would have to face intolerable unhappiness. Fortunately, the student survived Christmas with the help of the college doctor and an organization which places over-seas students in people's homes during the holidays. By Easter his depression had lifted. He was cheered up by the warmer weather and the lighter evenings. He was beginning to socialize and to familiarize himself with British culture and, importantly for him, he was beginning to be able to concentrate. His tutor phoned me in the last week of term and said he was likely to pass his exams and could return home with a sense of success rather than failure.

Here there may be a case for advocacy. Ali might consider a referral to a cultural support group which would provide advocacy for good accommodation and resources plus general improvement.

Student success is dependent on a great many different factors. A fear of success can interfere with academic progress. Difficult relationships with parents and emotional factors can get in the way of intellectual achievement. Anxiety about studying and things which happen in students' lives can impede progress, and institutions sometimes operate in ways which are unhelpful to the task of being a student.

In conclusion, we all have to learn to manage the internal and external conflicts of daily experience in our professional and personal work. Counsellors, like students, need support, as well as education and supervision. Although specific types of support come through groupwork and peer support, membership of advocacy associations which represent our own individual interests may be useful. Counsellors can also bring benefit through networking with mediators in conflict management services. These services have wide experience of the community and social situations in which people work towards social justice.

Counselling may be a wailing wall but it is certainly a force for individual and social change.

References

Bick, E. (1968) 'The experience of the skin in early object relations.' *International Journal of Psycho-Analysis 49*, 484–486.

Klein, M. (1929) 'Infantile anxiety-situations reflected in a work of art and in the creative impulse.' *International Journal of Psycho-Analysis 10*, 436–443.

Further Reading

Bell, E. (1996) *Counselling in Further and Higher Education: Counselling in Context.* Milton Keynes: Open University Press.

Bion, W. (1959) 'Attacks on linking.' *International Journal of Psycho-Analysis 40*, 308–315.

Coren, A. (1997) *A Psychodynamic Approach to Education.* London: Sheldon Press.

Halton, W., Heyno, A. and Noonan, E. (1988) *Student Success and the Institution.* Conference papers. London: City University.

Heyno, A. (1996) *Adhesive Learning, Culture and Psyche in Transition: A European Perspective on Student Psychological Health.* Conference paper. Rugby: Association for Student Counselling.

Heyno, A. (1994) *Pelvic Affiliation in a Perspex Society, Student Sexuality in a Changing Environment: Implications for College Staff.* Conference paper. London: Kings College London.

Klein, M. (1923) 'The role of the school in the libidinal life of the child.' *International Journal of Psycho-Analysis 5*, 312–313.

Klein, M. (1946/1963) *Envy and Gratitude and Other Works.* London: Virago.

Laufer, M. (ed) (1995) *The Suicidal Adolescent.* London: Karnac Books.

Meltzer, D. (1973) *Sexual States of Mind.* Perth: Clunie Press.

Meltzer, D. with Harris, M. (1986) *Family Patterns and Cultural Educability.* Perth: Clunie Press.

Noonan, E. (1983) *Counselling Young People.* London: Methuen.

Salzberger-Wittenberg, I., Henry, G. and Osborne, E. (1983) *The Emotional Experience of Learning and Teaching.* London: Routledge.

Spurling, L. and Noonan, E. (1992) *The Making of a Counsellor.* London: Routledge.

CHAPTER 6

Ending Bullying and Managing Conflict in Schools

Val Carpenter

I was challenged by the Milton Keynes Network to End Bullying, when I worked with them on the related language we use. This inter-agency network extended their thinking around bullying-related issues to take a holistic approach that encompasses many issues that contribute to bullying. They encouraged me to look at the term 'anti-bullying'. When I reminded myself that the words we use inform our thinking on issues, I recognized that the term 'anti-bullying' is in itself problematic. 'Anti' means to oppose someone, an attitude or opinion, to rival, so its use assists in setting up a climate whereby bullying can flourish. Within a competitive and violent society, being against something or someone (anti) is tantamount to being an invitation to be combative. Bullying comes straight out of such a culture. This chapter describes our work in seeking to prevent bullying.

A multi-oppression approach

The National Coalition Building Institute (NCBI) is an international leadership training organization dedicated to ending mistreatment of all. We train people from every field in the leadership skills of welcoming diversity, prejudice reduction, intergroup conflict resolution and coalition building. Our multi-oppression approach addresses every issue because we recognize that we will not end one area of mistreatment unless we end them all. People need the opportunity to make the connections between their own experience and that of others who are different to themselves. This is one of the reasons why our training models are particularly well suited to working with young people and adults on ending bullying.

As a member organization of Mediation UK, we have run workshops at the national conference for the past six years. These experiential workshops demonstrate how we can empower individuals to take initiatives for their own and others' rights by integrating the social justice commitments of political activists with the skills of dispute resolution practitioners. This strengthens awareness of the importance of emotional healing to reduce embedded prejudices and intergroup tensions.

Bullying can be just the usual name calling and abusive behaviour you would find in the average playground. But it can be because of a person's origins or beliefs. In fact *any* difference is a 'good' reason for one to pick on another. Who hasn't been singled out for their size, the fact that they wear glasses, have curly hair, freckles or a name that can be changed into something others think comical? Indeed, who has never targeted someone else in similar ways?

Most, if not all, of us have at some time been bullied. When we realize the sense of powerlessness our experiences brought, we can begin to understand how survivors feel and so to assist them to stand up for themselves. Moreover, most, if not all, of us have at some time in our life bullied. This does not make us 'bad' *per se*, but it does give us the ability to empathize with the perpetrator in order to understand and change what is going on for them. Theories of cycles of abuse – sexual abuse, child abuse, battered women – suggest that a bully now will once have been on the receiving end of mistreatment.

However, in NCBI we recognize that none of us are born a bully, racist or sexist, for that matter. We have to learn oppressive and damaging behaviour. Bullying is a learned response from adults, and the adult world is rife with bullying – in the home, the workplace, in education, in politics.

Scapegoating

Not to address ourselves to the wider picture leaves us scapegoating young people as the problem. They are not. The culture of our society is the problem. Every time young people get blamed for becoming bullies, that is, demonstrating they have learned the lessons society teaches, we are involved in scapegoating, which is in itself a part of bullying. We scapegoat when we feel bad about ourselves, and rather than own these feelings we hit out at others.

Neighbourhood young people took to hanging out in a residential cul-de-sac. The neighbours were incensed at the noise and crime. Finally, they went to the press to complain. The 'hordes' of young people turned out to be half a dozen. NCBI was called in to build bridges, and in listening to both groups it became clear that there was in fact no recent increase in neighbourhood crime, but that residents had an increased fear of it. The adults' response had been to hit out at suitable targets, the young people. However, the adults' stories told of *other times* they had been robbed or attacked by people on the streets. The young people, meanwhile, talked about having nowhere to go and being moved on as if they were criminals. 'We might just as well be criminals if that's all they think of us,' said one.

We are taught to hit out at others if we have been hurt. How many of us were encouraged to 'give as good as you get' by well-meaning parents? How many of us have espoused the same strategy with our own young ones? It is a strategy of no win–no win, that aims low for the immediate short-termism, that perhaps can leave a person feeling a bit better about themselves because they hit out harder than the original transgressor, but which actually sends both perpetrator and recipient on the downward spiral of low self esteem.

John's Mum is a lesbian. Classmates keep telling him his Mum is 'queer' and, with two Mums, they can't be a real family. Unlike John's family, theirs are the 'real families'. John professed to both his Mums that he took no notice and anyway, 'who cares about them?' However, beneath this front John was really hurting and he had taken to demanding money from a smaller class-mate. In the exchanges between John and his unlucky target for attention, John would say, 'anyway, you shouldn't be in this class, you're not big enough'. The place that he had been hurt – being told his family somehow wasn't enough – was exactly the place where he was hitting out at someone else.

Our schools' workshops start with a contract for the day. Invariably, a young person will put his or her hand up and offer 'no bullying' as a ground rule, to be quickly followed by 'including the teachers'. Bullying is a two-way process, and adults need to start with themselves in tackling the problem. One teacher provides an example:

> Steve was in despair following a staff training session on bullying. He left the training and immediately witnessed three teachers ignore a group of boys fighting and two girls attacking another with racist taunts. 'Then I walked into the staff room to be greeted by colleagues teasing each other. I'm at my wits' end to know where to start, or how. Videos, packs, reading lists, and T-shirts are all very well, but no one is being encouraged to look at their own behaviour. The truth is none of us know what we can do practically in any of these situations – other than resort to punitive action, let alone know how to translate our policy into a whole-school practice.'

The problem was all too evident. The staff needed help with their own experiences of bullying, and the powerlessness it left them with, before they could begin helping the students.

Bullying is endemic in society. Unless we recognize the extent of the problem we will not be effective because we will only attempt piecemeal responses. Implementing a whole-school peer leadership training programme means we are engaged in a systemic strategy that gives access to the skills for welcoming diversity, reducing prejudice and conflict resolution *to everyone*. A cohesive strategy can have a major impact on the culture of the organization, whilst operating an effective organizational team-building resource.

The first step is to encourage everyone to welcome and celebrate diversity – theirs and others. Allowing everyone to be welcomed because of, and not in spite of, their various identities replaces feelings of arrogance, shame or fear with a sense of real pride. When we feel respected we can relate to others with respect. The workshops are upbeat and always engender lots of laughter as staff and students quickly become excited by the prospect of creating a campus which is welcoming and 'home' to everyone.

Prejudicial attitudes arise when one takes in misinformation, often in the form of simplistic generalizations, about a particular group. Every distorted piece of information concerning another group is stored as a literal recording, very much like a record or CD.

Participants are asked to explore their first thoughts towards particular groups. With each taking a turn in pairs, one partner says the name of the group; the other partner, without hesitation, says his or her first uncensored thoughts. Sharing these thoughts in a large group, it soon becomes apparent that everyone has internalized negative recordings about other groups.

Once participants have aired many of the negative feelings towards their own groups, they can then more readily express authentic group pride. Many find that releasing the emotionally charged intragroup stereotypes allows them to overcome any resistance to claiming group pride.

A fundamental tenet of the NCBI prejudice reduction model is that human beings have to be mistreated systematically before they will mistreat others.

As we get mistreated as youngsters we often have no opportunity to heal or talk through what has happened to us. If we stay silent and carry the hurt around, it will come out later in an inappropriate way, often in the form of bullying. The NCBI approach takes this understanding and builds in the opportunity for healing. Every participant gets the chance to identify and heal the source of their own mistreatment, providing an effective intervention strategy since it is directed at the origins, rather than the symptoms, of mistreatment, enabling us then to make a decision of integrity.

Telling our stories

The most effective way to communicate the impact of discrimination is through the sharing of personal stories. When a person is afforded the rare opportunity to give voice to the experience of injury, the tale commands the group's attention and the stories are always compelling. Often, the listener is stirred to recall parallel experiences, which provide a strong identification with the storyteller. The purpose of personal storytelling is not to reduce all tough intergroup issues; however, one of the most effective ways to communicate a universal principle is to present the issue in human terms.

Several participants get the chance to share their experience of past mistreatment. This often becomes the turning point of the day because people begin to warm to each other as their humanity is unlocked by what they hear. Maryam, a 15-year-old young woman, recounted times when she had been hurt because she is shy. Many in the group were visibly moved as they listened, and as soon as the session had finished several of her classmates, including two who regularly picked on her, started for the first time to relate to her in a friendly and interested way.

Primary-level children are equally responsive, even though at first they might interpret 'past hurts' to be more physical than emotional. It takes a while before they may be ready to move on from recalling broken limbs and stitched heads to talking about the ongoing effect of being targeted for their names, race or what they look like. But when they do, it becomes an unforgettable experience for everyone. Staff are also spellbound and are often surprised we can hold the children's attention for each other for so long. Effective communication occurs because each member has a chance to speak and to listen.

Often it is impossible to listen to the painful experiences of others unless one is also afforded the opportunity to express one's own painful experiences. A climate is created that allows every participant to convey important information, and so there is a mutual investment in listening well. By listening to each other, groups come to the understanding that their experiences are more similar than they are different, therefore they are willing to work on behalf of each other:

> Leroy had been taunting other youngsters. His Dad, a single parent, is unable to afford the expensive trainers which many of his friends wear, and other youngsters were taunting him. He told his story, cried a bit, others did too, and they gave positive feedback for his courage in telling it. He sat down and then listened to Daren, who has a speech impediment, tell his equally moving story of how he gets mistreated

because he has a physical difference. When people were appreciating Daren, Leroy stood up and shakily said, 'I'm one of the people who calls you names, and I'm sorry I didn't realize it hurt as much as that, I won't do it again, and I won't let anyone else.'

This part of the workshop programme opens doors to many strong and lasting alliances.

Adultism and schools

Ten years ago schools struggled to mention bullying in case acknowledgement of it was perceived as admission of a serious problem and affected a school's reputation. We would ask the staff if there was a problem with bullying. Invariably we were told 'No!' As the day progressed, staff would come to us privately and say 'You know, this work is really going to help us with the bullying that goes on here'. Now bullying is openly discussed and every school is required to produce an anti-bullying policy.

However, like all other organizations that have an equal opportunities policy, many are struggling to translate their paper policy into a whole-school community practice. Often there is a description of what constitutes bullying, a checklist of what behaviour is or is not allowed, and penalties for bullies. Policies adorn walls and they may or may not be read, but they invariably depend on adult intervention.

Adultism

The core problem is that young people are undervalued because of adultism, the mistreatment of young people by adults. Within adultism there is an assumption that only adults will be able to take charge, make change, have the power to act, and so on. Actually it is a false premise.

Most bullying happens in the playground, toilets and on the school journey – all scenarios where school staff are not usually present. We need the very people who are present, young people, to be able to take action to intervene, to nip it in the bud.

NCBI's experience is that it's often the young people that have the ability to come up with the sharpest and most creative one-liners that stop the mistreatment in its tracks; responses that most of us only dream of in the bath or in the middle of the night three weeks after the event! Rukshana, a 13-year-old young woman, wears glasses and gets called 'four eyes'. After giving vent to her hostilities she turned to the person role-playing the perpetrator and with a sweetness and gentleness that absolutely floored the adults in the room, responded with: 'But if I didn't wear my glasses I wouldn't be able to see how beautiful you are!'

Three principles underlie NCBI skill training programmes. The first principle is dismantling the strangely consoling myth that bigots and people responsible for perpetuating various forms of discrimination are an unreachable, distinctive and fundamentally different group. The unsettling broader picture, that all of us harbour prejudices, is rarely considered. A measure of the self-righteous condemnation in reaction to another's bigoted comment may be traced to one's own insecurity. It is often easier to condemn another person than it is to face one's own prejudicial attitudes.

Approaches which stress a focus on the bully, as if 'the bully' is somehow different from the rest of us, set up a mythology of bullies. The bully becomes the other, an ogre who is unlike the rest of us. There is something wrong or lacking in this 'other' person. Painful as it may be, an effective strategy for intervention is built on reaching for a common humanity with those who express bigotry.

The second principle is adopting the attitude that prejudicial remarks are a call for help. When we bully others it is often an attempt to feel powerful ourselves, not to notice how frightened we feel, or a way to be popular and gain admiration from our peers. However, peer leadership programmes can change the culture so that it becomes cool to be a proactive champion of others.

Healing prejudicial recordings

So much attention is diverted to stopping the offensive comment at all cost that little consideration is given to the underlying forces which generate the behaviour. Expressions of bigotry have their origins in recordings of fear or injury. To stop a person from saying something bigoted may curtail an isolated effect but it does not address the underlying cause – the recordings which prompt the comments. Such recordings are healed by airing them. Instead of acting to silence the person, a more effective strategy is to employ a range of techniques designed to assist the healing of recordings, such as humour, careful listening and respectful questions.

The third principle is acknowledging that in attempting to heal the prejudicial recordings of others we must begin by tending to our own healing. Bigoted comments often trigger a reliving of our own painful experiences and thereby confound clear thinking in the present moment. In order to assist someone else, preliminary attention must be given to healing our own disturbing memories. Once the hostile feelings evoked by an oppressive comment are released we are better able to intervene and produce a number of creative responses.

The aim of NCBI programmes is to empower young people to respond and to take action against bullying, either for themselves or on behalf of the person targeted. The punitive action of adults only teaches the bully not to get caught again. Since punishment does not change attitudes, the goal of interventions is to offer skills and build people up to feel they have a sense of power and an investment in working for change.

Amelia, a ten-year-old, has red hair and freckles, and had been targeting Elena, a Jewish girl in her class. Other classmates however, called Amelia 'carrot head'. In the final session she got the chance to give vent to her hostilities and yell out how bad she feels when other children say these things about her. Once she had had a chance to think about the different strategies she might use, instead of not knowing how to react her response was a confident: 'Yes, I *am* different because of my hair. Has anyone tried to make you feel different too?' At the end of the workshop she and other young people said how good it had been to be able to share their feelings.

Most young people bullied at school tell no one either because they think nothing will happen or because they believe it will just compound the situation. Although they do not like it going on, most feel they do not have the confidence or skills to intervene.

Feelings of powerlessness create the reluctance of many people to work against bullying. Providing everyone with practical skills which give them even a small sense of control over their environment is the first step towards achieving greater institutional changes.

Vincent was an angry young man who kept interrupting as I was struggling to demonstrate the NCBI process for making effective interventions. His concern was that this process was a waste of time, and belittling. 'Yeah Val, that's all very well, but if anyone calls me "nigger", I'm not going to waste time on them, I'm just gonna take 'em out.' He was trying to communicate something really important to me and I decided to give him the space he was seeking. I asked him to tell me more, what had led him to think that would be a good move?

We all heard his story of being racially abused and beaten by white peers and adults. A large African-Caribbean heritage young man, who can look much older than his 15 years, many people behaved as if they were frightened of him. His response was to act frightening. He went on to tell of the many painful occasions he had been teased and abused.

I knew I had to address the daily reality for Vincent and his friends. I talked about the viciousness of racism, and then asked, 'Who would like to feel really good about themselves?' A sea of hands shot up. 'And who would like to feel really powerful?' Another sea of hands. I told them I wanted to teach them skills so that they could feel powerful *and* not have to hurt anyone.

After he vented his hostilities, Vincent was cheered on by everyone as he went on to make a great intervention: 'Hey man, what on earth did they do to you?'

When we know we can change someone we feel *really* powerful. (A self-reflective issue with which all caseworkers in the 'change business' need to be concerned.)

For many the issues are so overwhelming that it has been difficult to know how to begin. Often the greatest obstacle to taking action is the sense that individual initiatives have a minimal effect in light of the enormity of the problem. NCBI's strategy to overcome this key obstacle is to train teams of students and staff who reclaim power by leading concrete, replicable prejudice workshops in their school or college settings. By coaching this group to think of themselves as campus-welcoming diversity and prejudice reduction champions, we build a team that becomes a catalyst to effect deeper institutional changes.

Campus champions in welcoming diversity

Developing peer leadership teams to conduct welcoming diversity and prejudice reduction workshops is an effective organizational strategy and an effective teaching method for training campus leaders. When participants come to a training programme with the assumption that they are preparing to lead prejudice reduction workshops, their learning is both more rapid and more profound. The planning and conducting of the workshops reinforce the learning. The effective leading of campus prejudice reduction workshops requires each peer leader to be open to examining and working through his or her own prejudices. Thus the peer leadership team operates on the principle that one learns best by leading.

School or college life offers a powerful opportunity for human beings from diverse backgrounds to learn how to live together. By developing deliberate, systemic plans of action that foster healthy intergroup relations among all members of the campus community, it can become a model of good practice for our increasingly polarized society.

To change the culture of an institution we need a strategy that moves beyond piecemeal crisis intervention to foster an academic climate that views the diversity of the campus population as a valued learning resource. The peer training programme offers a constructive preventive alternative to crisis intervention.

School counsellors could also benefit by taking NCBI training and joining in our workshops, as they could learn more about how the deep emotional problems with which they are concerned can be caused by, or contribute to, the experiences of discrimination which we seek to prevent. Reciprocally, if students show prolonged pain on self-disclosure about discrimination, we might suggest to them that they should consider talking confidentially with their school or some other counsellor. NCBI supports and models co-operative networking.

Further reading

Bersag, V. (1989) *Bullies and Victims in Schools*. Milton Keynes: Open University Press.

Brown, C. and Mazza, G. (1992) *Peer Training Strategies for Welcoming Diversity on School, College and University Campuses*. Washington, DC: National Coalition Building Institute International, available from National Coalition Building Institute, Leicester.

Department of Education (1994) *Bullying: Don't Suffer in Silence. An Anti-Bullying Pack for Schools*. London: HMSO.

Munro, S. (1997) *Overcome Bullying – For Parents*. London: Piccadilly Press.

Community Education Development Centre (CEDC) (1996) *Tackling Bullying: Schools, Parents and the Community Working Together*. London: CEDC.

Useful addresses

Anti-Bullying Campaign

10 Borough High Street
London SE1 9QQ
Helpline: 0171 378 1446

Childline

A confidential 24 hour phone line for young people in trouble or danger
Helpline: 0800 1111

Kidscape

152 Buckingham Palace Road
London SW1W 9TR
Tel: 0171 730 3300

Kingston Friends Workshop Group

Quakers Meeting House
78 Eden Street
Kingston upon Thames KT1 1DJ
Tel: 0181 547 1197

National Coalition Building Institute, England

PO Box 411
Leicester LE4 8ZY
Tel: 0116 260 3232

National Coalition Building Institute, International

1835 K Street NW, Suite 715
Washington, DC 20006, USA
Tel: 001 202 785 9400

National Society for the Prevention of Cruelty to Children

43 Curtain Road
London EC2A 3NH
Helpline: 0800 800500

CHAPTER 7

Disability, Disabled People, Advocacy and Counselling

Colin Barnes

This chapter will address two principal questions: do disabled people need advocacy and counselling services and, if so, what form should those services take? It is divided into three separate but inter-related sections. The first examines two theories of disability: the traditional individualistic medical approach and the more recent socio-political perspective generally known as the 'social model of disability'. Drawing on the latter, the second section explores the process of disablement and its implications in terms of the advocacy and counselling needs of disabled people. The final part provides a critical evaluation of the growth of the advocacy industry and the self-help movement. It is argued that because of the increased complexity of the disability experience in late capitalist society, some disabled people may need access to specialist advocacy and counselling services, and that these services can best be provided within a social model framework by user-led organizations.

Changing perceptions of disability

There is overwhelming evidence that in most industrial and post-industrial societies the majority of disabled people experience severe economic and social disadvantage (Barnes 1991; Berthoud, Lakey and McKay 1993; Daunt 1991; Martin, Meltzer and Elliot 1988; Zarb 1995). In the broadest sense, there are two explanations for this disturbing state of affairs. The first, and the older of the two, is known as the 'individualistic medical' or simply the 'medical' model of disability. The second, and more recent, is generally referred to as the 'social model' of disability.

The former model finds expression in official definitions such as the World Health Organization's International Classification of Impairments,

Disabilities and Handicaps. Here, 'impairment' denotes 'any loss or abnormality of psychological, physiological, or anatomical structure or function'. 'Disability' is 'any restriction or lack (*resulting from an impairment*) of ability to perform an activity in the manner or within the range considered *normal* for a human being' and 'handicap' is a 'disadvantage for a given individual, *resulting from an impairment or a disability*, that limits or prevents the fulfilment of a role that is *normal* (depending on age, sex, social and cultural factors) for that individual' (Wood 1980, pp.27–29; emphasis added).

This and similar definitions are criticized for a variety of reasons, but mainly because they legitimate the view that perceived impairment is the cause of disability and the multiple deprivations associated with it. Here disability is the property of the individual; a 'personal tragedy' which can only be resolved by medical or rehabilitation intervention centred on the site of the problem – the disabled person (Oliver 1990, 1996).

Within this context, psychological adjustment to becoming disabled is usually explained in terms of 'bereavement', 'loss' or 'stage' theories. These maintain that the disabled individual must mourn the loss of his or her non-disabled status and in so doing pass through a series of emotional stages, such as shock, denial, anger and depression, before successful adjustment can take place. Movement is sequential, generally one-way, and the passage through each stage is usually determined by a professionally determined time frame and agreed criteria.

A product of the 'psychological imagination' dating back to Freud, Piaget and Erikson, such schemes continue to dominate medical and related professional thinking (Lenny 1993). This is despite the fact that there is little, if any, empirical evidence to substantiate their validity and a growing body of research showing that not all disabled people view their impairment(s) or the onset of disablement negatively (Campbell and Oliver 1996; Campling 1981; Morris 1989, 1991; Oliver and Hasler 1987; Sutherland 1981; Shakespeare, Gillespie and Davies 1997).

An important factor explaining the continued hegemony of these approaches is their professional and political expediency – both at the individual and structural levels. If individuals fail to achieve the anticipated professionally agreed goals, then the failure can be attributed to the disabled person's perceived inadequacy – whether it be physically or intellectually based, or both. The 'expert' is exonerated from responsibility, professional integrity remains intact, traditional wisdom and values go unquestioned, and the existing social order remains unchallenged (Barnes 1990).

The challenge to the medical model emerged in the 1960s and 70s with the politicization of disability by disabled people, their organizations and the emergence of what, today, is commonly known as the social model of disability. Building on personal experience rather than academic insights, the social model was initiated by a small but influential group of disabled activists (Union of the Physically Impaired Against Segregation (UPIAS) 1975, 1976).

In 1975 UPIAS, an organization controlled and run exclusively by disabled people, made the crucial distinction between impairment and disability. The former, in common with the traditional medical approach, relates to individually based bio-physical conditions; the latter is about the exclusion of disabled people from 'normal' or mainstream society. Thus disability is 'the disadvantage or restriction of activity caused by a contemporary social organization which takes no or little account of people who have physical impairments and thus excludes them from participation in the mainstream of social activities' (UPIAS 1976, p.14).

This definition was later broadened to accommodate all impairments – physical, sensory and intellectual – by other organizations of disabled people, such as the British Council of Organisations of Disabled People (BCODP), which is Britain's national umbrella for organizations controlled and run by disabled people (Barnes 1991) and Disabled Peoples' International (DPI), the international equivalent of the BCODP (Driedger 1989). Both BCODP and DPI were formed in 1981. The disabled writer Mike Oliver (1983) later referred to this new-found emphasis on the way society is organized as an explanation for disabled people's individual and collective disadvantage as the 'social model of disability'.

The social model is therefore a focus on the environmental and social barriers which exclude disabled people from mainstream society. It makes a clear distinction between impairment and disability; the former refers to *biological* characteristics of the body and the mind, and the latter to society's failure to address the needs of disabled people. It is a concerted attempt to draw attention to those aspects of disabled people's lives which can and should be changed – environmental and social barriers. It is not a denial of the importance of long-term illness or impairment(s), appropriate medical or psychological intervention or, indeed, discussions of these experiences. Nor is it an assertion that once the various barriers have been removed the problems associated with chronic illness or certain types of impairment will disappear – they will not. And, contrary to the recent assertions of some disabled and non-disabled writers (Crow 1996; Morris 1996), I have never met anyone or read anything that suggested otherwise.

Disability and disabled people

Nevertheless, for most non-disabled people becoming disabled is something to be avoided at all costs. Yet the process of disablement, or coming to terms with impairment and disability, is undoubtedly a relatively common experience. Recent official figures suggest that 40 per cent of the British population aged over 18 report having at least one 'long-term illness' or 'disability' and, in contrast to previous estimates such as the 1988 Office of Population Censuses and Surveys (OPCS) Disability Surveys (Martin *et al*. 1988), the figures are virtually the same for both women and men (Central Statistical Office 1996). It is unlikely, however, that the majority of these people would willingly identify themselves as 'disabled' unless they really had to.

This is hardly surprising given the degree of oppression and stigma encountered by disabled people in Western society. It is important to remember here that the social exclusion of disabled people is not a feature of all known societies. There is ample evidence that many, often less technically and socially complex societies, have responded positively to what we might consider as their disabled members (Hanks and Hanks 1980; Ingstad and Reynolds Whyte 1995). The oppression of disabled people is neither natural nor inevitable.

Yet throughout recorded history Western society has been clustered around a materialistic and hedonistic value system which, in a variety of ways, has prioritized individual self-interest and the pursuit of bodily and intellectual perfection. Its foundations lie in the ancient world of Greece and Rome; societies which were built upon slavery and characterized by patriarchy, elitism and violence. Indeed, the Greek quest for bodily and intellectual perfection, which can be traced back to 700–675 BC (Dutton 1996), was evident in proscribed infanticide for children with perceived abnormalities, in education, the Gymnasium and in competitive sports (Barnes 1991, 1996; Garland 1995).

In Greek culture, perceived abnormalities were associated with weakness, impotency and/or the outcome of divine retribution for sin and wrongdoing. Furthermore, following their conquest of Greece, the Romans absorbed and passed on much, if not all, of the Greek legacy to the rest of the known world as their empire expanded. Hence several of these traits are reflected in Judaean/Christian religions – often seen as the principal source of contemporary Western moral values (Giddens 1989). Biblical text is replete with references to impairment as a punishment for sin.

These ideas permeated both the culture of the Dark Ages and the medieval period, and were given a new-found legitimacy by the coming of capitalism and its accompanying ideologies: liberal utilitarianism and scientific rationality (Barnes 1991; Oliver 1990). Thus the nineteenth century witnessed the emergence of 'disability' in its present form. This includes the systematic individualization and medicalization of the body and the mind (Armstrong 1983; Foucault 1975); the exclusion of people with apparent impairments from the mainstream of community life into all manner of institutional settings (Scull 1984) and, with the emergence of 'social Darwinism', the 'eugenics movement' and, later, 'social hygiene', scientific reification of the age-old myth that, in one-way or another, people with any form of physical and/or intellectual imperfections pose a serious threat to Western society.

The logical outcome of all this was the proliferation of eugenic ideals throughout the Western world during the first half of the twentieth century (Jones 1987; Kevles 1985), and the systematic murder of thousands of disabled people in the Nazi death camps of the 1930s and 40s (Burleigh 1994; Gallagher 1990). It is important to remember, too, that Marxist communism is firmly rooted in the material and ideological developments which characterized eighteenth and nineteenth century Europe, and that many of its principal protagonists, both in Britain and overseas, embraced eugenic ideals as an essential corollary of the utopian hope for a better society. As has been well documented elsewhere, the legacy of much, if not all, of this remains with us today.

Indeed, the importance and desirability of bodily perfection and intellectual ability are endemic to Western culture. They find expression in genetic engineering, pre-natal screening, selective abortion, and the withholding and/or rationing of medical treatments to children and adults with perceived impairments; institutional discrimination against disabled people in education, employment, welfare systems, the built environment and the leisure industry; and the proliferation of 'able bodied' values and the misrepresentation of disabled people in the media (Barnes 1991, 1992, 1996).

Hence to be a disabled person means to experience a particular and pervasive form of social oppression or institutional discrimination. The problem is significantly more complex for disabled women, disabled people from minority ethnic and racial backgrounds, and disabled lesbians and disabled gay men. This is because in addition to disability they often experience other forms of institutional prejudice such as sexism, racism, heterosexism and institutionalized homophobia. There is little wonder, then, that for many people, coming to terms with the process of disablement and the ascription of a disabled identity can be a profoundly difficult and emotional experience.

However, in Britain as in most Western societies, there has, since the 1940s, been an unprecedented growth in service sector employment. This is attributable to several factors, including the decline of traditional manufacturing industries, the setting up and subsequent marketization of state welfare systems, enhanced consumerism and, of course, rising expectations among the general population in terms of civil, legal and social rights. A major feature of this development has been a huge expansion in advocacy and counselling-type services for all sections of the community, but particularly so for those who are perceived as the most vulnerable. The legacy of oppression summarized above, and the subsequent denial of many of the rights that the non-disabled public take for granted, ensure that disabled people are numbered among those groups.

Disabled people, advocacy and counselling

Advocacy

In the broadest sense, advocacy is about exerting influence within conventional structures of power. It is the presentation of arguments in support of a particular case, policy or reform by an individual or group to those with appropriate power and influence. The aim is to elicit some kind of favourable change, either for the advocate(s) themselves or for those they represent. Although they may take a variety of forms, there are only three types of advocacy – professional, voluntary and self – each of which has a relatively long history within the disability field.

Since at least the nineteenth century, disabled people have been surrounded by a veritable army of professionals and pseudo-professionals. Doctors, clinical psychologists, nurses, social workers, physiotherapists and others have, over the years, constructed their professional identities upon their supposed knowledge of disability: a knowledge which goes far beyond what would be considered appropriate medical or rehabilitation intervention. Sanctioned by the state and steeped in a culture that is necessarily wedded to the individualistic medical approach to disability, they form one of the most formidable barriers to disabled people's individual and collective empowerment.

This is evident by the fact that despite the rhetoric of advocacy, partnership and user involvement which permeates much of the most recent literature on professional intervention, professionals and their organizations have continually failed to support and implement policies designed to enhance disabled people's empowerment and have embraced those which compound their disadvantage. The 1986 Disabled Persons (Services, Consultation and Representation) Act, for example, instructed local authorities to consult and collaborate with organizations of disabled people in the planning and delivery of services. With one or two notable exceptions, this has not taken place (Bewley and Glendinning 1994; Warburton 1990). Most professionals welcomed the introduction of the 1990 NHS (National Health Service) and Community Care Act, because it expanded their role as gatekeepers to, and controllers of, community-based services. As with all present disability legislation, this Act is based on the medical model of disability and effectively ignores the call from disabled people and their organizations for a more holistic and realistic view of disabled people's needs (Barnes 1991; Finkelstein and Stuart 1996; Wood 1990). In short, professionals and the organizations they represent, whether they be in the state or voluntary sector, are dependent upon disabled people's continued dependence for their livelihood. Thus they are not, and never can be, independent of the system under which they operate and therefore their role as advocates is severely limited.

In many ways a similar situation exists for volunteers working for traditional disability organizations and charities. In the main these are organizations for disabled people controlled and run by non-disabled people. From the nineteenth century onwards, these organizations have claimed the moral high ground and, in the public mind at least, acted as advocates for various sections of the disabled community, if not the disabled population as a whole. Like their state-sponsored equivalents, they exist solely because of disabled people's perceived inadequacy and, in a variety of ways, have perpetuated this myth in order to justify their very existence. Probably the most obvious example is the way in which they exploit traditional myths and fears about impairment and disability through their fundraising activities and advertising campaigns (Hevey 1992). Moreover, besides continuing to promote and sponsor segregative facilities for disabled people, such as special schools, residential homes and so on, they did not provide meaningful support for the campaign for anti-discrimination legislation until the early 1990s, when it was clear that the campaign was unstoppable.

Furthermore, less than a month after the 1995 Disability Discrimination Act (DDA) entered the statute books, six of the largest charities, one of which is the Royal Association for Disablement and Rehabilitation, an umbrella organization for other similar organizations, elected to work with the government to implement the new law. The DDA is strongly opposed by organizations controlled and run by disabled people because it falls far short of what is needed to eradicate the problem of discrimination (Barnes and Oliver 1995; Gooding 1996; Northern Officers Group 1996).

It is this general failure of state and voluntary organizations to articulate the needs of disabled people as they themselves perceive them that has precipitated the recent and unprecedented growth of the self-advocacy movement. It is important to remember here that speaking for ourselves is something we all do every day of our lives and disabled individuals are no exception; they have been doing just that for centuries (Davis 1993). However, the legacy of oppression summarized above has meant that those voices have rarely been heard. This is no longer the case due to the politicization of disability by the recently emerged disabled people's movement.

In Britain the roots of self organization can be traced back to the 1890s with the formation of the British Deaf Association (BDA) and the National League of the Blind (Pagel 1988). But the movement really took hold in the post-1939–45 years, with the struggles for independence by disabled inmates in residential institutions during the 1950s and early 1960s, and the setting up of the Disablement Income Group by two disabled women in 1965 (Campbell and Oliver 1996). Inspired by events overseas – notably, the self-advocacy movement in Sweden (Williams and Shoultz 1982) and the setting up of user-led services by the American Independent Living Movement (De Jong 1983) the following decades saw an unprecedented growth in collective awareness and a proliferation of self-help groups and user-led organizations such as the Spinal Injuries Association (SIA) and the Derbyshire Coalition of Disabled People (DCODP).

Initially, the primary aim of these groups was to enable members to solve their problems themselves and not have them solved for them. One of their key functions was the provision of peer support services, including information, advice and peer counselling; indeed, the first Disablement Information and Advice Line was set up by disabled activists in Derbyshire in 1977. But because of the extent of the problems faced by members and the opportunities these organizations provided for them to express their views, a further aim quickly emerged: to identify the needs of the membership as a whole and to articulate them, both to statutory agencies and political parties, at both a local and a national level (Oliver and Hasler 1987).

Hence the disabled people's movement grew substantially during the 1980s and 1990s. For example, at its inception in 1981 the BCODP comprised seven member organizations; in September 1997 it represented 123 organizations, with a membership of over 300,000 disabled individuals (BCODP 1997). These range from large national impairment-specific organizations, such as the BDA and the SIA, to local coalitions and small groups, such as the DCODP. This growth is entirely due to disabled people themselves and was achieved without extensive financial support from either government or from traditional organizations for disabled people. The overwhelming majority of organizations of disabled people exist on a shoestring. Yet their influence has been unquestionable.

At the national level, besides leading the campaign for disabled people's rights, the BCODP and its member organizations have advocated a number of initiatives which benefit the disabled population as a whole. Probably the most significant example is self-operated personal assistance schemes. These enable a disabled person to employ a personal assistant (PA) or 'carer' to do the things they cannot do for themselves, thus eliminating their dependence on family, friends or the more expensive state-run services. The arguments for such schemes led directly to the setting up in 1987 of the hugely successful Independent Living Fund, and the introduction in 1996 of the Community Care (Direct Payments) Act, which enables local authorities to provide funding directly to the disabled individual wishing to employ a PA.

Other important initiatives include the development of Disability Equality Training (DET) programmes for disabled people, policy makers, professionals and employers, and the disability arts movement. Unlike disability awareness training, which is structured around the functional limitations of specific impairments, DET centres on the various social and environmental barriers confronting disabled people and strategies for their removal. Disability arts is a form of cultural advocacy produced by disabled artists, poets and musicians which provides an appropriate context for both disabled and non-disabled people to contemplate a disabled lifestyle. The spread of DET and the growth of disability culture is fundamental to the transformation of passive and dependent disabled individuals into active advocates of meaningful social change (Morrison and Finkelstein 1993).

The increase in direct political action by disabled activists provides another example of the growth of self advocacy among the disabled population. Frustrated by the pace of change, an increasing number have been taking to the streets in increasingly large numbers to draw attention to the problems disabled people face. Since the Rights not Charity march of July 1988, there have been a growing number of public demonstrations and civil disobedience campaigns by disabled people and their supporters up and down the country against a range of issues, including inaccessible transport, an inaccessible environment, the exploitation of disabled people by television companies and charities, and the poverty which accompanies impairment. In order to focus the public's attention on these and other injustices, disabled people are now prepared to risk public ridicule, arrest and even imprisonment (Campbell and Oliver 1996).

Counselling

Given the above, do disabled people need counselling services? The short answer is 'yes'. Everyday life in late capitalist society is increasingly complex and insecure; consequently many people, disabled or otherwise, may need some form of counselling or social support at some stage in their lives. It is also important to remember that disabled people are not a homogeneous group. While some have little difficulty in coming to terms with impairment and disability, others do not. So some form of specialist services is needed. In the broadest sense, these may be divided into two groups: formal counselling sessions provided by professionally trained counsellors in a formal setting, and the more informal counselling and advice-type services provided by peers and voluntary workers in the user-led organizations described above. Here I am concerned with the former.

It is clear that disabled people are no longer willing to put up with what professionals think is best for them. For instance, a recent review of counselling for people with acquired impairments due to injury found that most respondents felt that mainstream counselling services provided by psychiatrists and psychologists had little relevance to the issues raised by their new-found status. Yet nearly all felt that some form of counselling or emotional support would be beneficial for the newly disabled person (McKenzie 1992).

It is notable, too, that most professional counselling is provided by non-disabled people. Whilst there are arguments for and against disabled people being counselled by disabled counsellors – on the one hand, disabled counsellors may be viewed as too subjective, bringing their own experiences to the counselling table and on the other, non-disabled counsellors may be seen as too objective or distant because they have no personal experience of disablement – at present there is little choice. Disabled people find it very difficult to become professionally trained. Inaccessible premises, failure to provide training materials in accessible formats such as Braille and tape, and lack of understanding on the part of non-disabled tutors all contribute to the difficulties disabled people wanting to become counsellors encounter (Withers 1996). Since many disabled people do want counselling by trained peers, there is an urgent need for change in counselling training programmes.

Additionally, disabled people only have limited access to professionally trained counsellors. Often counselling services are only available in inaccessible premises and some counsellors are reluctant to do home visits. Also, counselling, unless it is provided by the NHS, is expensive, and more often than not disabled people do not have the money to pay for it. Even some of the larger voluntary organizations offering professional counselling services to disabled people and their families, such as the Association for Spina Bifida and Hydrocephalus, now charge commercial rates (Withers 1996). This means that disabled people have to go without or look to the often equally effective informal-type services provided by the user-led organizations discussed earlier.

But whatever form counselling takes, Joy Oliver, a professional counsellor, argues that its focus must be one of very consciously giving control back to the disabled person and enabling them to empower themselves through practical, emotional and social means. This is necessary as many disabled people have had difficult and often painful experiences at the hands of the medical and allied professionals, or in their families and interactions with the non-disabled world. Oliver rejects stage theories and suggests that there are several ways of enabling disabled people to empower themselves. These involve a humanist psychology and person-centred approach which enable people to explore their own situations and circumstances and the meanings these have for them.

Oliver's work with counsellors working directly with disabled people suggests that the social model of disability is one of the most effective ways of enabling disabled people to empower themselves. It helps them to see that many of the difficulties encountered are not impairment related, but the result of the way our society is organized. This attitude can and does empower the disabled person. Hence she maintains that all counselling training programmes should include some form of DET (Oliver 1995).

Conclusion

Clearly, the emergence of the disabled people's movement and the social model of disability has had a major impact on advocacy and counselling services for disabled people. Sadly, the need for such services is likely to stretch well into the twenty-first century. It is also evident that these services can best be provided within a social model framework and a user-led perspective. Therefore, sufficient resources must be made available to develop and expand these services further. Failure to do so will simply ensure that the dependency-creating culture of the past will continue to dominate the future.

References

Armstrong, D. (1983) *The Political Anatomy of the Body*. Cambridge: Cambridge University Press.

Barnes, C. (1990) *Cabbage Syndrome: The Social Construction of Dependence*. Lewes: Falmer.

Barnes, C. (1991) *Disabled People in Britain and Discrimination: A Case for Anti-discrimination Legislation*. London: Hurst and Co., in association with the British Council of Organizations of Disabled People.

Barnes, C. (1992) *Disabling Imagery and the Media*. Derby: BCODP.

Barnes, C. (1996) 'Theories of disability and the origins of the oppression of disabled people in Western society.' In L. Barton (ed) *Disability and Society: Emerging Issues and Insights.* London: Longman.

Barnes, C. and Oliver, M. (1995) 'Disability rights: rhetoric and reality in the UK.' *Disability and Society 10*, 1, 111–116.

BCODP (1997) Personal Communication, 17 September. British Journal of Organisations of Disabled People.

Berthoud, R., Lakey, J. and McKay, S. (1993) *The Economic Problems of Disabled People.* London: Policy Studies Institute.

Bewley, C. and Glendinning, C. (1994) 'Representing the views of disabled people in community care planning.' *Disability and Society 9*, 3, 301–315.

Burleigh, M. (1994) *Death and Deliverance: Euthanasia in Germany 1900–1945.* Cambridge: Cambridge University Press.

Campbell, J. and Oliver, M. (1996) *Disability Politics: Understanding Our Past, Changing Our Future.* London: Routledge.

Campling, J. (1981) *Images of Ourselves: Women with Disabilities Talking.* London: Routledge and Kegan Paul.

Central Statistical Office (1996) *Social Trends.* London: Central Statistical Office.

Crow, L. (1996) 'Including all of our lives: renewing the social model of disability.' In C. Barnes and G. Mercer (eds) *Exploring the Divide: Illness and Disability.* Leeds: The Disability Press.

Daunt, P. (1991) *Meeting Disability: A European Perspective.* London: Cassell Education.

Davis, M. (1993) 'Personal assistance: notes on the historical context.' In C. Barnes (ed) *Making Our Own Choices.* Derby: BCODP.

De Jong, G. (1983) 'The movement for independent living: origins, ideology and implications for disability research.' In A. Brechin and P. Liddiard (eds) *Handicap in a Social World.* Milton Keynes: Hodder and Stoughton in association with the Open University Press.

Driedger, D. (1989) *The Last Civil Rights Movement.* London: Hurst and Co.

Dutton, K. (1996) *The Perfectible Body.* London: Cassell.

Finkelstein, V. and Stuart, S. (1996) 'Developing new services.' In G. Hales (ed) *Beyond Disability.* London: Sage in association with the Open University Press.

Foucault, M. (1975) *The Birth of the Clinic; An Archeology of Medical Perception.* New York: Vantage Books.

Gallagher, H. (1990) *By Trust Betrayed: Patients and Physicians in the Third Reich.* London: Henry Holt.

Garland, R. (1995) *The Eye of the Beholder: Deformity and Disability in the Graeco-Roman World.* London: Duckworth.

Giddens, A. (1989) *Sociology.* London: Polity.

Gooding, C. (1996) *Disability Discrimination Act 1995.* London: Blackstone Press.

Hanks, J. and Hanks, L. (1980) 'The physically handicapped in certain non-occidental societies.' In W. Philips and J. Rosenberg (eds) *Social Scientists and the Physically Handicapped.* London: Arno Press.

Hevey, D. (1992) *The Creatures Time Forgot.* London: Routledge.

Ingstad, B. and Reynolds Whyte, S. (1995) *Disability and Culture.* Berkeley, CA: University of California Press.

Jones, G. (1987) *Social Hygiene in the Twentieth Century.* London: Croom Helm.

Kevles, D. (1985) *In the Name of Eugenics.* New York: Alfred A. Knopf.

Lenny, J. (1993) 'Do disabled people need counselling?' In J. Swain, V. Finkelstein, S. French and M. Oliver (eds) *Disabling Barriers – Enabling Environments.* London: Sage in Association with the Open University Press.

Martin, J., Meltzer, H. and Elliot, D. (1988) *The Prevalence of Disability Among Adults.* London: HMSO.

McKenzie, A (1992) 'Counselling for people disabled through injury.' In *Social Care Research: Findings No. 19.* York: Joseph Rowntree Foundation.

Morris, J. (1989) *Able Lives.* London: The Women's Press.

Morris, J. (1991) *Pride against Prejudice.* London: The Women's Press.

Morris, J. (ed) (1996) *Encounters with Strangers.* London: Women's Press.

Morrison, E. and Finkelstein, V. (1993) 'Broken arts and cultural repair: the role of culture in the empowerment of disabled people.' In J. Swain, V. Finkelstein, S. French and M. Oliver (eds) *Disabling Barriers – Enabling Environments.* London: Sage in Association with the Open University Press.

Northern Officers Group (1996) *The Disability Discrimination Act: A Policy and Practice Guide for Local Government and Disabled People.* Sheffield: Northern Officers Group.

Oliver, J. (formerly Lenny, J.) (1995) 'Counselling disabled people: a counsellor's perspective.' *Disability and Society 10,* 3, 261–281.

Oliver, M. (1983) *Social Work with Disabled People.* London: Macmillan.

Oliver, M. (1990) *The Politics of Disablement.* London: Macmillan.

Oliver, M. (1996) *Understanding Disability: From Theory to Practice.* London: Macmillan.

Oliver, M. and Hasler, F. (1987) 'Disability and self help: a case study of the Spinal Injuries Association.' *Disability, Handicap and Society 2,* 2, 113–126.

Pagel, M. (1988) *On Our Own Behalf: An Introduction to the Self organization of Disabled People.* Manchester: Greater Manchester Coalition of Disabled People Publications.

Scull, A. (1984) *Decarceration* (2nd ed) London: Polity Press.

Shakespeare, T., Gillespie Sells, K. and Davies, K. (1997) *The Sexual Politics of Disability.* London: Cassells.

Sutherland, A. (1981) *Disabled We Stand.* London: Souvenir Press.

UPIAS (1975) *Policy Statement.* London: UPIAS.

UPIAS (1976) *Fundamental Principles of Disability.* London: UPIAS.

Warburton, W. (1990) *Developing Services For Disabled People.* London: Department of Health.

Williams, P. and Shoulltz, B. (1982) *We Can Speak for Ourselves.* London: Souvenir Press.

Withers, S. (1996) 'The experience of counselling.' In G. Hales (ed) *Beyond Disability.* London: Sage in association with the Open University Press.

Wood, P. (1980) *International Classification of Impairments, Disabilities and Handicaps.* Geneva: WHO.

Wood, R. (1990) 'Care of disabled people.' In G. Dalley (ed) *Disability and Social Policy.* London: Policy Studies Institute.

Zarb, G. (1995) *Removing Disabling Barriers.* London: Policy Studies Institute.

Further reading

Brandon, D. with Brandon, A. and Brandon, T. (1995) *Advocacy – Power to People with Disabilities.* Birmingham: Venture Press.

Davis, A. (1989) *From Where I Sit: Living With Disability in an Able Bodied World.* London: Triangle.

Douglas, M. (1966) *Purity and Danger.* London: Routledge and Kegan Paul.

Gramsci, A. (1971) *Selections from the Prison Notebooks.* London: Lawrence and Wishart.

Hunt, P. (ed) (1966) *Stigma: The Experience of Disability.* London: Geoffrey Chapman.

Macfarlane, I. (1979) *The Origins of English Individualism.* Oxford: Basil Blackwell.

Nicholli, O. (1990) 'Menstruum quasi monstruum; monstrous births and menstrual taboo in the sixteenth century.' In E. Nuir and G. Ruggiero (eds) *Sex and Gender in Historical Perspective.* Baltimore: Johns Hopkins University Press.

Rieser, R. (1992) 'Stereotypes of disabled people.' In R. Rieser and M. Mason (eds) *Disability Equality in the Classroom: A Human Rights Issue.* London: Disability Equality in Education.

Ryan, J. and Thomas, F. (1987) *The Politics of Mental Handicap* (revised edition). London: Free Association Books.

Shakespeare, T. (1994) 'Cultural representations of disabled people: dustbins for disavowal.' *Disability and Society 9,* 3, 283–301.

Tooley, M. (1983) *Abortion and Infanticide.* New York: Oxford University Press.

Useful addresses

British Journal of Organisations of Disabled People (BCODP)

De Bradlei House, Chapel Street
Belper, Derbyshire DE56 1AR
Tel: 01332 295551 Minicom: 01733 828195
Fax: 01773 829672

CHAPTER 8

Couples Counselling

Gillian Walton

Working with couples, or with an individual, whose prime concern is a current relationship which is experienced as problematic, is something of an art form. To do it successfully and effectively involves having a substantial tool kit of skills from a variety of disciplines. Besides advocacy, counselling, systemic family therapy and mediation, there are teaching, knowledge of history, sociology, literature and, perhaps above all, the skill of having been able to put oneself in the role of service user.

Couples therapy lies at a nodal point between many other disciplines, and the effective couples counsellor needs to have the imagination, power of lateral thinking and lightness of touch to move between them. This is not to say that marital therapy is not a separate and special discipline in its own right; it is. Working with couples is beginning to emerge as a separate and legitimate way to approach people in trouble as a primary intervention when once it was tagged on to individual, group or family therapy.

Perhaps this was not surprising since couples present in a multiplicity of roles – as individuals in trouble (sometimes emotionally ill), as parents bringing worries about their children, as children of their own parents or with concerns about their experience of other family members. They present with concerns about work, with confusion about the difference between role and person, or with questions about the organic basis of sexuality and sexual functions. Sometimes they feel oppressed by the pressures of their professional lives and working environment. The examples I shall give illustrate how these complex issues impinge on the couple relationship and lead to it being used as the gateway through which many people enter counselling.

Development of couples counselling

In my view it is impossible to locate couples work exclusively in any one theoretical area, and this stems partly from its origins as a profession. The first people to write about their work with couples in the UK were from the Family Discussion Bureau (FDB). They began to be active after World War II, in the early post-war period when, as after World War I, there were very significant changes, in particular regarding the role of women in families. These changes had become enshrined in law in the nineteenth century in the Married Womens' Property Act and continued in the twentieth century with female emancipation (not fully implemented until 1928), and their impact on national consciousness was growing.

The post-war education reforms, reforms in health care and the concomitant social mobility, and changes in long-established communities gave family and marital breakdown an increasingly high profile. The incidence of divorce was increasing and families were easier to limit in size. Most of the original members of the FDB – later to be known as the Institute of Marital Studies and now as the Tavistock Marital Studies Institute – were social workers. Some later trained as Jungian analysts, but all had experience of working with families on a practical as well as a psychological level. The titles of their early books emphasize the social work origins, for example, *Social Casework in Marital Problems* (Bannister 1955). These workers were pioneers, moving resolutely against the trend of individual psychoanalysis which, by and large, saw concentration on marriage or relationships in a patient as a means of avoiding the real work of psychoanalysis.

Since those early years, the influence of classical and mainstream psychoanalytic theory has been added to with the early works by Klein (1975a, b). Particularly influential was the object relations school, together with Bowlby (1969) and his work on attachment theory. Henry Dicks, a psychiatrist who had a particular interest in couples, produced his book *Marital Tensions* in 1967. In it he explored the hypothesis that the marital relationship, partly because of the societal significance of a legal underpinning, was a place where people could, within a safe container, explore some of the unconscious issues which preoccupied them. Dicks (1967) was particularly interested in projective systems within marriage. Perhaps the nursery rhyme 'Jack Spratt' provides a simple illustration of this basic theory of projection within a couple relationship:

Jack Spratt could eat no fat
His wife could eat no lean
So between the two of them
They licked the platter clean.

Jack Spratt ate only lean, Mrs Spratt ate only fat. Together they were content, each doing something of value for the other. Only when tastes changed would there be any difficulty, and at this stage possibly the couple might look for counselling.

The marriage guidance movement

The marriage guidance movement, like the FDB, came from a concern about how people lived in a society, and in an important way had some of its roots in advocacy. It came to birth pragmatically, to address concerns which had arisen in the earlier twentieth century about perceived changes in marriage and family life, such as those mentioned above. The concept of 'companionate marriage' was beginning to be recognized as early as 1909 and took root as the century progressed. This, I suggest, had a profound effect on the way couples were treated therapeutically.

Marie Stopes and some of the earlier radical feminist writers raised the matter of power issues between men and women. In its early days the marriage guidance movement was especially concerned with education, particularly in the sexual area. Essentially its early workers were educators and communicators who facilitated discussion about intimate matters and so empowered people, and especially women, to take control of their own lives in the light of their expressed needs, especially in the most intimate areas of sexuality and fertility.

At first marriage guidance counsellors always saw couples singly, and only married couples. I can only think that although it became enshrined as a therapeutic principle that couples should not be seen together, it arose from some sense of fear on the part of the worker of being swamped, or from the premise that a couple consisted of two very separate individuals whose worlds overlapped only on a conscious and pragmatic level and whose best interests were probably going to be conflictual.

Training and trainees

The growing emphasis on the companionate marriage, the gradual development of a body of theory devoted specifically to work with couples, and the introduction of concepts from family therapy, have all contributed to a change of practice in couples work. In tandem with all the changes have come the development of a new profession of marital therapy and training programmes which have both reflected and led the field.

In an interesting way, the development of the marital and couples counselling profession has provided in itself a means through which its practitioners can gain a professional status where some of them might not have expected to do so. The qualifications for work in this field have not historically been based only on academic qualifications, although many practitioners are highly qualified in this way, but on the life experience of the would-be trainee. This has been a means of empowering people, especially women, to aggregate this life experience and to use it as the basis of further learning.

The training programmes for marital work vary from institution to institution. Relate, formerly the National Marriage Guidance Council, still trains volunteer counsellors free of charge in return for their working with service users. The training is partly based on a distance learning model, with six residential weekends during the course. The Tavistock Marital Studies Institute offers a diploma in Marital Psychotherapy at the end of a three-year part-time course. Its roots lie in psychoanalytic psychotherapy and trainees are required to be in intensive psychotherapy or analysis themselves. London Marriage Guidance has a three and a half-year diploma course based on psychodynamic principles, externally validated by an academic institution, and is the only couples course currently accredited by the British Association for Counselling. As well as the psychodynamic base, the London Marriage Guidance course explicitly integrates systems thinking with the psychodynamic.

Whether implicitly or explicitly, it is, I would suggest, impossible to view the couple as an entity for therapy or counselling in isolation from the family system or, indeed, to view any family system in isolation. It is essential to be aware, too, of the societal framework in which this system operates. The couple must be seen as part of an interlocking system contingent upon other social systems. It is helpful if trainees for marital work have the knowledge, experience and maturity to accommodate this, and the flexibility to take in a variety of approaches to couples work.

Methodology and who are the couples

Counselling, while it is a distinct discipline, will embrace advocacy and mediation also, for the very reasons previously mentioned. Nobody arrives at a counselling session with no context, and it is the role of the counsellor to take account of the context and to make sense of what people talk about in the light of the growing experience the counsellor has of working with them.

Couples who bring their marriages or very close relationships to a counsellor are acting with great courage. It is much easier to bring oneself and metaphorically throw bricks at the absent partner and so preserve the illusion at least that it is all the fault of the other. While of course the partner's complaint and his or her pain are attended to and taken very seriously by the counsellor, arguably the most important quality of any couples counsellor (second to the ability to be empathic) is the ability to be neutral and to build up a picture of interaction with any absent partner. Neutrality is of course very important when both partners are present. Inevitably many couples in conflict wish to draw the counsellor in as advocate for their own point of view, and when there are three people in the room with the complex relationships involved, it is a real art to preserve the therapeutic space necessary for thinking.

Couples are generally working on central or core issues. They often broadly cluster around two sets of polarities: the first is concerned with love and hate, masculine and feminine, intimacy and isolation, and the second involves addressing these systems: intrapsychic, interactive and intergenerational.

Love and hate, basic human emotions stemming from passion and very close to one another, are present in most couples in conflict, although when the conflict has been present for a length of time the emotions can become cold rather than being hot and the hate can turn to a sense of indifference, inertia or resignation. Gender issues, masculinity and femininity are present in all people and are issues with which all couples struggle. Generally, couples chose one another at an unconscious level to work on these issues and the counsellor needs to be very aware of the meaning of this for him/herself. The closeness/distance polarity is universal. It has to do with how people normally defend themselves and it is a healthy area for exploration. Where the difficulty to achieve a comfortable place is based on more deep-seated and painful experiences, couples often seek help to make sense of it.

To address the second of these systems involves an understanding of individual psychological development and psychopathology in order to have a sense of the individual make-up of each person. Counsellors are trained to attend to their own responses to couples and to interpret them in the light of couples' inner world and experience. For instance, if a counsellor feels judgemental or opinionated having heard a partner's story, having first taken account of that aspect of his or her own make-up, it might then be possible to see this as a feeling induced by the particular person and almost certainly part of his/her inner world.

Possibly he or she was used to being judged or criticized from an early age; is self-critical and critical of others. The interactional system is in the room if both partners are present and can be experienced by the therapist. Fighting, indifference, criticism, denigration, over-compliance, over-caring and crowding with withdrawal, to name but a few of the dynamics between couples, can be observed and understood by the counsellor. These provide a window into the wider experience of the couples – into other social relationships, at work and, perhaps above all, in their families of origin.

The intergenerational issues connect the intrapsychic and the interactional. The couple's inner world and inner figures from the deep unconscious are projected primarily on to the actual people with whom the primary relationships are experienced, above all the parental couple. The combination of the archetypal mother and father, masculine and feminine, and the experience of the actual relationship with the parent forms the template for the choice of partner.

One of the most important tasks a couples counsellor faces is to help the partners in the couple to distinguish between what is attributed to the actual partners and what comes from the unconscious or from earlier experience of a parent. Perhaps the link between this process and advocacy and mediation is that in helping couples to distinguish between these phenomena, the counsellor is facilitating them to take more control of their lives and to make a protest where it is appropriate. The aim of all therapy is a search for truth, and work with couples is no different in this respect.

For counsellors working psychodynamically an essential basis is self knowledge, for only to the extent to which it is possible to be honest with ourselves is it possible to help couples move forward in this search. The most important means of communication is from the unconscious, in the use of transference and counter-transference. While personally very much favouring a psychodynamic model, my bias is towards one that is flexible enough to be eclectic for the reasons discussed earlier. Basic skills of listening, empathy and summarizing are the bedrock in creating a therapeutic environment. Systemic interventions, such as reframing, use of metaphor, active intervention to raise or lower affect and prescriptive suggestions, are especially useful in working with couples, as are use of art work and sculpting.

In couples work, when two people are present this is a very complex task for one counsellor who, except in work with couples of the same gender, is inevitably at risk of seeming to be allied to or having a greater sympathy with the partner of the same gender. Where the focus of the case is in this area, there is a strong clinical indication for using conjoint therapy – that is, a couple, preferably a heterosexual couple, working with the client couple. Experience suggests that the unconscious issues emerge more quickly and powerfully in this setting, and it has the additional advantage of providing on-the-spot supervision of one or other for the therapist couple. A colleague pair can model couple communication; in the counter-transference they can provide insight about the interaction of the couple; gender issues can be explored more safely and a very effective therapeutic container can be provided.

Couples where there is a very strong projective system in operation, or who are in a state of great distress, can find an effective advocate in one of the therapists, even if there is hostility experienced in the relationship with the other. In that sense one of the therapist pair can act as advocate for the partner and enable him or her to be heard. Deep and fundamental issues can of course be addressed in couples work where there is one counsellor, and especially those concerning the early three-person relationship, Oedipal issues, sibling rivalries and sharing. The counselling room is often the first situation in which it emerges as safe to be part of a threesome and that in itself is a transforming experience.

I shall give examples of work with two couples, one seen by a counsellor working alone and the other in conjoint therapy.

Michael and Rachel

Michael and Rachel came into therapy fearing that their four-year-old marriage was on the point of breaking down. The sexual relationship had not existed since the birth of their son, James, three years earlier and the degree of Michael's anger was frightening Rachel, who responded by immersing herself in mothering James. The couple had met at university, been instantly attracted and lived together soon afterwards. Their marriage had followed after about two years and James had been conceived unintentionally. Michael is from the Antipodes. He is the youngest of six children and his mother left home suddenly when he was very small. He did not see her again for many years, and he experienced his father as cold and punitive. Rachel is the younger of two sisters, always the rebel and aware that her father in particular favoured her more compliant sister. Her escape from her family was through an academic life and Michael's was by leaving his country of origin. Both had experienced severe psychological distress in the past, and in the present there was a strong fear of breakdown which they defended against by a bright, strong demeanour.

As they arrived for sessions they would enquire about the health of the therapist, remark on the décor or the weather. This was how they had both learned to cover up the neediness they both felt. By making an effort to please, Rachel was trying to avoid being ignored or passed over by the therapist as she had been by her parents in favour of her sister, and Michael was trying to avoid the abandonment he had experienced earlier. These intergenerational issues had been further revived by Michael's rejection by Rachel's family, who do not approve of him, and by his rejection by Rachel in favour of James. Rachel's need for control in her present family, thereby focusing strongly on James to the exclusion of Michael, was driven by the wish not to be the excluded one as she had been in her family of origin, but rather to project this onto Michael.

The intrapsychic issues of fear, sense of wretchedness and, above all, fear of dependency were stirred up by the arrival of James, as they frequently are when new babies arrive, and these also contributed to the interactive issues in the relationship. The main interaction was fighting and bickering which effectively meant that intimacy was being successfully avoided. Painful though this was, it had the effect of reducing the danger of them becoming attached and dependent. If they avoided this, they might also avoid the abandonment or exclusion they each most feared and had experienced earlier.

Bearing in mind the complexity of the analysis of the case, it was important that the worker bore in mind the importance of maintaining neutrality and of interpreting to the couple what were their fears in this area. Work on the interaction was carried out, together with empathic listening to their stress.

At first there was a very strong positive transference which the couple clung to as a defence against being disapproved of or rejected by the therapist, but this gradually loosened, especially when they missed a session and the issue of paying for it was raised. Once basic trust had been established it seemed important to do some active parenting of these two quite regressed partners while still affirming them as an adult couple. The sexual area had been brought as an early problem, and on exploration it transpired that James was being used as a 'distance regulator' by sleeping in their bed.

In the session the partners discussed how they might alter this and this discussion empowered them to become the couple, with James as the third person, and so to return to their original vision of themselves as the powerful couple which they had on first meeting. Not surprisingly both Rachel and Michael were in working environments which felt oppressive, and as they became more assertive as a couple and as sex was resumed they were able to approach their work more effectively. In the counter-transference it was important that the female counsellor, while being an accepting motherly figure, could be challenging and strong enough to model for the couple the possibility of experiencing conflict and surviving it. It was fairly long-term work, and the closure involving the withdrawal of the counsellor from the threesome, leaving the couple as the effective unit, was a very important part of the therapeutic process.

Pat and Geoff

Pat and Geoff are a couple in their late 50s who are facing retirement. Geoff is a minister of religion who has had an active ministry and been a strong influence on many others. He is an extrovert man with a warm manner and a twinkle in his eye. Pat, his wife, is quiet and seems depressed and worried about retirement, both on her own behalf and on his. She has devoted herself to being supportive to Geoff and to their four successful, now grown-up, children and is now beginning to want to develop her own career as a painter of some talent.

It transpired that the couple have not had any sexual contact for ten years and this is assuming more importance now that they are facing being alone together more. Geoff feels angry about this and blames Pat. Pat finds it very difficult to talk about sexual matters and wonders if there is a physiological basis to the problem, since she has experienced pain on intercourse in the past.

This couple were seen in co-therapy by a male and female co-therapy pair. Although Geoff was consciously wanting to express his sexuality, the female therapist had little sense of this in her counter-transferential response to him and the male therapist felt equally sure of Pat's ambivalence. In systemic terms, this suggested that the ambivalence about sexual expression might be shared and that one partner, Pat in this case, might be expressing it on behalf of both partners. Pat's withholding was her way of making a protest about her feelings about being abused by the Church system by which their lives had been gripped, as well as by Geoff, who seemed to want her now that he was losing his grip on his job. On further exploration it emerged that Geoff was not sexually confident and that he had suffered from premature ejaculation in the past, leaving Pat unsatisfied. This couple, who were very competent in all ways and whose life had been devoted to looking after other people, had not found it possible to ask for the help they needed, a common phenomenon in the caring professions.

In this case there was an intergenerational aspect, as both Pat and Geoff's parents were involved in public life. The relationship between the institution of the church and the institution of marriage has been explored by Mary Kirk and Tom Leary in *Holy Matrimony* (1994), and this has application to similar professions which absorb those who work in them. It is helpful for practitioners to be aware of this, and Pat and Geoff's therapists explored with them the relationship between the church and their marriage and how in particular they had used it to conceal the part of themselves they found difficulty in expressing. Using a behavioural programme, they were able to resume their physical relationship, to explore their own desires and preferences, and to ask for things rather than always giving and feeling resentful underneath.

Working in depth with couples requires extensive practical knowledge, skills, training and supervision. Although counsellors may use advocacy and mediation skills, advocates and mediators would not have the relevant experience to help couples at this level. However, couples counsellors might well suggest that one or both partners would benefit by attending mediation subsequent to a course of counselling. It is important that professionals from all disciplines are well informed about each other's particular expertise and value the contribution colleagues can make.

References

Bannister, K. (1955) *Social Casework in Marital Problems: The Development of a Psychodynamic Approach.* London: Tavistock.

Bowlby, J. (1969) *Attachment and Loss.* London: Hogarth.

Dicks, H. (1967) *Marital Tensions – Clinical Studies Towards a Psychological Theory of Interaction.* London: Routledge.

Kirk, M. and Leary, T. (1994) *Holy Matrimony.* London: Lynx Publishing.

Klein, M. (1975a) *Love, Guilt and Reparation and Other Works 1921–1945.* London: Hogarth.

Klein, M. (1975b) *Envy and Gratitude and Other Works 1946–1963.* London: Hogarth.

Further reading

Burgoyne, O. and Richards, M. (1987) *Divorce Matters.* London: Penguin.

Useful addresses

London Marriage Guidance Council

76a New Cavendish Street
London W1M 7LB
Tel: 0171 580 1087
Fax: 0171 637 4546

Relate Marriage Guidance (administration)

The Warden's House, 46 Crowndale Road
London NW1
Tel: 0171 380 1463

CHAPTER 9

Family and Elder Mediation

Yvonne Joan Craig

Tony and Jill were fighting over her mother, Agnes, with chronic arthritis who lived with them, invading their privacy and dominating their children. Tony began locking Agnes in her room at weekends. Jill, considering separation, asked her social worker for help, who became involved with family counselling and mediating, as well as advocating disability support for Agnes, in order to prevent family breakup.

This chapter considers what family and elder mediation can offer in this area of 'public issues and private pain' (Becker and MacPherson 1988), suggesting where casework should include counselling and advocacy, or when these should be the first, or perhaps only, referral. The chapter briefly describes salient aspects of some of the major organizations involved, and case illustrations are given.

Social advocacy for family solidarity and bonding, at a time when it appears increasingly fragmented, is currently causing problems for caseworkers, as well as being promoted by groups concerned about remoralizing society (Parton 1994).

Others prefer wider definitions of cohabiting partnership as a preferred relationship norm, and Lena Dominelli and Eileen McLeod in *Feminist Social Work* (1989) are among many women caseworkers who point to the unjust exploitation of women in keeping families intact.

Janet Finch and Jennifer Mason, in *Negotiating Family Responsibilities* (1993), stress that most people only acknowledge moral guidelines, not strict rules, and that 1983–89 research showed that there was no consensus about dealing with family conflict. A requirement for mediators is that they avoid persuasion as 'moral agents' (Siporin 1992) in 'moral management' (Hudson 1995), as do caseworkers in domestic disputes, including those in possible elder abuse, where concern for an exhausted 70-year-old carer has to be balanced with that for a demented 90-year-old parent.

There is also ambivalence about the use of legal advocacy regarding divorce, separation and visitation rights for children, as this has been viewed as an adversarial rather than amicable way of dealing with sensitive relationships, as general advocacy may be sometimes (Chandler 1990), although Christine Piper has written about the value of legal remedies in an earlier chapter. Nevertheless, the Lord Chancellor has institutionalized counselling and mediation within the new divorce legislation, offering these processes as recommended first options, on a voluntary basis, to broken families.

From the social constructionist perspective, these recent developments have also been seen as a cost-saving way of providing superficial second-class justice (Freeman 1984), which leaves untouched the deeper socioeconomic infrastructural causes of family disintegration, including poverty, poor housing and pressures of dual employment. In this view images of parents as guilty failures are constructed to offset those of a failing society.

There is strong feminist pressure for the use of both social and legal advocacy in the protection of families who suffer from domestic abuse, as is shown in the women's refuge movement and police domestic violence units. Also, the pioneering work of Age Concern's Action on Elder Abuse (AEA), relating to the plight of vulnerable elders who are mistreated at home and in institutions, points to the need for legal protection. Nevertheless, in this area also there is evidence that counselling and mediation can play supplementary roles in finding the least painful ways of separating or reconstructing conflicting relationships (Knight 1992; O'Leary 1996; Terry 1997).

To add to this complexity, advocacy organizations such as the Carers' National Association also offer training courses in counselling and mediation as well as advocacy, while a Relate caseworker is called a 'mediator counsellor' in a recent book (O'Hagan 1986, p.219). So boundaries overlap in practice, and caseworkers may become involved with various roles and skills in response to the needs of service users.

They may have a problem, as did the social worker in the introductory case, about whether to maintain unifying support or to refer to separate agencies. However, as Agnes, Jill and Tony wanted to keep family troubles private, their caseworker used her advocacy, counselling and mediation skills, but was supported in these through networking with local services and consulting with their workers.

The growth of family mediation services in the United Kingdom

In American family mediation, which developed earlier, many lawyers became mediators, but in Britain advocacy, mediation and counselling have been shaped separately, although always self-critically (Davis 1988).

However, in support of the argument that mediation can be safely complemented with legal advocacy and counselling, it is significant that it was in the Bristol Family Court that conciliation services were pioneered in the late 1970s (Parkinson 1986). Probation officers, then called divorce court welfare officers (Howard and Shepherd 1987), took training in mediation and counselling, and worked with family solicitors in the context of what are now called Family Proceedings Courts.

The alliance between mediators and solicitors has also been formalized outside the court system through the development in 1982 of a Solicitors Family Law Association, promoting mediation by lawyers. This was joined in 1988 by the Family Mediators' Association, where there are joint professional partnerships to ensure legal rights are maintained but in a more therapeutic setting.

Here these two elements of empowerment are held together in the view that serious family conflict calls for crisis intervention: 'conciliators can be catalysts for constructive planning during this crisis period ... The crisis theory of mental health...suggests that if sufficient support is available, the crisis can be an opportunity for change' (Parkinson 1986, p.127). Crisis management means negotiated casework (Barber 1991).

Family mediation has also been developed in another framework by workers associated with another Bristol initiative which established the first out-of-court conciliation service there. They evolved the most comprehensive social model using trained volunteers, and eventually paid qualified workers, in establishing the national voluntary organization, National Family Mediation (NFM) in 1992, founded in 1981 as the National Family Conciliation Council (Fisher 1990), as was the Scottish Association of Family Conciliation Services (Garwood 1990).

NFM is the main agency chosen by the last Lord Chancellor for offering services to those affected by the new divorce legislation. It is also concerned with children's rights to be involved in family decision making about visitation and other issues, and has pioneered specialist counselling courses on this (Dasgupta 1996). In addition it has developed extensive codes of practice and lists of conciliation competences in collaboration with the other main agencies involved (Fisher 1990, pp.165–170).

Although NFM works with solicitors, the roles of its mediators are kept discrete. Marian Roberts, the NFM training officer, considers that for mediators to practise therapeutic intervention raises 'grave ethical concerns within the field of family therapy itself' (Roberts 1990, p.15).

Simon Roberts, a legal anthropologist, considers that therapeutic intervention in trying to 'correct pathological elements in the relationship' is 'fraught with serious hazards, and is potentially extremely harmful when practised in close association with attempts at joint decision-making' (Roberts 1988, pp.145, 149).

This discussion is at the core of issues about referring cases of family and intergenerational conflict to mediation or counselling. Simon Roberts (1986) advocates mediation as a *minimal* form of social intervention at a time when agencies are felt by service users to be making intrusive and unwanted examinations of their lives. Mediation is offered as a voluntary, non-coercive, time and depth-limited process (Lindstein and Meteyard 1996).

It is recognized that counselling is important in family conflict, on a separate basis before, after or co-existing with mediation. An example illustrates this, although none of the cases in this chapter come from the agencies cited:

> Pam and Eric were a middle-aged couple married 12 years, with two young children. Eric had a small business, the failure of which kept him away from home and dependent on alcohol. Pam was a social worker emotionally exhausted by casework and family care. They quarrelled increasingly and decided to separate, wanting mediation for agreements about maintenance and visitation.
>
> Eric arrived drunk at the interview, saying he wanted alcoholism treatment and mediation. Pam wanted counselling. The mediators enabled the couple to negotiate their own agreements in a problem-solving not blaming way. These were ratified by lawyers, with external ongoing counselling.

This case illustrates the collaboration of mediators, counsellors and lawyers, and the couple learning to converse constructively, eventually negotiating reunion.

Domestic abuse

Mediation is generally inadvisible in situations involving domestic violence, especially when restraining orders fail (Buzawa and Buzawa 1996), although it can offer useful complementary interventions and preventive processes. Girdner (1990) advocates mediation for screening and its helpfulness in triaging cases: those benefiting; those harmed by it; those needing associated protection:

Naomi and Sam were involved in an abusive situation. She attacked verbally; he assaulted physically. For religious reasons, and as they both worked for a voluntary organization, they did not want the police to become involved. Lawyers suggested mediation, with the couple living apart. Eventually the couple decided to reconstruct their relationship, with a strict written agreement including warnings about future exclusion and non-molestation orders which mediators facilitated.

Jean Wynne refers to domestic violence in Chapter 12 on victims and offenders, which links with elder abuse, here considered later.

Developing British elder mediation

The multicultural Elder Mediation Project (EMP, for empowerment) of Mediation UK is recognized by social gerontologists (Craig 1992, 1994, 1996, 1997a) but less by health and social services.

The acronym EMP focuses on empowering older people in self determination, indicating that it is not an empire-building organization, although associated with the British Society of Gerontology, the Centre for Policy on Ageing, AEA and all the major ageing advocacy organizations.

EMP's modest aim is to model social dissemination of its ideas (Mohrman and Lawler 1984) through training workshops offered freely to all agencies concerned with older people, to community mediation services and to old people's clubs. Since 1991 many workshops have taken place, including ones in Asian and Afro-Caribbean clubs, as EMP has co-workers with Hindu, Jewish, Muslim, Sikh, Zoroastrian and Christian backgrounds.

As EMP's ethical principles are based on non-oppressive good practice, and as many disabled people are elderly, EMP also offers services to disability groups, supporting the British Council of Organisations of Disabled People and its RIGHTS NOW advocacy campaign.

EMP's main work, apart from its training workshops, is in practical mediation. As the demographic increase of elders leads to more associated ageing agencies, inter- and intra-organizational conflicts are bound to occur, as the next part of this section shows.

Organizational conflicts

As EMP supports, but does not compete with, other organizations, it can impartially mediate intra- and inter-agency disputes, prior to possible disciplinary action, which do not come within the province of unions (although their representatives may sometimes have roles).

Cases can involve bitter interpersonal disputes between chairs and officers of committees, staff hierarchies and in co-ordinating services internally and externally.

Often, misattributions, fuelled by insecurities, jealousies and gossip, are corrected in face-saving ways, affirming the positive contributions participants make to organizational welfare. This recalls the superordinate goals of their collective achievements, empowering them to find remedies for grievances through co-operative, if critical, negotiation of relevant rights and responsibilities.

Mediation, a transparent process, helps organizations to increase their own transparency and the respect, loyalty and solidarity of their staff and members (Acland 1990; de Dreu and van de Vliert 1997).

Working with AIMS

Age Concern's Advisory, Information and Mediation Service (AIMS), led by a lawyer experienced in housing law, is committed to mediation in appropriate situations, and its collaborative potential with legal advocacy. Residents struggle with contractual intricacies before and after signing leases, and conflicts occur when expectations are unfulfilled, increasing service needs are unmet and difficulties develop with overclose neighbours.

Conflicts between residents, and with managers and wardens, often refused earlier by the housing ombudsman, are referred to AIMS. The following case involved an EMP caseworker:

> Jim was a litigious tenant of a small housing charity who had for ten years been battling with it, the council, the ombudsman and his MP about unfair service charges, with no one conceding his demands. He sent AIMS a caseload of fine, faint writing on thin paper, requesting mediation. After hours of reading and contact with the charity's chairman, also elderly, mediation was arranged. Jim vented pent-up fury, seeing he caused the chairman equal distress. Mutual appreciation led to cooler problem-solving, and mediation enabled both to agree on adjustments, provided Jim stopped complaining and paid future bills regularly. Mediation resulted in two winners.

Mediating in the community

EMP's mediation with individual old people is especially valuable in the sensitive area of family troubles where, for instance, a single daughter aged 60 may be looking after an incontinent mother of 80, yet may be too embarrassed to discuss conflicts with kin, especially those who have a moralistic or suppressive approach (Mayer and Timms 1970).

We old people are generally concerned not to burden families, increasingly preferring to maintain independence in the community, despite sometimes having lonely and isolated lives. So relationships with neighbours are critical:

> Kathleen, a childless widow, lived in a slum area where local ideology sandwiched 'respectable' elders between 'problem' youngsters in small flats within old houses with insufficient soundproofing. Kathleen's life was made hell by an unemployed black youth playing rock music throughout the night. Her social worker suggested mediation. Both neighbours were visited, Marcus complaining of her racist taunts.

The neighbours had never conversed before, and when Kathleen realized that Marcus was orphaned, she sympathetically said she hated racism but was sleepless. Marcus said this had also troubled his granny, agreeing to stop musicmaking at night. Kathleen offered to buy him earphones for Christmas. She later phoned saying Marcus had come to Sunday lunch and did her shopping.

This story is typical of 80 per cent of cases in early mediation before conflict hardens and relationships congeal in embittered patterns, leading to different outcomes, as the next illustration shows:

> Viju and Usha, living in a multitenanted estate, had neighbours with addiction problems, previously evicted, who threw rubbish in their porch, spoiled window boxes and had male visitors throughout the night. The old couple complained to the council and local law centre, calling the police occasionally, nobody helping, but their local tenants' association suggested mediation. Their neighbours refused, complaining about curry smells, until Viju applied for an eviction order, when they begged for mediation. Through shuttle diplomacy, mediators recognized the couple wanted court action through fear of strategic temporizing, explained this to the neighbours, offering a counselling referral which they refused.

Mediation and elder abuse

Elder abuse is an increasing social problem; British writers (Biggs 1993; McCreadie 1991; Pritchard 1992) following American pioneers (Breckman and Adelman 1988; Pillemer and Wolf 1986) in recognizing unresolved conflict's contribution to complex aetiologies.

We old people, proud war survivors, loyally support families, bear neglectful, harmful behaviour and avoid reporting this to medical and social workers. Although some abusers have criminal pathology, others may be dysfunctionally over-stressed in complicated circumstances where the minimal intervention of mediation enables problem-solving not blaming ways of preventing recurrence:

> Tom, a grief-stricken widower, lived with his single-parent daughter. Working long hours she could not control her two boys' passion for gunshooting TV films. When Tom screamed for quiet, she shut him in a cupboard. Neighbours hearing his cries called the family doctor and he suggested the community mediation service might help. Mediation encouraged the daughter to apologize for hasty mistreatment, the boys to understand bereavement and offer to turn the volume down, and Tom to share his pension more generously with all three.

Social psychologists such as Karen Rook (1989) describe the importance of not violating relational norms through damage limitation, and *Communication and Relational Maintenance* (Canary and Stafford 1994) provides theoretical justification for viewing mediation as a co-operative process enabling people to reconstruct relationships.

Three other related books of interest to caseworkers with old people are *Communication, Health and the Elderly* (Giles, Coupland and Weimann 1990), *Interpersonal Communication in Older Adulthood* (Hummert, Weimann and Nussbaum 1994) and *Communication and Aging* (Nussbaum, Thompson and Robinson 1989). Each of these shows how the personal and social identities of old people continue to develop self worth and achievement if their relational processes are good. Mediation is one such dialogic and co-creative relational process (Buttny 1993).

Mediation is essentially an ethical process which Moody calls a 'micro level analysis of justice' (1992, p.53) between people, although his work also endorses egalitarian constructive communication as critical to the development of distributive justice or macro justice. From this perspective, mediation is an appropriate ethical process to use in contributing to the prevention of elder abuse because of its advocacy for social justice.

Also in relation to elder abuse, the empowering process of mediation is strengthening in helping old people to develop resistance to 'learned helplessness' (Seligman 1975), which too often characterizes us in dependent relationships, fearful of losing support. Its philosophy is portrayed in *Changes and Challenges in Later Life* (Craig 1997b) as affirming the abilities of old people to face problems and giving us confidence to deal with them:

Victoria had been to an EMP workshop in her library club where she enjoyed role-playing dealing with a dispute. Months later she rang saying she had become frightened by her son's growing aggressive financial harassment of his sister, suspecting his early use of drugs: should she talk with them as she had learned with EMP? Mediation was offered, but she wanted to try first. She took them out to a nearby park, listened while her son confessed to past drug debts, and helped them reach an agreement that her daughter would stop loans, her son would take counselling, and she would terminate their sub-tenancies in their flatlets in her home if trouble restarted.

Unfortunately, the most serious cases of elder abuse remain hidden, and physical, emotional, mental and financial harm damage people so severely that strong protection is required, difficult though it is to find that which is adequate and appropriate. However, mediation may have a limited role in screening cases, or also in negotiating agreements when practical reconstitution of caregiving is necessary.

Mediators, like all caseworkers, have much to learn about the tragic complexities of elder abuse, and this will be a continuing concern in EMP's future work.

The future of family and elder mediation

The organizations described are heavily dependent on personnel and funding, and EMP volunteers are ageing. EMP would be glad for one of the national organizations concerned with old people to incorporate elder mediation into their existing advocacy, counselling and other services, so that EMP could wither away, its social diffusion work done.

This would also be a practical model of one of the themes of this chapter, that these three processes and their shared and different skills can be generally integrated within social organizations, even though it is also important to maintain distinctly separate specialist associations which ensure high ethical standards, accredited good practice, and ongoing learning and training in their areas of professional competence.

It is in the best interests of older people, and all age populations, for competitive systems to be replaced by co-operative ones, and the interdisciplinary drive for collaborative caregiving (Hornby 1993) is a social objective which is fully consistent with that of mediation.

References

Acland, A. (1990) *A Sudden Outburst of Common Sense.* London: Hutchinson Business Books.

Barber, J. (1991) *Beyond Casework.* Basingstoke: Macmillan.

Becker, S. and MacPherson, S. (1988) *Public Issues and Private Pain.* London: Social Services Insight Books.

Biggs, S. (1993) *Understanding Ageing.* Milton Keynes: Open University Press.

Breckman, R. and Adelman, R. (1988) *Strategies for Helping Victims of Elder Abuse.* London: Sage.

Buttny, R. (1993) *Social Accountability.* London: Sage.

Buzawa, E. and Buzawa, C. (1996) *Do Arrests and Restraining Orders Work?* London: Sage.

Canary, D. and Stafford, L. (eds) (1994) *Communication and Relational Maintenance.* New York: Academic Press.

Chandler, S. (1990) *Competing Realities.* New York: Praeger.

Craig, Y. (1992) 'Elder mediation.' *Generations Review 2,* 3, 4–5.

Craig, Y. (1994) 'Elder mediation: can it contribute to the prevention of elder abuse and the protection of the rights of elders and their carers?' *Journal of Elder Abuse and Neglect 6,* 1, 81–96.

Craig, Y. (1996) 'Elder mediation project.' *Elders 5,* 2, 16–24.

Craig, Y. (1997a) *Elder Abuse and Mediation – Exploratory Studies in America, Britain and Europe.* Aldershot: Avebury/Ashgate.

Craig, Y. (1997b) *Changes and Challenges in Later Life.* London: Third Age Press.

Dasgupta, C. (1996) 'Child counselling.' *Family Mediation 6,* 1, 12.

Davis, G. (1988) *Partisans and Mediators.* Oxford: Clarendon Press.

de Dreu, C. and van de Vliert, E. (1997) *Using Conflict in Organizations.* London: Sage.

Dominelli, L. and McLeod, E. (1989) *Feminist Social Work.* London: Macmillan.

Finch, J. and Mason, J. (1993) *Negotiating Family Responsibilities.* London: Tavistock.

Fisher, T. (ed) (1990) *Family Conciliation within the UK.* Bristol: Family Law.

Freeman, M. (1984) *State, Law and the Family.* London: Tavistock.

Garwood, F. (1990) *Divorce, Counselling and Conciliation Services in Sweden and Scotland.* Edinburgh: Scottish Association of Family Conciliation Services.

Giles, H., Coupland, N. and Weimann, J. (1990) *Communication, Health and the Elderly.* Manchester: Manchester University Press.

Girdner, L. (1990) 'Mediation triage.' *Mediation Quarterly 7,* 4, 365–372.

Hornby, S. (1993) *Collaborative Care.* Oxford: Blackwell Scientific Publications.

Howard, J. and Shepherd, G. (1987) *Conciliation, Children and Divorce.* London: Batsford.

Hudson, J. (1995) 'No solution, thank you!' *Professional Social Work* March, p.4.

Hummert, M., Weimann, J. and Nussbaum, S. (1994) *Interpersonal Communication in Older Adulthood.* London: Sage.

Knight, B. (1992) *Older Adults in Psychotherapy*. London: Sage.

Lindstein, T. and Meteyard, B. (1996) *What Works in Family Mediation*. Lyme Regis: Russell House Publishing.

Mayer, J. and Timms, N. (1970) *The Client Speaks*. London: Routledge and Kegan Paul.

McCreadie, C. (1991) *Elder Abuse*. London: Age Concern Institute of Gerontology.

Moody, H. (1992) *Ethics in an Aging Society*. Baltimore MD: Johns Hopkins University Press.

Morhman, A. and Lawler, E. (1984) 'The diffusion of quality of life as a paradigm shift.' In W. Bennis, K. Benne and R. Chin (eds) *The Planning of Change*. New York: Holt, Reinhart and Winston.

Nussbaum, J., Thompson, T. and Robinson, J. (1989) *Communication and Aging*. New York: Harper and Row.

O'Hagan, K. (1986) *Crisis Intervention in Social Services*. London: Macmillan.

O'Leary, E. (1996) *Counselling Older Adults*. London: Chapman and Hall.

Parkinson, L. (1986) *Conciliation in Separation and Divorce*. London: Croom Helm.

Parton, N. (1994) 'The nature of social work under conditions of (p)modernism.' *Social Work and Social Science Review 5*, 2, 98–112.

Pillemer, K. and Wolf, R. (eds) (1986) *Elder Abuse*. Dover, MA: Auburn House.

Pritchard, J. (1992) *The Abuse of Elderly People*. London: Jessica Kingsley Publishers.

Roberts, M. (1990) 'Systems of selves.' *Journal of Social Welfare Law 10*, 1, 3–19.

Roberts, S. (1986) 'Towards a minimal form of intervention.' *Mediation Quarterly 11*, 25–41.

Roberts, S. (1988) 'Three models of family mediation.' In R. Dingwell and J. Eekelaar (eds) *Divorce, Mediation and the Legal Process*. Oxford: Clarendon Press.

Rook, K. (1989) 'Strains in older adults.' In R. Adams and R. Blieszner (eds) *Older Adult Friendship*. London: Sage.

Seligman, M. (1975) *Helplessness*. San Francisco: W.H.Freeman.

Siporin, M. (1992) 'The moral basis for a radical reconstruction of social work.' In P. Reid and P. Popple (eds) *The Moral Purposes of Social Work*. Chicago: Nelson-Hall.

Terry, P. (1997) *Counselling the Elderly and their Carers*. Basingstoke: Macmillan.

Further reading

Craig, Y. (1995) 'EMPowerment: not EMPire-building.' *Generations Review 5*, 1, 7–8.

Phillipson, C. and Biggs, S. (1992) *Understanding Elder Abuse*. London: Longman.

Useful addresses

Age Concern Action on Elder Abuse

Astral House
1268 London Road
London SW16 4ER
Tel: 0181 764 7648
Fax: 0181 679 4074

Age Concern Advisory, Information and Mediation Service (AIMS)

Walkden House
3–10 Melton Street
London NW1 2EJ
Tel: 0171 383 2006
Fax: 0171 383 3614

Elder Mediation Project

27 Ridgmount Gardens
London WC1E 7AS
Tel: 0171 580 9706

Mediation UK

Alexander House
Telephone Avenue
Bristol BS1 4BS
Tel: 0117 904 6661
Fax: 0117 904 3331

National Family Mediation

9 Tavistock Place
London WC1H 9SN
Tel: 0171 383 5993
Fax: 0171 383 5994

CHAPTER 10

Mental Health Advocacy

David Brandon

This chapter begins with a brief look at the long history of mental health advocacy. It examines the vigorous growth of a variety of different methods and some contemporary obstacles. It gives an example of one long-term psychiatric survivor, Rosemary, and finishes by detailing some possible future developments.

History

Perhaps rather surprisingly, mental health advocacy has been long established. As early as 1620, a pamphlet, now lost, called *The Petition of the Poor Distracted People in the House of Bedlam* was published (Brandon 1991, p.13). John Perceval, the lunatic son of the murdered British Prime Minister in the nineteenth century, called himself 'the Attorney General for Lunatics'. In 1841, he acted as a peer advocate for a Dr Pearce, then a patient in the criminal section of the Royal Bethlehem (Bedlam) Hospital (Brandon 1995, p.103). Four years later, along with a group of acquaintances, he founded the Alleged Lunatic's Friends Society. Its aim was to 'stir up an intelligent and active sympathy, on behalf of the most wretched, the most oppressed, the...helpless of mankind, by proving with how much needless tyranny they are treated' (Brandon 1991, p.19). Our ignorance of history means that such processes need re-inventing every few decades, usually repeating major mistakes.

MIND's important pressure group work, begun in the 1970s and 1980s, inspired by its director, Tony Smythe, focused initially on *legal advocacy*. A series of individual cases taken up by Larry Gostin and others tackled serious abuses in the services. Gostin took important cases, especially of patients incarcerated in the infamous Broadmoor special hospital, to the High Court and often on to the European Court of Human Rights in Strasbourg. His successes established basic rights for patients, particularly about consent to treatment, and had a major impact on the 1983 Mental Health Act.

Gostin also saw the need for different sorts of advocacy: 'persons working within the mental health services to ensure that recipients ... are not deprived of their rights as citizens under the current or proposed laws' (Gostin 1975, p.131). One consequence was the opening of a number of citizens advice bureaux based in mental hospitals (King's Fund 1986). Another important trend was the development of lawyers specializing in mental health issues – legal mental health advocacy.

The World Federation for Mental Health conference in Brighton in July 1985 was a major stimulant. Present was the world's best known psychiatric survivor, Judi Chamberlin, who warned of dangers inherent in partnership and co-operation with professionals (Chamberlin 1988, p.69):

> Those groups that did not exclude non-patients from membership almost always quickly dropped their liberation aspects and became reformist ... group members began to recognize a pattern they referred to as 'mentalism' or 'sane chauvinism', a set of assumptions which most people seemed to hold about mental patients: that they were incompetent, unable to do things for themselves, constantly in need of supervision and assistance, unpredictable, likely to be violent or irrational. (Chamberlin 1988, p.71)

Mixed together with this heady conference brew, important and enduring contacts were made with colleagues and patients, especially in the Netherlands, which had a much more developed advocacy system. There, already there were professional patient advocates in the vast majority of mental hospitals, as well as patients' councils. Pioneering services in Nottingham were not only based on visits to Holland but their first paid advocate, Wouter van de Graaf, was a well-known Dutch psychiatric survivor.

By 1987, the self-advocacy group, Survivors Speak Out (SSO) was demanding rights for mental health survivors. These stressed that mental health service providers

> recognize and use people's first-hand experience of emotional distress for the good of others ... A Government review of services, with recipients sharing their views ... provision of resources to implement self-advocacy for all users ... facility for representation of users and ex-users of services on statutory bodies ... full and free access to all personal medical records ... provision to all of full written and verbal information on treatments, including adverse research findings. (SSO 1988, p.8)

These demands characterized the flowering of a considerable self-advocacy movement, with groups in many major towns. At the same time MINDLINK developed, based on MIND's regional offices and run by service users. One of its main campaign points concerned moving away from chemotherapy to counselling.

Obstacles

The increasingly influential advocacy movement 'involves a person(s), either an individual or group with disabilities or their representative, pressing their case with influential others, about situations which either affect them directly or, and more usually, trying to prevent proposed changes which will leave them worse off' (Brandon 1995, p.1). Classically, Rose and Black argued that mental illness treatment should be replaced with models based on advocacy and empowerment:

> Traditional medicalised models of mental health treatment enhance the position of dominators and exploiters objectively ... Workers socialised into the power and false charity of medicalised models of care are similarly socialised into dominated power relationships with clients which are dependent upon the client remaining within the crushing, stultifying confines of the mental patient role. When an advocacy/empowerment practice asserts the oppression in that role, the fight for competing legitimacies erupts at every level ... (Rose and Black 1985, pp.188–9)

In the mental health arena, the movement has faced profound problems. As I know from experience as a long-time advocate and psychiatric survivor, it has been difficult for advocates to get taken seriously by the various professionals. Working in MIND, I found hospital managers readily dismissive of serious allegations of physical and psychological abuse by staff as 'I know she's saying she's been attacked but it's only a symptom of her mental state. She's just hallucinating again.'

Peer advocates, those with similar backgrounds to their service users, were in double jeopardy. For example, Perceval's criticisms of the new Northampton county asylum in the 1840s were attacked by a senior official. Quoted in a local newspaper, he commented that: 'his [Perceval's] sympathies with the insane are of a very morbid character and his judgement to the last feeble and weak' (Podvoll 1990, p.57). It was always considerably easier to blame and vilify the poor messenger than respond to an unpleasant message!

Shuresh Patel, a patient trying to establish advocacy in Lancashire in the early 1990s, also found his ideas ridiculed:

> Some senior staff called our proposed Patients' Council 'a witchhunt'
> … In taking up racism in a psychiatric setting, I was told it was my
> delusions. I was allegedly hearing things in my head. But on one
> occasion when called a 'Pakki' by a staff member, I had a witness,
> complained and he got disciplined. (Jack 1995, p.117)

Chamberlin's mentalism was only recognized as a serious problem much
later than racism or sexism.

These different examples indicate how the essential human nature and
credibility of both patients and advocates, arising partly from psychiatric diagnosis, are profoundly suspect. They are tied tightly to a vicious circle –
close to Catch 22. Any complaints are seen as further symptoms of the given
syndrome. Any protests against such stereotyping are perceived as still further evidence of the diagnosis.

The consequence of much labelling, especially from the increasingly om-
nipotent Diagnostic and Statistical Manual IV (DSM), is fundamentally inju-
rious and reductionist. It raises huge obstacles for contemporary
empowerment ideologies, inherently basic to advocacy practice, which involve a respect for individual autonomy. Walker, himself an American psychiatrist, writes:

> DSM teaches psychiatrists to lump and label rather than to split and
> diagnose. It teaches them to disregard important symptoms that don't
> fit conveniently in to a DSM list, to ignore patients … it has led to the
> unnecessary drugging of millions of Americans who could be
> diagnosed, treated, and cured without the use of toxic and potentially
> lethal medications. (Walker 1996, p.51)

Whatever the truth about treatment efficacy, these processes make effective
advocacy extremely difficult.

Methods

Advocacy grew from a wide variety of different roots. It was greatly influenced by an increasing suspicion of the authority base of the different health
professions, eroded through well-publicized scandals, mostly concerning
medical incompetence and neglect. This questioning of traditional authority
is one important consequence of the so-called 'information revolution' – the
growth in health and personal growth books, the World Wide Web and
greater coverage by the media. It is now much easier to check the veracity of
decisions made by professionals, especially regarding the use of psychiatric
drugs. For example, the Internet has some excellent coverage of psychiatric
drugs and their side-effects. The service user/patient is gradually turning

into an active consumer. He or she demands to understand and to be involved, not just to become a passive recipient for professional advice and intervention. 'Why are you suggesting this? What are the side-effects of this medication? What about ...?' The insecure professionals felt under attack and the new user movement felt that mediation was barely possible as they faced deeper trenches.

In the fresh climate, and on the strong backs of a few, often persecuted, pioneers, advocacy has become something of a favoured child, at least in lip service. Even the notorious special hospital system has accepted and adopted it. Susan Machin, a social worker, protested about bad practice at her place of work – Ashworth Special Hospital. She gave evidence to the Blom Cooper inquiry and became clinically depressed. 'I was going strong at work, but driving home in tears. My personal life was left in tatters.' Later she lost her job but was exonerated by an industrial tribunal (Cooper 1997, pp.18–19). Ironically, the Ashworth inquiry recommended a funded system of patient advocates, which was put into practice and led to the development of a patients' forum (Department of Health 1992). The growth of advocacy and patients' councils had incurred a considerable backlash by 1996, with allegations by the staff union, for example, that the patients were running Broadmoor hospital.

The relevant professions, such as nursing and social work, increasingly compete for the desired role, *advocacy by service professionals*. They seek to protect the service users against the oppressing institutions, which are most frequently their employers. Most commentators ignore the so obvious and fundamental dilemmas. Siporin (1975, p.9) argues that 'the social worker is a spokesman for the needy in our society, particularly for the poor and disadvantaged ... More recently this has been referred to as the social worker's advocacy role'. And, rather evangelically, '... nurses are in the best position to carry out the advocacy role' (Graham 1992, p.148). The function which was once despised and resisted, within a decade, becomes valuable enough to fight over!

There are deep tensions between advocacy within the service professions and the rapid growth of disability lawyers and lay advocacy by volunteers and people with disabilities themselves. The service professions have only very limited independence, as they operate, at least partly, inside the system. They run the risk of being either toothless reformers or becoming victims themselves.

One individual taking the full brunt of these dilemmas is the whistleblower. He or she is an insider pointing out the deficiencies in services, and often gets scapegoated as a reward. Organizations vigorously defend themselves against these sorts of criticisms. A *British Medical Journal* report entitled 'The Rise of Stalinism in the NHS' claims 'increasing evidence of secrecy, suppression of information and intimidation of staff who are critical of the effects of the NHS reforms' (*Independent* 1994, p.6).

Hunt's NHS whistleblowers' survey reflected:

> Typically the whistleblower would be told by colleagues that they were 'right', but that it was futile or too risky to complain ... for every whistleblowing case which the media highlights there are dozens of cases of staff who raise concern and then drop it when they understand what they are up against. For every case of a dropped concern there are thousands of staff who are aware of substandard practice, patient neglect and abuse, and inadequate procedures but who feel powerless to voice any concern. (Hunt 1995, p.20)

The virulent defence against advocacy allows much incompetent practice to continue and even flourish.

One basic tension inherent in bringing incompetence and neglect to full light is the dragon of confidentiality. Increasingly, NHS and social services staff sign so-called 'gagging clauses'. These place the need for confidentiality, about issues such as commercial and patients' confidences, over the need for professionals to report bad practice. This issue was highlighted by Graham Pink, the Stockport charge nurse, who published material about inadequate staffing levels as well as other deficiencies in a psycho-geriatric unit. Relatives of one elderly patient complained that she could be identified from the *Guardian* article, even though names were not used. Nurse Pink was disciplined on the grounds of a breach of confidentiality, although the same ethical code obliged him to bring to notice any unsatisfactory standards of care (Hunt 1995, pp.135–6).

Gostin was a pioneer of *citizen advocacy* (CA). In June 1981, the Advocacy Alliance, consisting of five major voluntary organizations, including MIND, was launched to set up CA schemes in three large hospitals. It sought

> to empower those who have been kept powerless and/or excluded ... Members of devalued groups are put in touch, on a one to one basis, with ordinary people who have their own place in the community and who will listen to their point of view, respect their wishes, and stand with them to defend their rights. Individuals who have been stigmatised, ignored and made victims by society are thus enabled to assert themselves and become active members of their communities. (National Citizen Advocacy 1988, p.3)

The core activity was to create matches between one volunteer and 'valued' advocate and one devalued protégé. Part of the chronic service difficulty was that 'valued' usually excluded those who were, or had been, mental health service users.

This growing movement always included few mental health survivors, being largely preoccupied with people who had learning difficulties. Those few CA groups working with survivors moved almost inexorably into peer or multi-advocacy. As we saw earlier, peer advocacy presents some peculiar problems but also some strengths. Peter Campbell, himself a long-term peer advocate, comments:

> Last autumn when I was compulsorily detained, I had a friend of mine, a fellow user, acting as an advocate … She was someone who was in complete sympathy/empathy with me. She knew the 'power trip' from the inside. It was 'inside' her too. She was emotionally involved which I saw as a plus. We were reciprocally involved. I expected that I would act as her advocate at some point. This strengthened us vis-à-vis the system. (Campbell 1995)

> There are considerable difficulties in acting as an advocate for a close friend although when it works, it can be particularly satisfying for both partners. (Campbell 1997)

This form of advocacy offers several constructive processes. It can involve a 'rite-de-passage' from psychiatric patient to citizen and a way, rather like Alcoholics Anonymous, of using and valuing previously stigmatized experiences. As Campbell describes, it can provide a potentially reciprocal experience, whereby the present service user can see him or herself in the role of advocate. It usually involves very great passion and empathy, which needs harnessing. Its particular problems are the possible 're-clientization' of the advocate, a great danger as we saw with Perceval; that the problems of the advocate will be worked on rather than those of the service user; and the failure to develop relevant skills: the overlapping of close friendship and the need for effective advocacy can be difficult (Brandon 1994, pp.218–224).

CA has faced attempts over the years to provide a straitjacket to protect its presumed purity. The vast manuals and workbooks produced became over-prescriptive. Campbell worries about similar attempts to 'professionalize' peer advocacy which might undermine its passion and fix it like a fly in aspic. There are great tensions between the drive for increased efficacy and the chaos:

> Is there a way to provide the necessary support without some sort of professionalised take over? What are the tensions between formal and

> informal structures? What about the influence on networks? Some people's networks are already dominated by survivors. Survivors have similar experiences and backgrounds. Is that feeling of common experiences real? In a way there is a legend of collective experience when people's experiences of distress and service use may be, in reality, extremely different. (Campbell 1992)

Arising out of the tensions between relatives and survivors, there has been a tendency to neglect the role of *family advocacy*. This is understandable but extremely unfortunate. In most service user groups, families are the most vociferous advocates, but the major issue is – for whom do they speak? Sometimes their own suffering and concerns dominate the process of speaking out.

A relevant comment from across the Atlantic:

> The family movement in the United States has grown fast and has so much credibility because they are middle-class respectable people and they are not mentally ill. The family movement puts total reliance in the medical model, especially genetics. There is this new drug out and they're volunteering their kids, who are usually mature adults, to try it out. On an individual level I can understand families have been through a lot and suffered a lot and have their own issues. I wish they would stay organized as a support group around their issues but they don't. They see themselves as representing the consumers because 'we speak for people who can't speak for themselves'. (Quoted in O'Hagan 1993, p.35)

I experienced great difficulties in living with a father-in-law with Alzheimer's Syndrome, and making his case to the various professionals – doctors, nurses and social workers. The feeling over four long years was of not being listened to, making no impact on the professionals or services. We were advocating for him but being neglected ourselves:

> Without our agreement or any discussion, we had become 'carers'. No one at all tended to our grief or distress because we weren't the clients. We were invisible. We would have to break down psychiatrically and become clients in our own right, to be seen and heard. There was some possibility of real support and help but in order to receive it we had to be seen as co-operative, open and compliant. I had to share fully my wounds and vulnerabilities to compete effectively with many unseen others in the lottery for help. (Brandon in Jack 1997)

We were compelled to advocate primarily for ourselves as our family survival was threatened. Eventually we pressed hard for his exclusion, removal to mental hospital.

Framework

It is fascinating that although much has been published about mental health advocacy, relatively little is written about the necessary process and skills. In contrast to the legal profession's close attention to detail, the lay advocate is simply supposed to get on and just do it with virtually no relevant training. I have broadly adapted Bateman's (1995, p.60) various stages of the advocacy process:

- *Description* of the situation: issue(s) requiring advocacy is presented or uncovered. Where possible encourage *self advocacy.*

- *Instructions*: What do you want done? The person is helped to formulate ideas for action and present his/her own case, with the help of *family advocacy* (?)

- *Information*: getting relevant data, researching the facts given by the client with legal, policy or relevant procedures. Discussions with relevant professionals and organizations.

- *Feedback*: analysing the data gathered, forming a judgement about the best course, discussing with the person, taking further instructions; *lay advocacy.*

- *Negotiation*: negotiating with those able to change the situation in the person's favour; gain support and even *advocacy from the service professionals.*

- *Litigation*: use of formal appeals and other mechanisms to achieve objectives if negotiation is not successful or is inappropriate; *legal advocacy.*

- *Collective action*: working with others in similar situations to change the systems creating the problems; *collective advocacy.*

Let's take an example from Rosemary's situation:

Rosemary *described* in some detail the four years of her life spent going in and out of compulsory psychiatric detention, variously diagnosed as having depression and 'borderline personality disorder'. She was discharged about 18 months ago with no implemented care plan or organized follow-up. She wanted to explore a series of possible complaints against the authorities. She settled on a complaint over a serious attack made on her by a male patient while in a medium secure psychiatric hospital. She contacted her solicitor and *instructed* him to pursue redress.

We sought further *information* about the case from other professionals and research sources, as well as providing material about academic courses she might want to follow. We gave *feedback* to Rosemary about various possibilities. She *instructed* us that she wanted to meet with a 'friendly' psychiatrist to explore her DSM diagnosis, to provide a possible second opinion, as well as to resume her life as a student. Access to relevant university courses was *negotiated*, as was the meeting with the psychiatrist. She also received legal aid to pursue *litigation* about the attack in hospital.

Rosemary had been going through a period of exhaustion and challenge in her life. She got on a psychiatric conveyor belt through repeated overdosing, mainly of insulin because she has diabetes. This prolonged and dreadful experience destroyed any confidence she had left. It cost the health authority well over £250,000. Much needed was a more flexible and mediatory system rather than the medicalized juggernaut, unable to listen and respond to her needs. Rosemary concluded that a pleasant holiday and some counselling would have been much cheaper and more appropriate. Advocacy became necessary because the system would not accept mediation or even respond to letters.

Conclusion

So far, lay mental health advocacy has been rather chaotic and disorganized, in the authentic tradition of Perceval. As it gains power, influence and investment, there is a great danger of arid professionalization. Previously the danger came from burnout by a few devoted advocates. Standards of support varied wildly and widely.

Now we have moved from persecution to the more deadly dangers of co-option; from being hated outsiders to becoming just another part of the service. For example, the NHS task force published a code of advocacy practice, albeit drafted by service users (NHS Mental Health Task Force User Group 1994). Our own local authority also recently published a handbook detailing various principles, alongside a code of practice (Cambridgeshire Social Services Department 1997). On the one hand, we congratulate them for an enlightened interest; on the other the burglars are busily designing the locks. These various regulatory demands risk neutering the impact of advocacy by enforcing constipated discipline and excluding righteous passion. Only when service users influence the whole nature of the 'game', will it be worthwhile keeping to the rules.

References

Bateman, N. (1995) *Advocacy Skills.* London: Arena.

Brandon, D. (1991) *Innovation without Change?* London: Macmillan.

Brandon, D. (1994) 'Peer advocacy.' *Care in Place 1,* 3, 218–224.

Brandon, D. with Brandon, A. and Brandon, T. (1995) *Advocacy – Power to People with Disabilities.* Birmingham: Venture Press.

Brandon, D. and Jack, R. (1997) 'Struggling with Services.' In I. Norman and S. Redfern (eds) *Mental Health Care for Elderly People.* Edinburgh: Churchill Livingstone.

Cambridgeshire Social Services Department (1997) *Advocacy Handbook.* Cambridge: Cambridgeshire Social Services Department.

Campbell, P. (1992) Personal communication. June.

Campbell, P. (1995) Personal communication. February.

Campbell, P. (1997) Personal communication. September.

Chamberlin, J. (1988) *On our Own.* London: MIND.

Cooper, C. (1997) 'A risk worth taking.' *Community Care,* 10 July.

Department of Health (1992) *Report of the Committee of Inquiry into Complaints for Ashworth Special Hospital.* London: HMSO.

Gostin, L. (1975) *A Human Condition.* London: National Association for Mental Health MIND.

Graham, A. (1992) 'Advocacy – what the future holds.' *British Journal of Nursing 1,* 3, 148–150.

Hunt, G. (1995) *Whistleblowing in the Health Service.* London: Edward Arnold.

Independent, The (1994) 'NHS staff subject to a "reign of terror".' 16 December.

Jack, R. (ed) (1995) *Empowerment in Community Care.* London: Chapman & Hall.

King's Fund (1986) *The Advice and Representation Project at Springfield Hospital, 1982–1985,* No. 59 project paper. London: King's Fund.

NHS Mental Health Task Force User Group (1994) *Advocacy: A Code of Practice.* London: National Health Service.

National Citizen Advocacy (1988) *A Powerful Partnership.* London: NCA.

O'Hagan, M. (1993) *Stopovers on my Way Home from Mars.* London: Survivors Speak Out.

Podvoll, E.M. (1990) *The Seduction of Madness.* London: HarperCollins.

Rose, S. and Black, B. (1985) *Advocacy and Empowerment – Mental Health: Care in the Community.* London: Routledge & Kegan Paul.

SSO (1988) *Self-Advocacy Action Pack – Empowering Mental Health Service Users.* London: Survivors Speak Out.

Siporin, M. (1975) *Introduction to Social Work Practice.* London: Macmillan/Collier.

Walker, S. (1996) *A Dose of Sanity – Mind, Medicine and Misdiagnosis.* New York: Wiley.

Further reading

Goffman, E. (1968) *Asylums – Essays on the Social Situation of Mental Patients and Other Inmates.* London: Penguin.

Useful addresses

MIND

Granta House
15–19 Broadway
Stratford
London E15 4BQ
Tel: 0181 519 2122.

Survivors Speak Out

34 Osnaburgh Street
London NW1 3ND
Tel: 0171 916 5472.

CHAPTER 11

Substance Use Counselling

Graz Kowszun

Introduction

Since the dawn of civilization, all around the world, most people have used mood-altering substances. There appears, however, to have been an enormous increase in levels of drug dependency in the second half of this century. For instance, in 1955, there were 367 registered drug addicts in Britain, while in 1993 there were 27,976.

The drugs people have used have been intended, in the main, to perform a positive function for the user. Such purposes include recreation, ritual, inspiration, healing and escapism. Occasionally, drugs are used for reasons that are not so directly positive, for instance to counteract the negative effects of other drugs. The Sunday lunchtime alcoholic drink to alleviate Saturday night's hangover, otherwise known as the 'hair of the dog', is a prime example. Further, people who are physically dependent on a particular substance may or may not be aware that they are continuing to maintain its level in the bloodstream in order to avoid unpleasant withdrawal symptoms. Barbara Gordon (1979), in her well-known autobiographical novel *I'm Dancing as Fast as I Can* describes poignantly how little understood was her tranquillizer addiction and the problems caused by the over-prescribing of benzodiazepam (valium) in the 1960s and 70s.

In this chapter, I shall be using the term 'drug' or 'substance' interchangeably to refer to alcohol and other mood-altering chemicals, regardless of whether they are legal and/or medically prescribed or not. This is because, like most people working in the field, I believe questions of legality obscure rather than illuminate discussions of substance use and abuse. For instance, about one million people take ecstasy, a class A illegal drug, every week. Drug taking carries risks. Yet if we examine morbidity figures, annual figures for drug-related deaths in the UK are: 100,000 (tobacco), 15–30,000 (alcohol) and 150 (heroin). Ecstasy, in the last eight years, has led to a total of 48 deaths. Hence, on morbidity ratings, it is one of the safest drugs to use. None-theless, conviction for possession of ecstasy carries stiff penalties, while possession of tobacco and alcohol by adults is completely legal.

Patterns of drug use vary enormously. They can be measured, chaotic or anything in between, solitary and communal, celebratory and habitual. From licking the skin of the Colorado River toad to encourage hallucinatory visions, to quaffing a pint of fermented cereal down at the local pub to gain popularity as 'one of the lads', our substance-using patterns can be understood only in their socio-political context (Griffiths and Pearson 1988).

In the final century of the second millennium, where geographical and social mobility is so prevalent, the norms of various sub-cultures have intersected and clashed. Within this arena, battles for power and control are being fought as Western capitalist states have sought increasingly to define who can authorize or prohibit the production and distribution of alcohol and other drugs, while others make a living by growing opium poppies or coca plants and selling these for illicit exportation. The subtleties and paradoxes emerging from these culture clashes can sometimes tax our understanding (Robinson 1979). Consider, for example, how this man may feel:

> Vijay wants to rent a flat with his 19-year-old white English girlfriend, Alice, who has been ordered to leave home by her heavy-drinking father because she admitted taking ecstasy at a party. Alice wants Vijay to come to a rave with her and he realizes that that will involve him considering whether he should try any dance drugs himself. Meanwhile his father is being severely admonished by Vijay's elderly hookah-smoking grandfather over in London on a visit from Pakistan, just because he suggested a visit to a pub. Used to respecting the life experience and views of his elders, Vijay does not know who to ask for advice.

In Britain, alcohol use is officially sanctioned for those over the age of majority, who can maintain the appearance of orderly conduct in public. What happens in private is a different matter, as alcohol is often implicated in domestic violence and child abuse (Kinney and Leaton 1978). Some drugs are completely illegal despite having some beneficial properties (e.g. LSD, cannabis), while others are closely controlled through a system of prescription (e.g. tranquillizers, morphine). Unofficially, the alcohol industry appears increasingly to target teenagers and children with its sweet and deceptively strong concoctions. Thus although those using dance drugs (ecstasy, LSD, amphetamines and cannabis) tend not to drink much alcohol at the same time, nonetheless most alcohol is consumed by the young.

Meanwhile, young people, especially those whose past has featured abuse and neglect, and whose present consists of poor job prospects and little legitimate stimulation, are finding the short-term high of heroin or crack cocaine readily available, while the elderly may over-use prescription drugs or alcohol. Psychologists have long used the acronym PIG to identify the Problem of Immediate Gratification, and while the expectations heaped on to mood-altering substances are seldom realized, they remain far more motivating and encouraging than the abstract deterrent of a criminal record or imprisonment.

In recognition of the decisive influence of supply on demand on illegal use of class A drugs, especially heroin and cocaine, British governments have tended to put resources into international efforts to stem drug production and trafficking, as well as encouraging police to prioritize catching major drug dealers (Department of Health 1994). The same strategy is clearly not applied to licit drugs. While tranquillizers are now socially censured, antidepressants such as Prozac are regularly prescribed. According to the British Medical Association, almost half of all drugs prescribed by doctors in the United Kingdom are psychoactive drugs or drugs which affect the central nervous system. In the past, alcohol could only be purchased at strictly licensed premises; now it is easily available in supermarkets and corner stores. An ambivalence about substance use is clearly widespread.

Attitudes of counsellors, supporters and helpers

Support workers tend to be sensitive, empathic, non-judgemental and self-aware, attributes which are selected and fostered during training and job selection (Frank 1991). However, given the levels of cultural bias and the politically sensitive nature of issues of substance use and misuse, an in-depth examination of our own patterns of substance use over our lifespan may uncover surprisingly unfounded assumptions and judgements, as well as personal motives and patterns of which we were previously unaware. Additionally, the process of systematically monitoring our substance use can provide invaluable insight into the possible embarrassment and reluctance service users may feel when examining their patterns of drug use.

Supporters may find it hard to allow a service user to feel ambivalent about changing a lifestyle that has gains as well as detrimental effects for them. Because there is some limited validity to stereotypes, they are tempting to impose on those who use our services. Thus, typically, the greatest substance use is among men aged 15–25. This tends to tail off as the responsibilities of dependants take over in the late 20s and 30s, though this applies less to those engaged in an alternative lifestyle, for example, as lesbian or gay.

Some professions and occupations seem to support heavy ongoing drug use. In terms of alcohol, the high risk occupations include the army and navy, journalism, medicine and, of course, alcohol workers (Plant 1979).

Problematic substance use is more likely to develop following times of crisis and major loss. Those who come from a family where substance use was either absent – such as many British-born Muslims – or particularly heavy – such as children of heavy drinkers – are known to be at higher than average risk of developing problems related to substance use (Murray and Murray 1991).

However, whilst there may be more drug problems among young white men, people of all ages – women, men and the transgendered as well as all ethnic groups – may experience functional and dysfunctional substance use. Therefore service users, regardless of their presenting problem, may or may not be experiencing difficulties as a result of their substance use, and their patterns of use may or may not impinge on these difficulties.

Consider the following example. Had you been helping or counselling Jenny, what might have alerted you to the real nature of her problem?

> Ever since her ex-lover had suddenly died, Jenny had been finding it increasingly difficult to leave her flat, particularly during the day. Finally, she decided to consult a counsellor. They spent several months exploring her feelings about being bisexual, her fears of death, the dynamics of her childhood and her relationship with her previous partners.

Although she valued the deeper self-awareness this gave her, the acute anxiety she felt when going out did not abate. Her doctor referred her to a psychologist, with whom she worked cognitively and behaviourally on what was perceived as agoraphobia and panic attacks. After several sessions, Jenny grew wary that this psychologist was homophobic and broke off the relationship. She became increasingly despondent and felt more and more suicidal.

A supportive male ex-lover invited her to visit him on his farm in the United States. For several days, she suffered acute anxiety, where she found herself shaking uncontrollably, could not eat and found her sleep fitful, with night sweats and terrible nightmares. Jenny became convinced she was seriously ill and prepared to return to England, only she could not face the journey. Then, after a week, she began to feel much better, more relaxed and started to sleep soundly.

Delighted but unable to understand the reasons for her increasing physical and emotional well-being, Jenny returned to England where, through a chance discussion with another volunteer, she became aware that her anxiety had actually been a physical symptom of alcohol withdrawal. Drinking about two bottles of wine every evening prior to her trip to the US, Jenny had wrongly attributed all her feelings of panic and depression to her psychological state. None of the professionals working with her had considered physical causes, though fortunately she had not been prescribed tranquillizers for depression, which would have potentiated the alcohol, making withdrawal much more severe and dangerous.

Knowledge

Once we are aware of our assumptions and judgements around substance use, we are in a position to absorb useful information about the range of drugs, their effects, the likely consequences on us physically, emotionally, legally and socially, and the currently available treatment options. This is available from local and national drug and alcohol agencies in the form of leaflets, videos, books and publication recommendations. Telephone consultations may also be extremely helpful. The Health Education Authority (HEA) has even brought out a CD-ROM, *D-Code*, featuring extensive information about drugs in the form of a quiz game (HEA 1997). It is not necessary to have full detailed knowledge, but a general overview of the main types of drugs and their effects facilitates confidence and credibility.

Whilst confines of space render it impossible to provide much detailed information, some general comments about useful ways to think about substance use follow.

According to the Diagnostic and Statistical Manual of Mental Disorders (American Psychiatric Association (APA) 1994), the major misused drugs are alcohol, amphetamines, caffeine, cannabis, cocaine, hallucinogens, inhalants, nicotine, opioids, phencyclidine, sedatives, hypnotics, anxiolytics, and medications such as muscle-relaxants, anti-depressants, analgesics and anaesthetics. Initial use of a particular drug is considered experimental and, if the person likes it, it may become recreational. Recreational use may remain harmless, though intoxication can be the cause of problems, directly for the user or for affected others.

> For instance, Simone is missing work when the after-effects following a weekend on speed (amphetamines) prove too much for her.

> Edward neglects his ageing, disabled mother for whom he is main carer when smoking marijuana joints (cannabis).

> Pauline lives in a rural area. She got drunk at a party, stayed the night, but did not realize her blood alcohol level was still dangerously high

the next morning. She was stopped for speeding, breathalysed and may lose her licence and consequently her job as a social worker having to travel to people's homes.

Problems with substances may not be the direct result of intoxication but the harm that that drug causes. This can be physical, social, legal and/or psychological, as illustrated in the vignette below:

Peter has been a widower for six years and is a single parent to a 12-year-old son. He has chronic bronchitis from smoking and a peptic ulcer from regular drinking. He also suffers from impotence as a result of his drinking. These physical problems are less significant than his deteriorating relationship with his son, who has been suspended from school for drinking at lunchtime. Peter was so frustrated, he thrashed his son and a neighbour who witnessed this reported him to social services. Luckily the social worker organized some family therapy, during which it emerged that neither father nor son had dealt with the loss of Peter's wife and that was an underlying psychological problem, which together they were able to confront.

Finally, drug use can lead to dependency of a physical or psychological nature if symptoms such as withdrawal symptoms, narrowing of social repertoire and loss of control of usage are present (APA 1994).

Whilst good information and understanding can make an enormous difference to the quality of service provision we can offer, we must also bear in mind that all health and social caseworkers need to stay within the limits of their competences, and service users can easily spot ignorance and fear in those purporting to help them.

Skills

With a constructive, open, warm attitude, and basic knowledge providing a foundation, supporters and counsellors could usefully acquire some skills to be of practical benefit to those with substance-related concerns.

First, communication and counselling skills are needed to develop an appropriate working alliance between the supporter and the service user. Good active listening skills; a respect for, and commitment to, autonomy, keeping sight of the humanity and underlying spirit of the service users; and the capacity both to empathize with them and to perceive the obvious without becoming critical, avoidant or collusive are very important competences to develop as a supporter. The skills of specificity, constructive challenge, intelligent and flexible focusing, and crisis management skills are also very important.

The skills to be able to assess the presence and nature of any substance-related problem can be acquired by a broad range of workers after a short course and access to consultative support. The mnemonic APPLE is a useful memory jogger: ask about the *amount* of substance used: over the last half day, week and month. Discover the *pattern*: what is taken and how the substance is used; where, when, with whom, what are the high and low risk situations. A regular substance-use monitoring diary is invaluable to help a service user spot connections and patterns. Explore the *presenting problem*: what is it and how may it be connected, or not, to the substance use. The *level of control versus chaos* in how substances are used is important to ascertain. The capacity to establish a working relationship is affected by the service user's capacity to form bonds, hold a sense of time and cope with less intense support or service provision. Finally, *evaluate dependence* to establish whom to refer for detoxification, to a dependency unit or to a residential facility, as a prerequisite for the user being likely to benefit from the services you offer.

A second important area to assess in relation to substance use is where in the process of change is the service user at present. Prochaska and Di-Clemente (1992) have developed a very useful model of this process which enables supporters to identify with the user what tasks are relevant and necessary at present to facilitate the process of change.

The first stage is called 'pre-contemplation' to underscore that the individual is not considering that he or she has a drug-related problem at this point in time. Service users in this phase may be difficult to help. Supporters may, however, find the person is able to move on as a result of a crisis, education, coercion, love or motivational interviewing (Miller and Rollnick 1991).

The next stage is 'contemplation', and at this time the user is weighing up the benefits and costs of their substance use. Support to do this consciously and in detail, with the supporter acknowledging the positive aspects of the drug pattern as perceived by the service user, helps them progress to the 'decision'-making phase. Respecting autonomy is vital here, for users need the foundation of determination and self-responsibility to put the decision into practice.

Substance users may decide they are unwilling or unable to change their drug use and consequently move back to pre-contemplation. Alternately, they may decide to take some 'action', thereby moving to the next stage of the process. Service users may need help to identify just what they want to change and what course of action to take. Egan's (1994) action-based model of counselling describes many useful skills around working with goals and strategies. Having changed the behaviour, the most demanding stage of the process is 'maintenance' of the change. Skills of relapse prevention are most usefully applied to support this process (Marlatt and Gordon 1985).

All being well, and a time span of maintaining the change for some two years or more is considered realistic with well-established dependence, the service user can now exit from the process of change, having successfully completed it. Lapses in this time can be useful learning experiences as long as they do not become relapses (when the individual gives up giving up, as it were). Some people do relapse and this may mean that an earlier stage in the process may have been inadequately addressed. Following relapse, people may become pre-contemplators again, or rejoin the process of change at an earlier point.

For example, Fatima works as a care assistant with the elderly, and her mother has just died. She is angry at what she considers neglect in the hospital where her mother died. Fatima would prefer not to work, but as she receives no paid leave she asks her doctor for something to calm her nerves, and is prescribed both anti-depressants and tranquillizers. Several months later, she wants to come off the tablets, but is worried she would not cope. 'The doctors have ruined my life now,' she asserts angrily to her colleague, Sonia, at work.

Sonia recognizes that Fatima is in the contemplation phase of the process of change, and that action may involve reducing her medication, some stress management work leading to a holiday perhaps, and some support around her bereavement, specifically to explore her anger and its causes. 'You are feeling vulnerable and also angry at doctors and you also want to be drug free,' she empathizes. This provides Fatima with the opportunity to explore her concerns and 'contemplate' the benefits of 'reclaiming her life' and the costs, what she might need in order to make the necessary changes.

Advocacy, counselling and mediation in working with substance use issues

The sooner people whose substance use is becoming problematic are supported to tackle the issues constructively, the easier it is to change patterns. A worker, volunteer or friend with good self-awareness, a facilitative attitude (which includes a deep commitment to individual autonomy and the capacity to respect the limits of support), coupled with limited training in skills and information, can make all the difference. Hopefully this chapter has demystified the bogeyman of addict/alcoholic, which are terms that distance us from those who need our respect and humane 'carefrontation'.

Different approaches to counselling have their place in working with substance-related issues and what may lie underneath them, but attention to the specifics of the drug use on a behavioural level must be a priority in any support system.

An advocate working with someone whose substance use is considered problematic can do much to support that individual. For instance, a good employer should have an alcohol and drugs policy, covering all levels of staff equally and of which all employees are aware. This avoids the extremes of collusion, whereby colleagues deny or cover up the problems, or punitive approaches, whereby employees in difficulty are summarily dismissed. Advocates can get information and lobby for such a policy and ensure it is implemented correctly. In this way, substance abuse which is affecting the work is tackled directly and constructively, through an agreement whereby the employee actively engages in treatment, which may involve paid time off work, and keeps their job.

A person's substance use may be the cause or excuse for complaints from neighbours, and local community mediation services may be able to unravel the specific nature of the problem and whether and how drugs play a part in it. Disputes between families or partners may focus, justly or not, on the substance use of a party to that dispute:

> Geraldine has become physically dependent on opiates and is worried that if she seeks any help she may lose custody of, or even contact with, her children. She loves her children enormously and is deeply committed to taking responsible care of them, despite her drug use. An informed advocate can do much to see that she gets the community care services she needs to maximize her chances of keeping her children. This may be through effective child care support and a programme of stabilizing and gradually reducing her drug use alongside individual counselling and a drug-using parents' support group.

Self-help groups are another vital source of support. Groups such as Alcoholics Anonymous (AA) or Narcotics Anonymous (NA) provide crisis befrienders who can be rung day or night when an individual is in dire straits. They have a philosophy which many find comforting and a structure of activities that may provide emotional support, companionship, insight and an alternative way of spending time. Mainliners, a charitable organization working with drug users around issues of HIV and AIDS, promotes self help through support groups and communication through a newsletter.

There are relevant national helplines and, of course, the Samaritans will talk to people who are feeling desperate. However, given the ignorance, ambivalence and shame surrounding drug users, self-help groups are often a preferred option. In big cities, there may be AA and NA informal sub-groupings for those experiencing particular forms of oppression, such as lesbian and gay people or people of African descent. Sometimes other support networks may provide the particular understanding of our identity and advocates can suggest speakers who are invited to give information and impart skills related to substance use. Such networks include co-counselling, groups for people with disabilities, ethnic groups, support groups for survivors of childhood abuse, *Big Issue* homeless networks, and so on.

Conclusion

It is very easy to avoid dealing with people who may be experiencing problems and who are using drugs. It is simple to deny that the substance use is at all relevant or to insist it is the sole cause of all the individual's difficulties and therefore refer them automatically to specialist services. To remain engaged in a relationship with the user, to respect their right to self-determination, to explore with sensitivity and openness in detail with them the interface of the different issues with which they are grappling is much more challenging. To offer people the opportunities and support to decide what they are willing and able to do to tackle the problems, and what the consequences of that decision may be, requires that we as counsellors and supporters take the risk to be present, curious, compassionate, involved and affected by the experience. It can be very painful and it can also be deeply rewarding as we see people change, grow and become stronger and more hopeful.

I have found substance users a diverse and generally delightful group of people to work with, and in the process I have found out much about myself and the way our society works. I hope the discussion above helps you discover how rewarding it can be to be a catalyst, however small, in the process of changing our relationships to ourselves, each other and the substances we use to alter our world views.

References

APA (1994) *Diagnostic and Statistical Manual of Mental Disorders. DSM-IV.* Washington, DC: American Psychiatric Association.

Department of Health (1994) *Tackling Drugs Together. A Consultation Document on a Strategy for England 1995/1998.* London: HMSO.

Egan, G. (1994) *The Skilled Helper.* Pacific Grove, CA: Brooks/Cole.

Frank, J. (1991) *Persuasion and Healing.* Baltimore, MD: Johns Hopkins University Press.

Gordon, B. (1979) *I'm Dancing as Fast as I Can.* New York: Bantam Books.

Griffiths, R. and Pearson, B. (1988) *Working with Drug Users*. Aldershot: Wildwood House.

HEA (1997) *D-Code*. CD-ROM. London: Health Education Authority.

Kinney, J. and Leaton, G. (1978) *Loosening the Grip: A Handbook of Alcohol Information*. St Louis, MS: The C.V. Mosby Company.

Marlatt, A. and Gordon, J. (eds) (1985) *Relapse Prevention*. New York: Guilford Press.

Miller, W. and Rollnick, S. (1991) *Motivational Interviewing*. New York: Guilford Press.

Murray, A. and Murray, R. (1991) 'The role of genetic predisposition in alcoholism.' In I. Glass (ed) *The International Handbook of Addiction Behaviour*. London: Routledge.

Plant, M. (1979) 'Learning to drink.' In M. Grant and P. Gwinner (eds) *Alcoholism in Perspective*. London: Croom Helm.

Prochaska, J. and DiClemente, C. (1992) 'The transtheoretical approach.' In J. Norcross and R. Goldfried (eds) *Handbook of Psychotherapy Integration*. New York: Basic Books.

Robinson, D. (1979) 'Drinking behaviour.' In M. Grant and P. Gwinner (eds) *Alcoholism in Perspective*. London: Croom Helm.

Further reading

Velleman, R. (1992) *Counselling for Alcohol Problems*. London: Sage.

Useful addresses

Alcohol Concern

Waterbridge House
32–36 Loman Street
London SE1 0EE
Tel: AC: 0171 928 7377

Alcohol Counselling and Prevention Services

34 Electric Lane
London SW9 8JT
Tel: 0171 737 3579 (training)

Alcoholics Anonymous

GB General Services Office
PO Box 1, Stonebow House
York
Tel: 01904 644026
London region: 0171 352 3001

Useful addresses

The Big Issue

Albion Place
Galena Road
London W6 0LT
Tel: 0181 741 8090

Health Education Authority

Hamilton House
Mabledon Place
London WC1 9TX
Tel: 0171 383 3833

Institute for the Study of Drug Dependence

Waterbridge House
32–36 Loman Street
London SE1 0EE
Tel: ISDD: 0171 928 1211

Mainliners (self-help for those affected by drugs and HIV)

38–40 Kennington Park Road
London SE11 4RS
Tel: 0171 582 5434

Narcotics Anonymous: 0171 351 6794

National Drugs Helpline: 0800 77 66 00

National Smoking Education Campaign Office

Trevelyan House, 30 Great Peter Street
London W1P 2HW
Tel: 0171 413 2622

Prisoners' Resource Service

PO Box 3689
London NW1 8QP
Tel: 0171 267 4446

Project LSD (a lesbian, gay and bisexual drugs project)

Box 9, 136–138 Kingsland High Street
London E8 2NS
Tel: 0171 288 1111

Release (advice and information on legal- and drug-related problems)

388 Old Street
London EC1V 9LT
Advice Line: 0171 729 9904
Helpline: 0171 603 8654

The Samaritans

0171 734 2800 (central London)
0345 90 90 90 (nationwide: calls charged at local rate)

Teachers Advisory Council on Alcohol and Drug Education

2 Mount Street
Manchester M2 5NG
Tel: 0161 834 7210

CHAPTER 12

Victim Offender Mediation

Jean Wynne

Advocacy, counselling and mediation

The difference between advocacy, counselling and mediation within the context of the criminal justice system is that whilst all three aim to help offenders, the methods and interactions with offenders are quite different. This chapter describes the development of victim offender mediation and its relationship to advocacy and counselling, illustrated by case histories.

Advocacy requires speaking on behalf of, or promoting the interests of, offenders. This places advocates in a hierarchical relationship in that offenders are dependent on the advocate's performance to achieve their goals. In the criminal justice system offenders usually have legally trained advocates to defend them or to mitigate sentence at the court hearing. Probation officers also have roles as advocates when preparing the offenders' pre-sentence reports, which provide the background information, including the circumstances leading up to the offence, for the court.

In contrast, counselling does not involve promoting the offenders' interests to others; rather, it is a way of working privately with offenders. Counsellors use listening skills to help offenders to understand better their problems and so try to work out solutions to those problems themselves. In counselling the relationship between counsellors and offenders is not hierarchical rather it is more a partnership. Probation officers use counselling skills during their supervision sessions with offenders on probation, but do not enter into a full counselling relationship. They have to maintain the hierarchical nature of their relationship with the offender because of their duty of supervision during the probation order or parole licence.

Mediation, on the other hand, combines elements of advocacy and counselling but is quite different to both. Mediation means working neutrally with both parties in a dispute or, in the context of criminal justice, with victim and offender to resolve some of the effects of the offence. The aim is to restore the parties, as much as possible, to how they were before the offence took place. The focus is on the parties themselves and what they want to achieve from the mediation process. The mediator's role is to enable them to achieve this. Counselling skills may be used when listening to victims and offenders individually, but there is no attempt to work with them on a long-term therapeutic basis. The intervention is short-term and strictly focused on the offence and its after-effects, and how these can be put right.

The mediator visits each party in turn, usually at their homes, to find out whether they are willing to enter into the mediation process. The mediator also assesses the safety of the process for both parties, and this assessment includes emotional and psychological safety as well as the purely physical. Offenders must admit the offence fully and accept responsibility for what they have done. If these criteria are fulfilled, the mediator will find out what the victim needs and what the offender can offer and whether these can be matched. There are a whole range of mediation possibilities, ranging from an exchange of information and apologies, via the mediator, to a face-to-face meeting between victim and offender culminating in a written agreement. The mediation continuum can include exchange of letters, audio or video tapes and practical work carried out by the offender on behalf of the victim. The relationship between the mediator and victims and offenders is that of a neutral facilitator not as an advocate or counsellor.

However, there may be some element of advocacy if the mediation work is carried out prior to the offender's court hearing. The court needs to know if anything has been agreed between victim and offender. The mediation service must ensure that a report of the mediation work is sent to the court. The difference between a mediation report and a pre-sentence report is that the mediation report concerns two people, victim and offender. Any advocacy has to ensure a balance between the interests of both these parties and what they have or have not agreed as the best resolution to the offence.

The development of victim offender mediation

Victim offender mediation practice actually began as part of probation officers' casework with offenders on supervision. The early mediation work was started almost simultaneously in Canada and the United Kingdom by probation officers working with offenders. They attempted to challenge offenders' perceptions of their behaviour through direct contact with the actual victims of their crimes. From these early experiments sufficient evidence was gained that mediation could benefit both offenders and victims. Whether probation officers were the best people to carry out this work, however, became one of the ongoing debates.

The move towards including victims in work with offenders was part of a general trend during the 1970s of including victims in the criminal justice process. It began to be recognized that victims, who should be a central feature, had in fact become excluded from the criminal justice process during the nineteenth and earlier part of the twentieth century. The court process now belonged to the offender and the only official place for victims, at court, was as witnesses in trials when offenders pleaded not guilty. When offenders pleaded guilty victims had no role at all and were usually not informed when the trial took place; nor did they receive anything to compensate them for their losses.

In response to this recognition some changes were made in terms of sentencing. The development of the compensation order was in direct response to the recognition that victims deserved some acknowledgement of their losses. It meant that offenders paid money, via the courts, directly to their victims.

Other forms of reparation for victims were provided through the development of the community service order, whereby offenders could pay their debt to society through unpaid work for their local community. In some areas direct reparation for victims by their offenders was tried out as a way of paying back. The Home Office funded an experimental project during 1985–87 when four reparation schemes were set up in England with the aim of diverting offenders from either court or custody by making direct reparation to their victims. Each scheme had a slightly different brief, and in the Leeds scheme the aim was to achieve diversion from custody for 200 offenders, during the period of the experiment, by carrying out some form of direct reparation (financial or practical work) for their victims. The mediation was undertaken prior to sentence and a report then went into court stating what had been agreed between victim and offender, and what had actually been carried out. This mediation work was then taken into account by the sentencer. Although the aim was reparation to the victim, a mediation process had to be carried out first in order to establish what the victim wanted.

Kevin's story

Kevin broke into Mary's house late at night when she and her children were in bed. The noise terrified them. Kevin ran off but was soon caught and charged. With several previous convictions for burglary he faced a prison sentence. The mediator asked Mary if there was anything Kevin could do for her. She agreed to meet with him to discuss reparation. The meeting was confrontational and Mary gave Kevin a hard time. Drunkenness was no excuse for her, nor was his shortage of money as she herself was on social security.

During the meeting Kevin offered to do some work for Mary. She felt this would be helpful as her garden was overgrown. They agreed that if he got a community service order he would do 40 hours of his work for Mary. Their agreement was put to the court and Kevin was given a community service order and carried out the gardening work for Mary. He said later that the meeting with Mary affected him more than anything else had done. Mary said she benefited from having the opportunity to off-load her anger on to Kevin. Eight months later he still had not re-offended. Mary, later, became a probation volunteer.

This type of mediation was, arguably, a form of advocacy for offenders in that the aim was to achieve a community sentence for offenders. This was one of the criticisms of these early mediation services, although they did achieve increased satisfaction for victims in the process (Marshall and Merry 1990). The mediators involved in these early projects were not trained counsellors and sometimes themselves felt unhappy in a role acting as advocates for offenders. The Leeds scheme and, by 1995, all five West Yorkshire Probation mediation units worked to ensure that mediation was not aimed at advocacy purely on behalf of the offender but rather represented an even-handed way of working with both parties. The West Yorkshire services have always trained mediators from the local community in order to ensure neutrality for victims and offenders.

As well as changes in sentencing and court procedures, victims' demands for better treatment in the criminal justice system, and the whole victims' rights movement, led to the formation of Victim Support schemes. These voluntary organizations have played a key role in providing advocacy on behalf of victims of crime at both local and national level. The role of Victim Support schemes is to provide advice and guidance for victims in coping with the aftermath of crime. At a national level they actively campaign to improve services and policies for victims and were instrumental in the production of the government's Victim's Charter in 1990.

This Charter, apart from improving court services for victims, has also meant that all probation services in England and Wales are now expected to contact victims of serious violent or sexual offences to offer information on the offender's release plans and also to report victims' concerns about the release plans into the decision-making process. Who should contact these victims constitutes an ongoing debate. However, West Yorkshire Probation Service has used the experience of its county-wide mediation units to carry out this new work on behalf of victims. The work involves advocacy on behalf of victims who wish a report to be prepared on their behalf. What has also become apparent is that some victims request mediation during the course of the Victim's Charter enquiry process. The West Yorkshire model does mean that victims have easy access to mediation as the mediator/enquirer is already trained. Once the enquiry is completed and a report prepared, the mediator/enquirer can visit the offender and offer mediation. This has already happened in several cases. One case involved two female victims meeting the man who burnt down their house after he had served ten years in prison.

Casework

Probation officers' casework with offenders requires them to challenge offenders' perception of how their behaviour impinges on others. This challenging can be done on an individual basis or during groupwork sessions with offenders.

> I only do commercial burglaries.

> It's the victim's fault because they left the window open so I'm doing them a favour teaching them not to leave it open.

> Everyone is insured so they get their stuff back.

These are common responses made by offenders when challenged about their behaviour and represents their need to distance themselves from any harm they have caused. Bringing in the victims' perspective is not easy for them to accept and the common reaction is to avoid eye contact with the person challenging them. They look up at the ceiling or down at the floor when any mention is made of their victims. It is difficult for them even to contemplate thinking about their victims because this will require them to accept they have done harm deliberately to others and they don't wish to see themselves in this way.

This can be a sticking point for probation officers' casework with offenders and is where mediation can help move the whole challenging process forward. Mediation offers more to offenders than accepting responsibility for causing harm to others. It also offers the possibility of trying to repair the harm and thus offenders can start to feel better about themselves. This raising of their self esteem is essential. Most offenders have low self esteem and telling them what awful people they are makes them feel worse and does not help to change their behaviour. By taking part in mediation with their victim, and having the possibility of trying to put things right for their victim, offenders can feel better about themselves. This means that the mediation process becomes an enjoyable one which offenders are proud of; they can talk with their friends and family about the efforts they have made. Braithwaite

(1989) calls this process 'reintegrative shaming'. Although the offender has been publicly shamed during the court process, the mediation enables the offender to accept the shame in a positive way and thus be more easily reintegrated back into the community.

John's story

John was convicted of an aggravated burglary committed with another. John had no previous convictions but was given a six-year prison sentence. The victim, an 80-year-old lady, was in her flat when they broke in and the other offender knocked her to the ground. John felt very bad about what happened. He asked his probation officer if there was anything he could do and was referred to the mediation unit. When the mediator saw John, in prison, he was coping badly and was feeling very depressed. He wanted to do anything he could to put things right.

The mediator then saw the victim, Peggy, who spent her time fundraising for her church. She was very interested in mediation with John and wanted to meet him. This meeting was arranged with the co-operation of a probation officer in the prison. The meeting enabled the full expression of emotions. Peggy told John that she forgave him. The only thing she wanted from him was for him to make good when he got out of prison. John made a sincere apology. A few weeks later John wanted to write to Peggy and Peggy wanted to write to John with things they had thought about since their meeting. A second meeting was arranged to enable a final closure of the case. Later Peggy also asked John's mother to come to tea with her. This was helpful to John's mother as she had suffered tremendous feelings of guilt. Lifting that burden of guilt meant that she would be able to take John back into her home more easily when he came out of prison.

Of course, this is only half the story because mediation can also be enormously empowering for victims. Through the mediation process victims are given a series of choices. Part of the after-effects of an offence such as burglary, robbery or assault is that victims feel vulnerable through a feeling of loss of control over their lives. They were not given a choice about the offence happening. The normal criminal justice process may leave them out completely and they are left feeling helpless. The mediation process means that they can choose whether to take part in mediation or not. They can choose what type of mediation they want, indirect or face to face, and they can choose what type of reparation they would like from the offender. Having a choice is empowering for victims in itself, but even more empowering can be the opportunity to challenge the offender, to be angry, and to know that the offender has heard their pain and anger.

The management of anger is an important part of the mediation process. If the victim remains angry to the point of being abusive throughout the assessment period, then a face-to-face meeting with the offender may not be appropriate. Offenders need to know that their victims are angry but there is a difference between controlled and uncontrolled anger. Safety for all parties is obviously of paramount importance and this is where the skill of the mediator, and the case supervisor, is demonstrated during the assessment process.

The type of mediation undertaken will depend on this assessment process and the safety considerations must include emotional and psychological, as well as physical, safety for both parties. In some cases it is not safe for victim and offender to meet, not because they might come to blows but because of psychological concerns, as illustrated by the following case example.

Michael's story

Michael was convicted of two counts of indecent exposure. He was given a probation order. The probation officer, in her casework with Michael, tried to get him to address what he had done and think about the effect on the victim, Sally, a woman 'postie'. The mediator offered mediation to Sally and Michael. Both were willing for some form of mediation to take place. However, Sally did not want to meet Michael again. The mediator and the probation officer agreed with her that a meeting was not appropriate. This was because Michael fantasized that Sally enjoyed what she saw. He was sure of this because she had come back to his house to deliver mail on a second occasion and so he exposed himself again. If Sally met Michael he would assume that she really liked him.

Michael was a loner who had no close relationships. The probation officer helped him to understand that because women smiled at him, or delivered to his house, they did not necessarily like him. Michael's difficulties were explained to Sally which helped her to understand what had happened to her. She wanted to make it clear to Michael that he was completely wrong in his perceptions of her. She wrote him a powerful letter saying how she felt about what he had done and making it clear what her feelings were about him. Michael cried when he read the letter. The destruction of his fantasy was painful for him but necessary if he was to address his faulty perception of relationships with women.

Sally was pleased that he had been so affected and felt empowered. The offence had left her feeling vulnerable and now she felt strong again.

The probation officer gained through the real challenge to Michael, and was able to continue the challenging work during the probation order.

This case example shows how redressing the power imbalance caused by the offence can help victims to recover. Many offences which involve a large amount of power imbalance can be difficult to mediate because of the care which needs to be taken to redress that imbalance. The more difficult cases to mediate involve the types of offence which may have the largest power imbalances, for example sexual assaults, domestic and racial violence, and offences involving very young or old victims (or offenders).

Probation officers preparing reports for court for offenders charged with assaults on their wives or partners, often find that offenders say they are very sorry and want to apologize. Probation officers can be in a difficult position because they need to know the truth, yet they may be perceived by victims as representing offenders. Victims of domestic violence are often terrified if they think an approach has come from their former partner.

There is a place for mediation here as a neutral mediator can offer to hear both sides separately in a neutral venue. If the couple are still living together and the husband or partner is not prepared to let his wife see the mediator independently, there is a clear message for the probation officer.

The case experience of the Leeds unit is that where the couple were already separated, not one of the victims wanted to be reconciled. The women used the mediation process to let their former husbands/partners know that the relationship was finally ended. These victims and offenders found that mediation helped them to end their relationship on a better note and to finalize their arrangements in a civilized manner. The mediation process helped the probation officers to work with offenders by confronting them with the absolute fact of their relationships' end. The officers were then able to focus on what had led the offenders to perpetrate the violence, to prevent it happening again in their future relationships.

Melvyn's story

Melvyn was charged with arson. After a row with his wife over her supposed adultery he set fire to the bedroom. Sarah fled the house. The mediator found that Melvyn was very sorry and wanted to make up with Sarah. She, however, said it was the final straw in their violent relationship and wanted him to know that this was the end. Through the indirect mediation process Sarah was able to say the things she needed to in order for Melvyn to begin to realize that it was finally over. Direct face-to-face mediation was not an option because of the safety element. Both Sarah and the mediator felt that Melvyn would attempt to use the mediation meeting to re-establish dominance over her by making threats.

The relationship between the probation officers and the mediation service has to be one of close co-operation and information sharing. With the permission of both victim and offender, information can be passed to the probation officer which is invaluable for working with the offender on offending behaviour. Offenders often do not tell the whole story or may not know the whole story and the information provided by victims is essential for confronting and challenging offenders with the effects of their behaviour. However, the benefits to victims of being included as equal partner in this process are now well documented (Marshall and Merry 1990; Umbreit and Roberts 1996; Wynne 1996).

One of the most devastating crimes, in its long-term effects on victims, is sexual abuse. The abuse of power has heart-breaking results for children and is compounded when the abuser is a close family member. Survivors of abuse may require long-term counselling to help them come to terms with what has happened to them, but mediation also has its place in assisting the healing process for other family members.

A child's story

A child, four, was abused by her uncle Thomas, a 17-year-old who babysat for her. Her distress alerted her mother and the child revealed what had happened. Thomas was sent to a young offender's institution. His probation officer referred him for mediation because none of the family had ever discussed the offence. His mother visited him in prison regularly and this led to conflict because she and her daughter, Janet (mother of the child), used to be very close and saw one another every day. Janet felt that her mother had let her down by visiting Thomas and no longer saw her mother.

The mediator was able to visit all the parties and effected two mediations. The first was between Janet and her mother, who fell into each other's arms and said the things they needed to say to each other. The second mediation was between Thomas and his mother to enable them to discuss the offence. During the mediation process Janet realized that she needed professional help and the mediator put her in touch with a counselling agency. At that point Janet's husband realized that he too needed some help. At no time was it intended that mediation should be carried out with the four-year-old child. We felt that the best way to help the child was to help the parents work through their grief so that they could act normally again with their daughter.

Mediation in casework is something that can have enormous benefits, but only if used in an ethical manner which follows good practice guidelines and experience. It is ironic that mediation practice was begun by probation officers in their casework with offenders. Today, many years' experience shows that probation officers are often not perceived as neutral by victims, unlike trained community mediators. Good practice now suggests that probation officers should not attempt to mediate their own cases but rather work in partnership with separate mediation service providers (Mediation UK 1994).

References

Braithwaite, J. (1989) *Crime, Shame and Reintegration*. New York: Cambridge University Press.

Marshall, T. and Merry, S. (1990) *Crime and Accountability*. London: HMSO.

Mediation UK (1994) *Guidelines to Starting a Victim Offender Mediation Service*. Bristol: Mediation UK.

Umbreit, M. and Roberts, A. (1996) *Mediation of Criminal Conflict in England: An Assessment of Services in Coventry and Leeds*. Minnesota, MN: University of Minnesota.

Wynne, J. (1996) 'Ten years' experience of victim offender mediation.' In B. Galway and J. Hudson (eds) *Restorative Justice: International Perspectives*. New York: Criminal Justice Press.

Useful addresses

West Yorkshire Probation Service

Leeds Mediation and Reparation Service
The Basement
Oxford Place Centre
Oxford Place
Leeds
Yorkshire LS1 3AX
Tel: 0113 243 5932

CHAPTER 13

Healthcare and Complaints Advocacy

A Campaign for Real Listening
and Patient Participation

Stephanie Ellis

Why is healthcare advocacy needed?

This chapter is written from my perspective as Chair of an inner city Community Health Council (CHC), although the views are my own. Advocacy schemes come in many forms, but are usually thought of as helping to ensure that the voices of those with special needs, who are all too easily ignored, are heard. There is a real danger, however, that advocacy has a marginalizing effect. We listen to people with advocates because we feel we should, rather than believing that what they have to say is important. It is too easy to dismiss, without thought, what they have said. Advocacy for people with special needs remains important, but remember, most of us go through times when we need help to ensure that our views are heard. Everyone needs an advocate at some stage in their lives.

Ranjit, a colleague rather than a friend, asked if I would accompany him when he went for a check-up at the hospital. He seemed worried but did not say what was wrong. While we sat on the bus I chatted about what I did whenever I went to see a doctor. I said I liked to write down what I wanted to say: symptoms and important questions (i.e. can I still have a drink while taking the medicine?). Ranjit was not impressed, and sat in silence that lasted all the way through the long wait outside the consultant's room. Half an hour later he came out of the doctor's room looking as worried as before. Although his English was good he had not understood what the doctor had said. He had a prescription but had no idea what it was or how often he had to take the medicine. At the pharmacy I asked the pharmacist to explain to him what he would be taking, and what the side-effects and so on might be. He did, and Ranjit came away looking much happier.

Going to the doctor had been traumatic for Ranjit: he found it impossible to have a meaningful conversation with the consultant. He was unable to listen properly to what was said and, judging by the consultant's cheery look when Ranjit left, it is unlikely that he had a clue about how his patient felt. Ranjit's career has been impressive and his job is high powered. He had never shown any signs of being anything other than very confident, yet he, like so many others, found that being a patient meant being unable to speak.

Most of us find that going to see a doctor ties our tongues and clears our brains of rational thoughts. It is a salutary experience, a useful reminder that advocacy is a universal need, and not 'just' for the 'deserving'. If ordinary people find any conversations with doctors disempowering, then how much more difficult will they find it to ask a question, never mind make a complaint? This is why the advocacy role undertaken by CHCs is so important.

What is healthcare advocacy?

This chapter is about the needs of the ordinary layperson dealing with healthcare professionals. People with special needs are considered in other chapters. Some of the people I am talking about will be patients, others will be carers, others friends and relatives. All can find talking to doctors disabling. Much of what I am saying applies, of course, to all forms of advocacy, but my own expertise is in healthcare situations.

I use the standard terms of 'advocate' and 'partner' – advocates endeavouring to help their partners either by speaking on their behalf or helping them to represent themselves. As in other forms of advocacy, the partnership may be a long-term arrangement, but it could also be quite short-term or indeed, as with the colleague I mentioned above, a one-off event.

Advocacy is, then, empowerment: enabling the partner's voice, views, wants and needs to be heard. The pressures of time will mean that it will often be a matter of the advocate representing the partner. The ideal helps the partner develop the skills and confidence to speak on their own behalf. However, I would argue that advocacy should surely also be about educating people, such as service providers, to realize the value of making the effort to listen to their clients, and to demonstrate that they have heard and valued that person's comments.

In the National Health Service (NHS), advocacy is often confused with translation and interpreting. This is unfortunate since they are very different needs. Interpreting services are necessary, and this applies not only to foreign languages but also to providing signing and Braille for those people with impaired hearing and vision who would benefit. It is essential that everyone has access to such services if they are needed to enable them to communicate.

However, I want to concentrate on advocacy. Advocacy is about ensuring voices are heard but, even more importantly, about ensuring others listen. Over the years my attitude to advocacy has changed: my concern is less with making voices louder and more about making the rest of us listen more carefully.

Listening as a passive activity is useless. Making reassuring noises merely tells the speaker that there is a life form (not necessarily intelligent) in front of them. Saying no more than 'I hear you' or 'I understand' is so meaningless as to be insulting. It is, in my experience, a way that people with MBAs use to ignore you: their sign that they cannot be bothered to listen to you. People will feel ignored, hurt and insulted by what they will see as a lack of genuine commitment to their needs.

Real listening is, of course, hard work: it means taking sufficient notice of what is said so that you can, and do, reflect back in your own words what you have heard. This demonstrates that you have listened. The rest is pretence. Listening, and acknowledging what has been heard, does not necessarily mean agreeing with what has been said; only that the person really has been heard, that the decisions have been taken whilst aware of these views. This is when advocacy works. Sadly, it is the rarest form of healthcare advocacy. These strictures also apply to the public consultations that are a feature of the NHS.

Advocating for the community

CHCs are the official watchdog of the NHS. There are some 100 CHCs in England and Wales. Anyone with a query, or a complaint, about healthcare services can either telephone or visit their CHC. The staff actively network with NHS officials, and so know who best to contact when wanting to find out more information. Most CHCs maintain a library of reference materials, as well as having stocks of healthcare-related pamphlets.

There will be three or four paid staff who help people with their enquiries, but there will be over 20 council members who are volunteers. We are part of the NHS in the sense that it funds us, but our remit is to represent patients' views about local services. The local authority, regional NHS office and local voluntary groups elect members, but we remain independent. There is little guidance about what we in the CHC must do, but all organizations within the NHS proposing to change their healthcare services must consult with us, and the health authority (whose job is to purchase healthcare services for its population) must meet with us at least once a year. Some CHCs see their role as a confrontational one: they believe that they are there to argue with the NHS. Sometimes this is necessary, but I would argue that it is usually more effective to influence than to shout.

CHCs are primarily concerned with patients' rights. *The Patients' Agenda* (1996), published by the Association of Community Health Councils for England and Wales (ACHEW), reflects this:

> The Patients' Agenda sets out a series of rights not included in the NHS Patient's Charter. Drawn up in consultation with Community Health Councils and patients' organizations, it highlights those areas where patients find their present rights are poor or non-existent and where reasonable expectations are not met.
>
> Since the Government launched the Patient's Charter in 1991 it has raised certain standards in the NHS, although sometimes at the expense of others. Most notably it has cut waiting times. Yet it could do far more to address important issues at the heart of the health service – equality of access to health care, the scope for patient participation on the basis of informed choice and the quality of care and treatment. These are the central concerns of the Patients' Agenda.
>
> Many of the standards listed in the Government's Patient's Charter are described not as rights but as expectations. An expectation, we are told, is a standard of service which the NHS is aiming to achieve, and which, in exceptional circumstances may not be met. Faced with this statement it is difficult to know how to respond when one of these expectations is not satisfied. (ACHEW 1996, p.1)

CHCs are not the only organizations which comment on NHS standards. However, whilst CHCs are primarily concerned with the needs of the local community, other organizations, such as the Patients' Association and the College of Health, take the national view. Then there are the plethora of voluntary bodies and charities, at local, regional and national level, that look at the NHS, usually at a specific aspect or particular illness. They make their own representations, also often in the form of advocacy – although tailored to their particular client group. I welcome this pluralism.

Part of my work in the CHCs has been about persuading the local NHS trusts (i.e. the providers of healthcare services) to see advocacy to be more than interpreting, and to see advocacy as helping rather than hindering them. I have also tried to get the NHS to understand the value of public consultation. Consultation is the reverse side of the coin to advocacy. Both are needed.

If advocacy is about ensuring voices are listened to, public consultation should be about making sure that the message is seen to have been heard. Consultation is too often seen, by even quite forward-looking organizations, as simply being an exercise *after* the planning process is finished to tell the public about proposals and get some feedback. Good consultation is far more than that. It is a tool for making the best decisions, and helping people to see that this has happened, by enabling them to participate. If service providers see their role as working in partnership with service users, then the services will improve (Winn 1990).

When I first joined the CHC we found ourselves faced on numerous occasions with a trust coming up with a proposal to change a service. There would usually be a neat row of options and we were asked to comment on these. None would be satisfactory, but if we suggested better ones we would then be told that these were too late for consideration. We were only involved at the end of the planning process, when the decisions had already been taken.

We appear to be persuading some of the NHS trusts in our area that it is better to discuss the issues with us earlier: it is then easier for all to spot what might or might not work. It also stops the rows that too often mar the public consultation meeting. We have therefore started regular 'keep in touch' meetings in which we and they can discuss informally possible developments before their planning becomes too fixated on any one option.

This is fine for the CHC, but we also want to see the public involved earlier. At the time of writing my CHC is considering two consultations. The first is about the future of in-patient mental health care provision. The second is about a community needle-exchange. Both have involved some acrimonious public meetings at which residents have expressed hostility to the proposals. In neither case had the NHS bodies responsible taken the time before the proposals were launched to talk to local residents. In the case of the needle-exchange this was despite the fact that the residents had been protesting about the users for some time.

The users of the mental health-care provision were lucky. They had been consulted on the proposals. The drug users were never, as far as I can tell, even asked what sort of facility they might want. These are not isolated incidents. Nor is it only the providers who make these mistakes. My doctor is about to move to a new surgery, provided for by the local authority. I know about this because I was at the meeting, two or three years ago, when this was decided. However, I doubt many of her patients are aware of this move. There has been very little announcement of it, never mind discussion. It was presumably not felt to be worth the bother to talk to the patients. This is despite the fact that I have had a number of discussions with the health authority about this issue and they have recognized that it needs to be improved.

CHCs collect many similar examples where patients or potential patients are not given the opportunity to comment on proposals which will affect their treatment. Persuading the NHS that it is worth talking to people and discussing plans as early as possible remains a struggle.

The process of consultation

There are other ways to improve consultations, and these include making them staged processes. The formal consultation at the end of the planning should at one level be just that, a formality, and one that marks the end of the process: the real engagement of the public should happen at earlier stages.

I am not saying that the formal consultation is a waste of time. It is a necessary and valuable part of the process – provided that its purpose is clearly understood: to be a demonstration that the earlier stages have taken place. It is not to introduce the proposals, but instead it should be the opportunity to demonstrate that all views have been heard and taken into account.

For a consultation to work, for it to be useful, it must go through the following stages:

- The proposals need to be introduced, with the context and available resources explained. This should be in the form of presentations as well as written reports.

- Then the public, whether as groups or individuals, should be given the opportunity to discuss and debate the principles, and look at possible options while they are still in a fairly flexible form. They should be able to contribute alternative ideas.

- The public should then be able to make more considered comments about the proposals.

When the consultation period is over, two more stages are needed:

- The publication of the responses. I am not talking about a vast print run, but there should be enough copies for the CHCs and local libraries, as well as there being a few copies to hand out at public meetings.

- A final meeting at which the consultation and the responses it generated are discussed, and the proposed way forward is explained in the light of the responses.

This model seems to me both straightforward and obviously beneficial. It enables the public to see how their views are listened to, to see how decisions are made. However, when you look at the resistance within the NHS to something as simple as printing the responses, it is evident that openness and the principles of participation cause senior officers a lot of unnecessary fear and worry.

In respect to the in-patient mental health proposals mentioned above, these involved expanding the wards at a psychiatric unit. The local residents were concerned about whether the patients would be a danger to them. However, when our CHC held a public meeting on this topic, it was interesting to watch several people become much happier just hearing that the planners were interested to hear their views. The NHS trust which runs this psychiatric unit has since created a local liaison group. Even their first meeting rapidly moved away from the original proposal and began to debate more general issues. The residents were already beginning to relax: being listened to reassured them.

It can be seen that many of these lessons about listening and participating are ones that apply to the NHS in regard to both advocacy and consultation: they go hand in hand. Advocacy enables the voices to be heard, whilst good public consultation ensures that people are confident that they are being listened to.

The CHC has a role as a vital conduit, enabling the public to reach the NHS and helping the NHS to reach the public, to become responsive to service users. CHCs can quickly identify the appropriate person and resources, and how to get hold of them. Because we are known to them they are more prepared to listen to what we say, and we recognize that one of our main roles is to act as a conduit for patients' concerns about the NHS.

Advocating for the complainant

The CHC's main source of information about patients' concerns comes from dealing with complaints. I serve on the Patients' Services Committee at my local NHS community services trust, and am also Secretary of the Patients' Association. As a result I have studied over a couple of thousand complaints. In my view there are three main reasons for complaints: communication, communication and communication.

Too many health service managers and professionals regard complaints as something that must be denied. Doctors seem to associate complaints with blame, and are more concerned with avoiding the consequences than trying to ameliorate them. They act as if saying sorry is admitting guilt, but this attitude is mistaken. They assume that the patient is going to sue, but surprisingly few complaints revolve around wanting to sue, at least not until they have been kept waiting by a ridiculously long complaints procedure. Some doctors also seem to assume that patients do not understand the problems and limits of medicine and surgery and expect every treatment to work out perfectly. I hardly know of any patients who think that. They are much more likely to appreciate that medicine is an art as much as a science. There is always a risk in undergoing medical treatment, for instance surgery or chemotherapy, no matter how skilled the doctor. The art of medicine is to reduce the risks wherever possible: but the risks never go away completely. Operations can go wrong. People react in different ways to drugs, and a drug that works beautifully on 10,000 patients may cause an unforeseen problem for another patient.

In my experience most patients expect doctors to do their best, but to feel remorse when treatments are not as successful as hoped. I still regularly hear of patients who were not given any explanation about the risks of a treatment, were not given enough information to assess the likelihood of success in different options. If the patients have not had an opportunity to understand the decisions made about their healthcare, it is not surprising if they express disappointment at poor outcomes.

Even if the patient is angry when realizing that a treatment has not been successful, it still does not mean that they will want to sue. In my experience what usually persuades the patient to sue is the feeling that the doctor does not care, has not recognized the patient's viewpoint. Indeed, I have seen several complaints in which the patient was quite explicit that had the hospital apologized they would have felt their complaint was dealt with: suing appeared to be the only way to force the hospital to recognize that the patient had suffered.

Apologizing is a very quick and effective way of dealing with complaints and avoiding being sued. Out of the dozens of complaints that I have monitored, at least 80 per cent could have been resolved by an apology. For example, I met Grace at the annual general meeting of the Patients' Association. She caught me over the tea break and regaled me with a long story about a court case in which she was suing a consultant. Listening to her I soon became aware that she did not have a leg to stand on, but that somehow her tenacity had enabled her to keep the case going far longer than was sensible. It was going to end in tears. She would never accept that her case was not sound.

I was amused to realize that I knew the consultant and so later was able to get his view of the events. Once prompted he was voluble about the time and money wasted on the case. He was furious about the four long, boring days he had spent in court. He could not comprehend how a ridiculous court case started by a vague, confused and very confusing woman should have run for so long.

The consultant is bright but does not see that he brought the case on himself: that it was his fault that he had to spend those four long, dreary days in court. His crime was that he did not apologize when Grace's husband died of cancer whilst on the operating table. He felt she was a fool because when he had described her husband as stolid, she had thought he was saying he was stupid. He knew she had misunderstood but instead of spending a few minutes comforting her, he stormed off saying he had better things to do. There is never anything better to do than apologizing to someone whose spouse has died under your care.

I met Grace about five years after her husband's death. I found her difficult to follow, narrow-minded and rather argumentative. None of these qualities endeared her to me. I did not enjoy her company. However, I am equally clear that she deserved to be listened to. She needed to be heard. She did not need an advocate to relay her concerns: she needed an advocate to help ensure that people would see that it was important to listen to her.

Grace, like most people, did not understand or care about the nuances of who to complain to or about, or what the procedures were. It is difficult for a service user to understand the differences between purchasing health authorities, hospitals and the clinics run by NHS community trusts. Such concepts were all irrelevant to her. She was right to ignore these. A patient should be able to lodge their complaint anywhere in the system, confident that it will be listened to and dealt with by the correct people.

Much of the work of CHC staff is about helping complainants. It takes time to help the complainant work through their worries and allow them to clarify their thoughts so that they can see more clearly what their complaint is about and how they can take it forward.

Patients think that it is easy to complain, that they can complain about any aspect of the service: not so. CHCs can give information as to whether service contracts provide for particular standards in each area. Complaining about general practitioners (GPs) is particularly difficult. If they have been negligent then the patient can complain, but if the complaint is that they have been rude or unhelpful then the complaint will not be heard. GPs are self employed: their contracts with the NHS do not stipulate that they have to be pleasant.

Complainants therefore need to know what they can complain about as well as how they can complain. CHC advocacy for complainants must therefore start by discussing these issues to enable patients to consider realistic options.

The complaints procedures used in the NHS were adopted following the Wilson Report (1994). while helping to standardize the way complaints are dealt with, these do little to address a fundamental flaw. Some complaints are to be judged as being real complaints while others are not. The complaint may be valid but if it is not a contravention of the terms of a contract then it will not be listened to. Helping complainants develop their cases is an important CHC task, although there are many other issues which seriously concern service users which are not addressed because of lack of resources. There is only so much three CHC staff and 24 members can do.

Advocating for the patient

Why should a patient need to have a complaint against the NHS before their voice can be heard? How can service providers get to hear what service users think of what is provided? I would like to promote one idea: focus groups, which are a simple way of enabling people's views on issues to be garnered.

It is a very simple idea. Patients are invited to join a small group, and are led through a structured discussion about some aspect of the service. Sometimes people with specific interests in the area are invited, but the idea works even better when a more disparate group is brought together. A facilitator is necessary to help tease out some of the issues that concern the members of the group, and he or she will enable the members to question some of the practices, and thereby improve the service. Focus groups allow people to make comments without feeling they are making a complaint. They provide a useful forum for gathering feedback on the service.

Many service users find it difficult to articulate their views. They find the language of the NHS bizarre and impossible to understand. So why should they make the effort? Yet it is right to say that as citizens we have a duty to make ourselves aware of how we are governed, what a service such as the NHS should provide, and how we can influence decisions about the provision of healthcare. However, with the best will in the world we cannot be interested in everything. There are enough problems in our everyday lives without having to look for more problems. I have been interested in healthcare provision for some time but I recognize that other people have other interests.

At one stage I assumed that the problem of low attendance at CHC meetings, and public meetings, was because of public apathy: only the really committed would come. I no longer see it in these terms: I know too many people who have attended such meetings but find the experience too difficult to understand. They cannot see any progress being made in addressing their concerns, so they move on to doing something where they can see that they are being effective.

There is plenty of rhetoric in the NHS about the desirability of listening to what people want and encouraging patient participation. Unfortunately, too often that is all that it is. Until the NHS develops a genuine commitment to working with its users, seeing it as a partnership, empty rhetoric is all it will ever be.

This chapter has focused on advocacy as being a primary role of CHCs. As part of this, one of the needs CHCs have pushed for is ensuring that the right sort of services are available. Counselling is an example of one of the services that is too often seen as an add-on rather than an integral part of healthcare within the NHS. Fortunately this attitude is changing and it is increasingly common to find GP practices which employ a counsellor: most seem to offer a general service, but some specialize in psychosexual, addiction, bereavement or other kinds of therapy. This is generally short-term counselling, but it is certainly a help.

CHCs can also provide enquirers with details of counselling services that are available. They officially focus on NHS provision, but most have extensive networks in the voluntary sector and can help identify where to look. The voluntary sector, especially in a large inner city area, can involve an extensive patchwork of services, helping, for instance, people with cancer, refugees, battered wives, dyslexic children, and so on. The standards can vary widely, and while CHC staff may have extensive contacts they are wary about being seen to endorse organizations about which they know little, and for which there is no mechanism for monitoring or for complaining about.

Our CHC is very aware of the unmet needs, such as for counselling, of many minority groups, including the homeless and those who suffer from some form of discrimination (for instance, racism, ageism or sexism). These people will be vulnerable to poor physical health and to depression, so health and psychological counselling can be helpful to them.

CHCs also have contacts with the mediation and conciliation services which are now being set up throughout the NHS. How this relates to assisting in dealing with conflicts between patient and doctor is explored in Chapter 15 of this book.

CHCs themselves can be seen as being mediators. They help mediate with service providers and the NHS, helping to create a framework in which discussions about the provision of healthcare can be held. The independence of CHCs and their comprehensive local knowledge of the NHS enables them to help people discover the advantages and disadvantages of a proposal, and discuss the options. Mediation, like advocacy and counselling, is a process of empowerment.

Nevertheless, CHCs give primacy to their image as an advocate for patients while also helping to educate them about the NHS. CHCs offer the opportunity to contribute to the debate on healthcare provision, so that rather than being passive receivers of the services, patients can enter into a dialogue about what they really want. They are therefore essential cornerstones of a citizen-based democracy.

References

Association of Community Health Councils for England and Wales (1996) *The Patients' Agenda*. London: ACHEW.

Wilson, A. (1994) *Being Heard*. London: Department of Health.

Winn, D. (ed) (1990) *Power to the People*. London: King's Fund Centre.

Useful addresses

Association of Community Health Councils for England and Wales

30 Drayton Park
London N15 1PB
Tel: 0171 609 8405
Fax: 0171 700 1152

The Patients Association

Union House
8 Guilford Street
London WC1
Tel: 0171 242 3460

CHAPTER 14

HIV/AIDS

Advocacy, Counselling and Mediation
with the Dying and the Bereaved

Bill Kirkpatrick

Much of my work during the past 15 years has been with those persons living with the challenges of HIV/AIDS, whether infected or affected. I have also been alongside many that were dying as a result of an opportunistic infection due to massive damage to their immune system; and I have been with their bereaved partners, families and friends.

Being involved in this work has caused me to recognize and accept that dying and bereaved persons are both suffering major losses. Therefore I believe it is crucial that I am able sensitively to hear and understand the meanings of their differing cries. These anguished cries are nurtured by loss; they are cries for supportive empathy, for understanding and for helping sufferers to find a meaning to their losses, and for something positive to emerge out of their dying and their grieving.

Certainly I am not there to moralize, to preach, to condemn or to proselytize. In my view that could be emotional or religious blackmail, not an act of acceptance or empathy.

My experience shows me that the roles of advocacy, mediation and counselling are nurtured through listening attentively with the whole of my person. I find they sometimes merge, but at other times develop in sequence, during the long supportive relationships I have with people.

Advocacy has a very long history: it can be found in the Hebrew and the Greek Bible. The *Oxford English Dictionary* (1986) defines the advocate as one whose profession is to plead the cause of justice – one who pleads or speaks for, or on behalf of, another as I often do if I am trying to help a family understand and accept a relative who has AIDS.

In the role of counsellor, I support sufferers through their deep emotional problems so that their sense of identity and meaning is maintained and developed, and not destroyed by the disease.

As a mediator, I am often asked to encourage the reconciliation of families, friends or lovers who are in conflict over HIV or AIDS.

Sensitive casework: the need for multiple skills

Clearly there is a need for the advocacy role in this area of care, especially with regard to various forms of discrimination, health and social care needs, home care and accommodation needs. In other areas such as gender and sexual orientation, and in areas of sex information and sex education in relationship to safer sex activities, there is a need to be involved in pressing for the rights and needs of those infected and affected by HIV/AIDS.

A crucial time for advocacy and mediation is when the person has decided that the quality of life is far more important than its length. When this is felt to be the case, the person may ask for no further aggressive treatments. In this situation the function for me is to be the advocate and mediator for the person too ill to speak for his or herself, or who may be in conflict with a doctor or family member, or to assist in writing the Living Will of the dying person. In such a situation I am very aware of the valuable gift of listening to the dying person and those who are significant to him or her.

This work is not just some aspect of caring, or the making of decisions by or with another person. It is making sure that no one usurps the needs, the rights and the humanity of the person who is entrusting him or herself to me as his/her chosen advocate and mediator. This depends on my ability to collect information, and to act on it appropriately. It further demands that I respect the other person and that I am ready to defend his or her rights.

There are other times when I am asked to go there not only for the dying person, but also for the partner. Especially if the situation between the families is difficult, if they are unable to accept the reality of the commitment, or if there is a common-law type of relationship between two men or two women, an advocate and a mediator may be necessary. Many times I have found myself in these roles for both the dying person and grieving persons. Also, bereavement casework often begins with pre-bereavement counselling.

If I am to be involved then it is essential that I be aware of the various ethical decisions to be made and their possible interpretation for all concerned. This is essential to any advocacy, mediation or counselling. This means having to be prepared to sacrifice my own life, in terms of continuous or crisis demands on my time and energy. In some instances, I face hostility from those who are antagonistic to HIV/AIDS patients and caseworkers; and this has occasionally meant putting at risk my ministry and health.

I am there by the request of the person and my prime function is to listen in such a manner that the other person will know he or she is being heard. This only occurs when I am unencumbered with my own self and my own needs. It means that I am free enough to enter into the silences of the pain of the other person without self interruption. This is the real work of counselling.

I am there in the recognition and acceptance that each and every person is created in the image of God, that each situation is unique and that my work is nurtured by the empathy of compassion. This is linked to a real awareness and understanding of the facts of each person's situation.

The following stories are all true, but names have been changed. They offer a glimpse of the many different roles nurtured by attentive listening, depending upon the immediate situation. Where possible, the prime function of my role is to empower the person seeking such assistance to become his or her own advocate, mediator and counsellor; and many people also think of me as befriending them, as being a 'soul friend'.

Peter's story

The phone rings, the person on the line is a very distraught father, demanding to know what hospital his son is in: 'I know that you know and that you are a priest'. I inform Peter's father I am not able to give him this information. His son, aged 30, has previously said that he does not wish his father to know where he is or his diagnosis. His father replies angrily that he will report me to my bishop. I reply that he is free to do so. Peter's father says he will make my life very uncomfortable. My reply is that I do understand his anxiety but that I am not at liberty to provide him with the information he is seeking without his son's approval. I ask him to try and understand and to be patient. I feel that Peter would agree to see him, but in his own time. Peter had earlier informed me that neither I nor any of the hospital staff or authorities were to get in touch with his family. He did not wish to have anyone to visit him, and he would get through his illness without help, other than that of the care team, and he included me in this team.

Peter had left home just after his sixteenth birthday for the first time. He was pushed out when he informed his family that he was gay. At that time his family was not prepared for such a revelation. Like so many young people Peter left for London, supposedly to stay with a friend. Within the week, during the early hours of one morning, he was arrested for soliciting in the Piccadilly area. Later that same morning he appeared before the local magistrate and was given a conditional discharge providing he returned home the same day. On his return home he was coolly received. However, a few days later an article appeared in the paper about boy prostitutes which included his picture, among several others. He was told to leave and that he was no longer a son. He returned to London with no money, no accommodation, no job and no social security. Peter saw no alternative but to return to selling his body for sex. He left the street scene after being introduced to a group of young male prostitutes who shared a flat.

Eventually someone offered Peter a pub job and after a series of such jobs he became a valet and did very well. His employer encouraged him to go to night school, training to be a chef. He eventually got into the catering trade and became a dinner party chef; for a hobby he was learning about antiques.

Two or three days after his initial phone call, Peter's father phoned again and asked after his son. I simply said that his son was trying to make up his mind and also taking in the ramifications of a diagnosis of AIDS. I suggested to his father that if he tried to pressurize Peter into seeing him before he was ready, they would never meet. It was crucial that the meeting was arranged on Peter's terms and in his timing. For about three months Peter's father phoned me two or three times a week. I would listen; I could feel his anxiety and his guilt. Each time Peter's father rang I would inform him of his son's general condition.

Nearing the end of the three-month period, Peter asked me whether or not he should see his father. I said 'it's your decision, only you can make it'. I asked if he would like to share anything with me that might help him to make his decision. Would he like to share any anxiety he might be having about a possible visit? Two or three days later, Peter said he would like to have a talk with me about his family, who he had neither seen nor heard from in the last 10 or 12 years. He asked what was the point of the proposed visit as they had thrown him out; so far as he knew, they had never tried to make contact with him. In the telling of his story he expressed a great deal of anger, revealing even more about himself and his life. Near the end of my visit he said, 'Father Bill [I believe this was the first time he had called me 'Father'] I would like to see my father, but no other member of the family, for about five minutes'. Peter then asked me to stay with him during the visit. I said I would meet his father at the hospital entrance and stay with them until the visit was over.

Peter's father rang the same evening, with the usual question: 'when am I going to see my son? You can't keep me waiting like this.' I informed him that his son would like to see him for five minutes only, and in my presence, in two days' time and that I would meet him at the hospital entrance. His father was naturally annoyed: 'only five minutes, after a six-hour trip and many weeks of waiting, hardly worth it'. I quietly said, 'your son has offered, it's now up to you'. I further suggested that, no matter how difficult it was for him, if he could follow his son's wishes this could be the opening up of the way for future visits and possibly a full reconciliation, if that was what all the parties really desired.

The meeting did occur. It was cool, each man testing the other out within the allotted time. Later Peter suggested to his father that he should go and catch his train. His father left saying, 'well, son, I will go and we'll meet again – that is, when you are ready'. I walked with the father to the hospital entrance. He was clearly upset, saying, 'I hope my son can forgive me and my family'. I returned to see Peter; he had obviously been crying and all he said to me was, 'he called me son, I would like to see him again'.

For a while Peter controlled his father's weekly visits by extending the time of the visits by a few minutes each time. Within three months after his father's initial visit, Peter said to his father, 'you could visit me whenever you wish'. Once he and his father began to communicate in depth, Peter then asked to see other members of his family. His mother had died some years previously. After Peter left hospital he eventually invited members of his family into his home, which plainly reflected his orientation.

Gradually, Peter became more disabled and made it quite clear that he did not wish to return to hospital. Recognizing he was going to need full-time care, he asked his father to move into his spare bedroom and to be prepared to care for him to the end. His father moved in and cared for Peter until his death, and prepared him for his funeral.

During his last months, Peter started receiving Holy Communion from his father who was a lay church deacon. He arranged and conducted his son's burial service according to Peter's wishes. I was asked to give the address and the committal prayers.

Clearly, by the time Peter died, a great deal of mutual healing had taken place between himself and other significant members of his family.

Mary's story

Mary has been living with the challenges of HIV/AIDS for about three years. She had been living in a friend's flat for five years. One day Mary was informed by the owner of the flat that he had sold it and she was given one month to find new accommodation. It was crucial for her to get a new flat, and as close to the treatment centre and the hospital, as soon as possible.

Mary's social worker and clinic doctor wrote to the housing department for assistance in finding such a flat as soon as possible because of her medical condition. Within three weeks Mary was given a fifth-floor flat in a rather run-down building with no lift and looking out on to railway tracks just outside her window. Mary had great difficulty getting about due to her breathing problems and had barely enough strength to do the most menial tasks of looking after herself.

A further approach to the housing authorities was made by the social worker, armed with full medical reports. In due course a meeting was arranged with a housing official, who refused to make any alterations. He said, 'your situation is all due to your own fault and your lifestyle – why should the state pay for them?' Mary broke down in tears when she heard this.

The social worker reported this meeting to her colleagues and the medical team. Later, Mary came to me asking, 'what can I do?' I said that if she wished, I would get in touch with my local councillor and the director of social services. She readily agreed. The medical and social care teams and I approached the councillor and the director of social services. Within ten days Mary had a new flat, ideally suited to her needs and within five minutes' walk of the hospital. The success of our joint efforts can be seen as a team effort on behalf of Mary.

Bob's story

John had just died; Bob, his partner of ten years, was with him, as were John's parents, who were not happy that Bob was there. They were accusing him of their son's murder.

Two weeks before he died John asked to see me privately, and part of the conversation was around my becoming an advocate and mediator, not only in the fulfilment of his wishes but also for Bob. He was well aware that his parents did not like Bob and he felt they would try to prevent Bob from having anything to do with the funeral service, which he and Bob had planned together, and would certainly try to prevent him from attending the funeral. John said, 'my partner loves me and has cared for me throughout my illness, something my family has refused to do. I know they want me to be buried privately with none of our friends attending, in their local cemetery.' He then said the family would insist that they had first rights in law. 'They want me taken away from those who they say "corrupted me".'

After many hours of trying to be alongside John's family, they informed me, 'we will decide the shape of the funeral, and Bob Smith can attend at a distance, but no comments are to be made about their so-called partnership'. Later I was told that while Bob was viewing his partner's body, John's parents had somehow got into their flat and destroyed any pictures of the two of them together. Bob's parents were incensed at this and the way John's parents were treating their son, having come to love John like another son. They could not believe that John's parents could act in such a way.

Bob's parents were determined that they and Bob would attend John's funeral and that they would acknowledge the committed relationship, love and care they had for each other. Through many hours of mediation, John's parents agreed that Bob and his parents could attend the funeral service, but not the wake afterwards.

Due to the fact of losing his partner of ten years, the pain surrounding his death and the agony caused by John's family, Bob soon became severely depressed and very reclusive. Not allowing anyone to visit him in his new accommodation, he quickly found after the funeral service that he could never go back to their home after what had happened there. Sadly, within six months, Bob committed suicide. His parents suffered a double bereavement and needed many hours of pastoral and specialist bereavement counselling.

Alfred's story

Alfred, aged about 27, had been in and out of hospital for about three years with various opportunistic infections. During his recent spell of hospitalization he appeared to be responding to treatment quicker than previously. He was looking forward to going home and spending the weekend with Tom, his partner of many years. However, during the middle of the week I was asked by the ward team to make a midnight visit to Alfred. Prior to seeing Alfred I had a meeting with the ward team to discuss the reason for their request for such a late night visit. After Tom's visit a couple of days before, Alfred had asked to see his consultant and a senior member of the nursing team, saying he wished to have no further treatment. The various members of the care team spent considerable time with Alfred but he refused to speak with any of them. Instead, he covered his face with his sheet and refused to come out from under the covers for anyone. The care team could not find Tom to see if he knew why Alfred had made such a decision.

When I walked into the room at about midnight, Alfred was completely covered up and lying there as though in a shroud. I sat down beside him and spoke quietly to him, saying 'it's Father Bill' and that I would stay for a while and that if he felt he could share anything with me, this would be confidential unless he stated otherwise. I could say this knowing we had a fairly good relationship. I sat there for about two hours without a word passing between us. He eventually started to make a slight movement towards uncovering his face just enough to have a glimpse of me and then covering up again. About an hour later he lowered the sheet just enough so that he could whisper something to me. This was so inaudible that I had to put my ear next to his mouth. Slowly his voice became more audible. He said he could trust me enough to tell me why he had decided to have no further aggressive treatment.

His partner had come in the other day, saying that he could no longer cope with Alfred's illnesses or the fact that Alfred's share of the money for the house mortgage had stopped. Tom said he was sorry, but he felt he must leave the house and the relationship because he could not cope anymore. Alfred then said to me, 'I felt it would be best if I died and that would solve Tom's problems, as my life insurance would pay off the mortgage and allow Tom to continue living in our home'. I assured Alfred that I felt something could be done to ease this situation and that I would do all I could. I asked him if I could meet with Tom and the full care team and put them in the picture: he agreed. I consulted with the nurse and the doctor before going home. Around eight o'clock that evening I went in to pay a visit to Alfred, who was sitting up in bed having a cup of tea with Tom. This was the result of the medical and other care teams discussing the relevant issues with both men, separately and together. A couple of weeks later Alfred went home with Tom, supported by the community care team. Between them both men were given various forms of assistance and their relationship regained its positive aspects.

These stories show me how valuable it is to have time just to sit and be and let the silences speak. I am sure that most acts of advocacy, mediation and counselling are nurtured through attentive listening and being prepared just to be there for the other person as a person.

Further reading

Curtin, L. (1979) 'The nurse as advocate; a philosophical foundation for nursing.' *Advances in Nursing Science 1*, 3, 1–10.

Kirkpatrick, B. (1988/1993) *AIDS: Sharing the Pain*. London: Darton, Longman and Todd.

Kirkpatrick, B. (1994) *Cry Love, Cry Hope: Responding to AIDS*. London: Darton, Longman and Todd.

Kirkpatrick, B. (1997) *Going Forth: A Practical and Spiritual Approach to Dying and Death*. London: Darton, Longman and Todd.

Kohnke, M. (1982) *Advocacy: Risk and Reality*. St Louis, CV: Mosby.

Marks-Maran, D. (1993) 'Advocacy.' In V. Tschudin (ed) *Ethics; Nurses and Patients*. London: Scutari.

Melia, K. (1986) *Everyday Ethics*. Edinburgh: Churchill Livingstone.

CHAPTER 15

Healthcare Decision Making and Mediation

Yvonne Joan Craig and Masana De Souza

It is said that there is a popular belief in the power of medical science to solve patients' problems, this authority becoming a source of moral and social regulation in 'unhealthy societies' (Wilkinson 1996). For patients this may be their gravest problem.

Women's views whether they have inductions or Caesarean interventions in childbirth may be discounted, and Britain's gynaecologists are facing record numbers of complaints and claims by patients.

Patients seek homeopathic or complementary medicine through anxieties about the harmful effects of chemotherapy and surgery. The pharmaceutical empire may advertise that 'natural' medicine is promoted by health industry followers of Ivan Illich's *Limits to Medicine* (1977), but there is genuine concern among orthodox practitioners, as well as patients, to explore expanding ideas about holism and healing. This is relevant to mediation, a process of individual as well as social healing (Folberg and Taylor 1984).

The medical model of healthcare (Radley 1994) has been experienced as inadequate, and insights from socioeconomics, psychiatry and spiritual dimensions are widely debated. Although there is gratitude for the technological advances of 'frontier medicine' (Hogg 1988) and the devoted commitment of healthcare caregivers, there is concern about ensuring individual participation in decision making, and about whose political power determines health policies, plans and strategies.

Public watchdogs such as Community Health Councils and the Patients' Association are safeguards, but this chapter considers the role of mediation in more directly empowering individuals in decision making about healthcare affecting their lives. As mediators are independent and impartial, they are also concerned about the rights, interests and needs of staff, who suffer from verbal and physical psychopathic attacks (Royal College of Nursing (RCN) 1994), and some unfounded complaints.

The first part of this chapter discusses mediation in relation to its use in a Family Health Service Authority (FHSA) setting and elsewhere. The increasing use of mediation as a first step in resolving complaints is being institutionalized following the 1991 Patient's Charter, although used informally in the past.

The second part of the chapter considers mediation in relation to nursing homes, intensive care, medical ethics and the developing area of decision making with regard to Advanced Directives or Living Wills.

Case studies illustrate the chapter, which concludes with showing the need for interdisciplinary collaboration in healthcare (Loxley 1997), and that advocacy, counselling and mediation all depend on communication skills to advance patient decision making and promote good healthcare (Williams 1996).

Healthcare mediation in action

In 1995 a London health authority was confronted with an ever-growing backlog of patients' complaints which still awaited local resolution before any subsequent appeals could be made at the higher stage of the existing complaints system, pending the establishment of a statutory mediation service.

The Newham Conflict and Change Project (NCCP), described in detail in Chapter 17 of this book, had a wide and trusted reputation for the excellence of its multicultural mediation services. Also, its manager, Masana De Souza, co-author of this chapter, had qualifications as a state-registered nurse as well as skills in practising and training others in mediation, plus extensive experience in preventive healthcare. This combination of factors influenced the choice of the NCCP for providing a model of healthcare mediation which could be utilized by a future statutory health mediation service, while more immediately dealing with the backlog of initial complaints.

The aim of this service was to assist in re-establishing the relationship and communication between health professionals and patients.

About the same time a nearby FHSA offered a year's contract to the NCCP for providing similar mediation services in respect of patients' complaints about general practitioners (GPs), dentists, pharmacists and opticians (although, interestingly, between 1996 and 1997, complaints processed were only about GPs).

As the NCCP's provision of services to these two health authorities, although being administered separately, was based on using similar processes of mediation and specialized training for its team, called health mediators, it is proposed here to merge illustrations and comments about the work done.

The health mediators, already skilled in general mediation, were given specialized training backed up by a manual which included a chapter on the reasons why patients complain about and sue doctors, based on an article in *The Lancet* (Vincent, Young and Phillips 1994). There were also copies of pro forma letters to patients and GPs, the latter indicating that eventual reports on mediations could not be used in any professional disciplinary processes, and that the mediators would respect confidentiality, even though patients might not. Information was also recorded about the rights of patients to bring a relative, friend or Community Health Council member, and those of GPs to bring a professional associate but not a legal representative.

Pre-mediation meetings with patients and GPs were arranged to explain the mediation process, answer questions and confirm that all parties gave informed consent to it. Mediator debriefing after sessions followed the usual NCCP pattern; records were kept, decisions were relayed to the health authorities and ongoing evaluations were made.

The following cases illustrate some of the work done:

> Mr W had recently had heart surgery, suffered from a weak bladder and restricted mobility, and received ongoing psychiatric care, which possibly contributed to the abusive and racist remarks he made about his doctor, who was Jewish. The doctor consequently refused to visit Mr W, who made an official complaint and wrote to his MP.
>
> During the long listening which the mediators gave to Mr W on a home visit, they learned that although he had meals on wheels and home help, he neglected cleanliness and eating. He appreciated the time and attention they gave to him, showing no aggression, but admitted that he was abusive to his doctor. He was also willing for the mediators to report to the health authority that he would welcome an assessment for residential care.
>
> After this visit Mr W withdrew his complaint but changed his GP, which resolved the problem without a full mediation being held.

A more serious complaint involving an allegation that a patient's death was caused by poor treatment was made by Mrs X, a relative of the deceased and his widow. A full mediation took place with the two doctors involved:

> Mrs X alleged that the termination of blood pressure tablets and prescription of steroids were faulty failures of administration which caused Mr Y's fatal heart attack. The doctors explained the danger of

the tablets for elderly people, and the need for steroids to offset the risk of blindness associated with temporal arthritis. Although Mrs X had doubts about whether there had been adequate monitoring of the drugs, she withdrew her complaint.

The doctors, Mrs X and the widow expressed satisfaction at the mediation, which had enabled them to discuss painful, sensitive issues in the presence of impartial mediators who maintained a calm and controlled, although sympathetic, atmosphere.

Two other cases, implicating the same doctor, concerned complaints about poor diagnosis and treatment. The first involved a second doctor also:

Mr and Mrs Z said that their brother's death from pneumonia was caused by the failure to diagnose and treat it earlier in hospital. The doctors had made home visits and gave antibiotics, warning that the situation was potentially serious as he was elderly. However, it was the family which arranged an emergency admission to one hospital shortly after the last visit, from which he was transferred to another where he died a week later.

The relatives complained that there was a failure to order X-rays on hospital admission. The doctors argued that the antibiotics they had given were the same as those given in hospital, and that in-patient care is only necessary when patients have other symptoms requiring intensive care, which did not appear to be the case during the last home visit. However, they agreed that, in retrospect, earlier hospitalization might have been a benefit, although probably not changing the treatment plan nor preventing the sad outcome.

The mediation helped to relieve the stresses and uncertainties of the situation and enabled the relatives to discuss issues in a more relaxed way so that they could consider whether they would accept the doctors' explanation and withdraw the complaint. The doctors hoped that this would take place and expressed satisfaction with the mediation.

The second case involving the same doctor concerned Mrs V's anxieties about breathing and heart problems, from which she complained she had suffered for six years without accurate diagnosis and treatment:

Mrs V felt she had 'lost six years of life' through inadequate care, but the doctor's medical records showed that in 1989 a university hospital check showed no heart problems, nor did tests before ear surgery in 1990. In 1991 the doctor gave her appropriate treatment for reported heart pains, but had no record of her mentioning breathing troubles then or in 1992. In 1995 he recorded this complaint, and an X-ray showed the heart was functioning normally, with some thickening of its tissue.

The mediation helped to bring out the differences between the facts and feelings about illness, and how fears can exacerbate a patient's anxieties and consequent ill health, especially when the heart and breathing are involved. The doctor said that he recognized that communication between himself and Mrs V could have been better, and she said that the mediation had helped her to understand her feelings and the situation more clearly. It appeared likely that she would not proceed with the complaint, but she changed her doctor.

In concluding this brief review of NCCP's work in health mediation, it is important to note that doctor satisfaction is a crucial element in making the process acceptable to the medical profession in the context of the developing statutory complaints system, even though the most vital issue is whether service users feel that it is fair and just.

The fact that local GP group practices are now asking NCCP to train them in communication and conflict management skills could mean, at its best, that patients and doctors learn to talk together constructively about problems at an early stage, so that grounds for complaint do not occur. It is to be hoped that the local confidence in health mediation which NCCP is successfully developing, will spread more widely.

Patient decision making in critical care situations

Institutions such as nursing homes have been called human 'warehouses' (Goffman 1961), and house not only frail elderly people but also younger ones with mental or physical disabilities. These patients have deep, often unmet, needs for sensitive understanding of their varied wishes and problems: so do caregivers, who are overworked, underpaid and undertrained by cost-cutting, time-saving management. The tensions and anxieties generated by competing interests are exacerbated by increasing privatization of National Health Service (NHS) institutions.

Through patient advocacy, formal complaints have increased (RCN 1992; United Kingdom Central Council for Nursing, Midwifery and Health Visiting 1994). However, in many situations sensitive inter-relationships between distressed patients and frustrated staff depend on delicate behavioural adjustments in which mediation skills can help, as the following case shows:

> Paul, aged 30, victim of a body-shattering car accident, resented his recent admission to a long-stay unit and the pain killers which made him sick. He pushed his black nurse away using racially offensive language; she forced the pills down him. Relatives informed the social worker, who used her mediation skills to enable Paul and the nurse to talk about the problem, expressing their mutual anger. When Paul was offered the choice of taking medication before sleeping instead of after meals, he agreed, and apologized to the nurse, who also said she was sorry she had been over-zealous in her duties.

This case may be regarded as a minor instance of the value of mediation which should have yielded to common sense, although this is always culturally conditioned (Geertz 1983, p.10) and subject to the uncritical thinking of which Adrian Furnham writes in his *Lay Theories* (1988). However, mediation is especially useful in some of the decision making involved in intensive care, where crises have to be negotiated between medical staff, patients and relatives.

Allison Murdach (1995) describes the important mediation role of medical social workers in decision making in nursing homes, which is affected by patient, family, clinical and other contexts. *Health and Social Care Management* (Whiteley, Ellis and Broomfield 1996) stresses the need for role clarification, stating that the critical task is conflict handling and negotiation.

Dr Michael Horan (1992) describes a case when he advocated hip-pinning surgery for a patient of 86, speechless, deaf and partially paralysed by a stroke for six years, who had fallen at home. He wanted to enable her to resume home life with one daughter, but a second one threatened litigation if he operated, saying her mother was too old. Dr Horan discussed the problem with his patient, who chose surgery despite the daughter's continuing threats of legal action.

So Dr Horan negotiated a medically ethical decision with patient participation, although, had independent mediation been used involving the litigious daughter, it is possible that her threat might never have been made.

Similar threats were made in a case more fully discussed in *Elder Abuse and Mediation: Exploratory Studies in America, Britain and Europe* (Craig 1997), where Long-Term Care Ombudsmen (LTCOs) acted as advocates and mediators:

> Carl, aged 30, was dying of AIDS, and his distraught parents were angrily watching a nurse trying to give an intravenous injection which made Carl scream in pain. They threatened to report the nurse for incompetence and malpractice, and said that their son wanted no

more life support to be given. The nurse said that only the (unavailable) doctor had authority to discontinue the treatment. The LTCO calmed the situation, saw that Carl was made comfortable, and sat down to listen in turn to them express and learn each other's views, giving first attention to the patient. Carl accepted the injection, the nurse agreeing to call a doctor so that the patient could negotiate about further treatment. The parents apologized to the nurse.

Although medical ethics committees are developing in the health infrastructure of the UK, these are more advanced in the US, where formal mediation processes are being advocated for complex cases.

Mediation and medical ethics

The argument for mediation in healthcare is based on improving existing medical models of paternalistic decision making which can disempower patients, particularly with the advent of telemedicine, who want to contribute to discussions and to limit the legalistic model of judicial intervention which determines what happens to those who are in situations of powerlessness. *Who Owns Our Bodies?* (Spiers 1997) is a cry often heard from the Patients' Association.

Also, the welcome emphasis on holistic medicine may carry its own dangers if the 'clinical gaze' (Foucault 1973) invades even more of our emotional and spiritual lives (Porter 1997).

Mediation is a realistic process for use in holistic medicine that depends on partnerships between patients and healthcare staff (Veatch 1991), and which aims to empower people in as much self determination and self management as possible. Hence the titling of the 1990 American Patient Self-Determination Act, which will be referred to later.

American use of mediation in adult guardianship is also developing, often by lawyers trained as conciliators, or working with them, to ensure that the legal rights of mentally incapacitated persons are upheld, yet providing a more sensitive, comprehensive process for negotiating whether guardianship is necessary, or to what extent (Craig 1997). In Britain Gordon Ashton (1997) describes the conflicts between risks and restraints, and empowerment and protection, which have to be negotiated in the care of old people with dementia: Bart Collopy (1992) in America suggests that mediation can play a useful role here.

It is significant that just as legal reform in the US and UK has contributed to the development of mediation in general, so its application to American medical ethics has been pioneered at the Institute of Public Law, University of New Mexico, where an investigative study revealed the potentials of mediation in a sample of 20 medical ethics committees (West and Gibson 1992), and where a relevant training manual was produced.

The study also showed clearly that conflicts between professional members of committees were as time-consuming, frustrating and serious as those involving patients and relatives. The research found complex networks of sources of professional power which affected staff and patients in disempowering ways, derived from authority, expert information, resource and referent control, coercive sanctions, moral, nuisance, habitual and personal pressures, plus other legitimizing strategies such as the decision-making process itself. This reinforces earlier findings and modern feminist ones (Sherwin 1992).

Although the study found that mediation in medical ethics issues was often informally practised in case conferences by social workers, counsellors and chaplains, and recommended that designated in-hospital workers should enhance their professional abilities by formal training in medical mediation, so that there was always one key person available when situations of conflict or uncertainty arose, the value of independent mediators was stressed.

Here it should be stressed that mediation acknowledges with respect, and in no way detracts from, the principal responsibility and authoritative knowledge of the consultants in charge of cases. However, it provides an opportunity for patients to learn about available optional and recommended treatments, to express their preferences and thus feel some ownership of the decisions eventually made by consultants, or consensually with the caregiving team, through mediation facilitation. It is also recognized that some patients do not want to know anything about the diagnosis, prognosis and treatment of their cases, and that they have the right to request that others make relevant decisions for them.

It is realized that these types of discussion take place informally in most hospitals which conform to good practice standards, although it can depend on consultants and staff power relations as to how patient participation in decision making is conducted. This is where the formal recognition and acceptance of mediation as a procedure for regular institutional use can simplify and normalize arrangements. It could also be useful in local research ethics committees, where chairing may need mediating skills, as in other areas.

Also, although this chapter is focused on patient decision making, it should be noted that well-established hospital mediation processes are valuable for dealing with those inter-staff conflicts which require conciliation but which do not come within the province of unions and professional associations. Mediation can thus make an important contribution to the hospital as a therapeutic community, where interpersonal conflicts are dealt with early in a problem-solving not blaming way before they fester into deeper unhealed stress-related malaise, the spreading infection of which it is much harder to check and heal (Craig 1996).

The future use of mediation skills in decision making about Advanced Directives or Living Wills (King 1996) will depend on how far healthcare professionals, especially GPs (Collins, Lightbody and Gilhooly 1997), and the British public follow the American example in developing legislation comparable to the USA 1990 Patient Self-Determination Act.

This Act is limited to not imposing any statutory obligation on patients to make Advanced Directives, but only requiring nursing homes and hospitals to give patients information about Living Wills and inviting them to consider making these. The Act expressly states that no pressure is to be put on patients, so as to safeguard them from commercial institutions wishing to protect staff from litigation, by misusing such documents to defend non-resuscitation or other near-death interventions.

In Britain, although there is an increasing call for better public education on the subject, led by organizations advocating old people's rights (Greengross 1986), the sensitivities and uncertainties of the area are well understood and respected. This adds to the reasons for making mediation procedures available, on a voluntary basis (as is always the case), to enable patients, relatives, and medical and nursing staff, as well as lawyers, to discuss issues in a way that is empowering to the patient. People are now beginning to make Advanced Directives, which most doctors will accept as legitimate guidance, even though there are no firmly established case law judgements on their use at the time of writing.

Whether Advanced Directives have been made or not, the importance of 'negotiating a good death' by patients, especially where discussion about continuing intensive care does 'not necessarily end in consensus' is stressed by Mary Bradbury (1996, pp.93–94). Sensitive use of mediating skills can be valuable here, although Tony Walter, referring to 'post-modern dying', suggests that many people seek to avoid any authoritarianism of hospital and pastoral management and prefer their own self-directing 'negotiation with each other' about the closing chapters of life (1996, p.202).

All of these issues concern the intimate yet philosophical concepts of personhood which are at the heart of good health and palliative care (Greaves and Upton 1996). It is recognized that the spiritual dimensions of counselling (Thorne 1990) have traditionally brought dying and bereaved people greatly valued comfort, as they feel emotionally accompanied through the transition between life and death.

It is significant here to remember that advocates, counsellors and mediators all share in collaborative casework responsibilities of what Elisabeth Whitmore and Maureen Wilson call 'accompanying the process' in 'participatory alignment' with people at all stages of development as they seek to transform the crises of life (1997, pp.57–74). So this chapter, in describing the potential of mediation, reinforces the book's concern for interdisciplinary co-operative caregiving in supporting people in healthcare decision making.

References

Ashton, G. (1997) 'The legal dilemma of risk and restraint.' *EAGLE 5*, April–May, 4–8.

Bradbury, M. (1996) 'Representations of "good" and "bad" death among deathworkers and the bereaved.' In G. Howarth and P. Jupp (eds) *Contemporary Issues in the Sociology of Death, Dying and Disposal.* New York: St Martin's Press.

Collins, K., Lightbody, P. and Gilhooly, M. (1997) 'General practitioners' attitudes towards Living Wills.' *Generations Review 7*, 2, 13–14.

Collopy, B. (1992) *The Use of Restraints in Long Term Care.* Washington, DC: American Association of Homes for the Aging.

Craig, Y. (1996) 'Patient decision-making.' *Journal of Medical Ethics 22*, 3, 164–167.

Craig, Y. (1997) *Elder Abuse and Mediation: Exploratory Studies in America, Britain and Europe.* Aldershot: Avebury.

Folberg, J. and Taylor, A. (1984) *Mediation.* San Francisco: Jossey Bass.

Foucault, M. (1973) *The Birth of the Clinic.* London: Tavistock.

Furnham, A. (1988) *Lay Theories.* Headington: Pergamon.

Geertz, C. (1983) *Local Knowledge.* New York: Basic Books.

Goffman, E. (1961) *Asylums.* New York: Anchor Books.

Greaves, D. and Upton, H. (1996) *Philosophical Problems in Health Care.* Aldershot: Avebury.

Greengross, S. (1986) *The Law and Vulnerable Elderly People.* London: Age Concern.

Hogg, C. (1988) *Frontier Medicine.* London: Greater London Association of Community Health Councils.

Horan, M. (1992) 'Difficult choices in treating and feeding the debilitated elderly.' In L. Gormally (ed) *The Dependent Elderly.* Cambridge: Cambridge University Press.

Illich, I. (1977) *Limits to Medicine.* Harmondsworth: Penguin.

King, N. (1996) *Making Sense of Advanced Directives.* London: Routledge.

Loxley, A. (1997) *Collaboration in Health and Welfare.* London: Jessica Kingsley Publishers.

Murdach, A. (1995) 'Decision-making situations in health care.' *Health and Social Work 20*, 3, 187–191.

Porter, S. (1997) 'The patient and power.' *Health and Social Care in the Community 5*, 1, 117–120.

Radley, A. (1994) *Making Sense of Illness.* London: Sage.

RCN (1992) *A Scandal Waiting to Happen.* London: Royal College of Nursing.

RCN (1994) *Violence and Community Nursing Staff.* London: RCN.

Sherwin, S. (1992) *No Longer Patient.* Philadelphia: Temple University Press.

Spiers, J. (1997) *Who Owns our Bodies?* Southampton: University of Southampton.

Thorne, B. (1990) 'Spiritual dimensions in counselling.' *British Journal of Guidance and Counselling 18*, 3, 225–232.

United Kingdom Central Council for Nursing, Midwifery and Health Visiting (1994) *Professional Conduct.* London: UKCC.

Veatch, R. (1991) *The Patient–Physician Relationship.* Bloomington, IA: Indiana University Press.

Vincent, C., Young, M. and Phillips, A. (1994) 'Why do people sue doctors?' *The Lancet 343*, 25 June, 1609–1613.

Walter, T. (1996) 'Facing death without tradition.' In G. Howarth and P. Jupp (eds) *Contemporary Issues in the Sociology of Death, Dying and Disposal.* New York: St Martin's Press.

West, M. and Gibson, J. (1992) 'Facilitating medical ethics case review.' *Cambridge Quarterly on Health Care Ethics 1*, 63–74.

Whiteley, S., Ellis, R. and Broomfield, S. (1996) *Health and Social Care Management.* London: Arnold.

Whitmore, E. and Wilson, M. (1997) 'Accompanying the process.' *International Social Work 40*, 1, 57–74.

Wilkinson, R. (1996) *Unhealthy Societies.* London: Routledge.

Williams, D. (1996) *Communication Skills in Practice.* London: Jessica Kingsley Publishers.

Further reading

Rambrogus, V. (1995) *The Deconstruction of Nursing.* Aldershot: Ashgate.

Useful addresses

Mediation UK

Alexander House
Telephone Avenue
Bristol BS1 4BS
Tel: 0117 904 6661

Newham Conflict and Change Project

Christopher House
Streatfield Avenue
London E6
Tel: 0181 552 2050/470 5505

CHAPTER 16

Stress Management and Counselling

Stephen Palmer

Introduction

In this chapter I cover recent models of stress and highlight the multimodal-transactional model which can be used to underpin stress counselling and stress management assessment and interventions (Palmer and Dryden 1995). To help counsellors and casework practitioners understand some of the issues involved with occupational stress, I shall discuss the major stressors that may be encountered in the average organization and consider how these can be reduced. I make suggestions regarding dealing with referrals.

Recent models of stress

The word 'stress' is probably derived from a Latin word, *stringere*, which means literally, to draw tight. It was sometimes used to describe hardships. Later it denoted effort or strain.

The psychological or interactive variable approach attempts to overcome the shortcomings of the earlier models of stress by focusing on the interaction between the external and internal worlds of a person. There have been a number of proposed psychological theories: the interactional and the transactional. The interactional theories focus on the fit between an individual and their environment (Bowers 1973), whereas the transactional theories of stress focus on the cognitive and affective aspects of a person's interactions with their environment and the coping styles they adopt or lack (Lazarus and Folkman 1984).

Lazarus and Folkman defined stress as resulting from an imbalance between demands and resources. They suggested that a person evaluates a particular demand, incident or ongoing situation. This initial evaluation is known as *primary appraisal* and involves a continuous monitoring of the environment together with an analysis of whether a problem exists (Lazarus

1966). If a problem is recognized then the stress response may be activated and unpleasant emotions and physical feelings may be experienced.

The next stage, known as *secondary appraisal*, follows when the person evaluates his or her resources and options. Only if the demands are greater than the resources does stress then occur. If the resources are greater than the demands then the person may view the situation as a challenge and not a stress scenario. It is the subjective, and not the objective, appraisal or assessment of any scenario that may trigger the stress response.

In *Counselling for Stress Problems* (Palmer and Dryden 1995), I described a psychological model of stress that I had been developing which explains how the stress response occurs and guides counsellors, casework practitioners and health professionals in the selection of suitable interventions which may help a person to manage or eliminate stress. The model is a modified version of the transactional model of stress proposed by Cox (1978) and Cox and Mackay (1981) which embodies Arnold Lazarus' (1989) seven interacting modalities consisting of: behaviour, affect, sensory, imaginal, cognitive, interpersonal and drugs/biology (known by the acronym BASIC I.D.).

How people react to a potential stress scenario is due more to their appraisal of it and their perceived abilities to cope or deal with it than the event or situation itself. A situation can be considered as a potential 'trigger' which may initiate the stress response but may not necessarily be the main cause of its activation. The multimodal-transactional model of stress has five discrete stages, and these are explained below.

In *Stage 1*, demand is usually perceived by the person to be arising from an external source in the environment, for example, Jayne has to give an important presentation to the board of directors.

In *Stage 2*, the person appraises whether she or he can cope with the problem or threat. If Jayne believes that she can cope, even if she is being unrealistic, then she may stay in the situation and continue to work on giving the presentation. If she perceives that she cannot cope, then at that moment she may experience stress. Often other factors are involved, such as family, social, cultural or organizational beliefs which she may have imbided over time and now strongly believes in. Therefore, if Jayne believes that she 'must' always give an excellent presentation an innocuous project may assume great importance.

In many cases dogmatic and inflexible 'musts' are internal and not external demands, as Jayne could choose not to hold on to the belief. Many people who suffer from stress cognitively appraise experiences as 'highly stressful' as a result of their attitudes and beliefs which distort the importance of a feared or actual event. If the person believes that she or he can deal with the situation then the stress response is less likely to be activated. However, if the person perceives that she or he does not have the coping resources to deal with the situation, then we move into Stage 3 of the model.

The appraisal of any given situation may occur almost instantaneously. For example, if Jayne thought 'Giving presentations is awful', or 'I can't stand it', or 'I'm going to fail to give an excellent presentation', she may very rapidly feel stressed as these could all constitute negative appraisals of a situation or negative predictions about the possible outcome, and will be sufficient to trigger the stress response. In some cases the appraisal does not have to be in a cognitive form, as sometimes a catastrophic image of the possible negative outcome of an event can also be considered as equivalent to its cognitive counterpart. For example, Jayne could have imagined a picture in her mind's eye of giving a bad presentation.

In *Stage 3*, psychophysiological changes occur. Taken together, these comprise what is generally known as the 'stress response' (Palmer 1997). There is usually an emotion or combination of emotions such as anger, anxiety or guilt. In some cases where a failure has occurred, the person can feel depressed. The person may also respond in a range of modalities, including the behavioural, sensory, imaginal, cognitive, interpersonal and biological/physiological components. There will probably be the minimum of behavioural and cognitive attempts to change the environment or escape from the situation and thereby reduce the demand. People with a range of skills may also use strategies taken from the other modalities too. For example, Jayne could have employed coping imagery (imaginal), communication skills (interpersonal) and relaxation exercises (sensory) to help her cope.

In *Stage 4* the person appraises whether the coping strategies applied are helping to deal with the demand or problem. Thus if Jayne perceives that she has successfully dealt with the presentation then she returns to a state of equilibrium and will no longer feel stressed. At this stage Jayne may have thought, 'I'm in control; I've prepared well; it was well received'. However, if she believes that her strategy is not helping to attain her goal she could remain stressed. Also, she may picture herself failing, which in itself becomes an additional strain in the situation. Actual failure to meet the demand is also detrimental if the person really believes that the demand 'must' be met in an acceptable manner.

Stage 5 involves the long-term feedback or feed-forward system. Interventions may be made by the person which may either reduce stress, maintain the status quo, or alter the external or internal demands. If these produce a positive outcome then the person may return to a neutral state of equilibrium. However, if over a period of time the coping strategies continue to be ineffective, then the person may experience prolonged stress, which could lead to burnout, ill health, or mental or physical breakdown.

Counsellors and other professionals can help service users to improve their coping skills and strategies and thereby to reduce or manage stress. It is worth noting that stress theorists and researchers consider the concepts of coping and control an important part of the stress process (Cox 1993; Dewe, Cox and Ferguson 1993; Lazarus 1966; Lazarus and Folkman 1984; Palmer 1996).

Applying a model of stress to counselling

So how would a stress counsellor, caseworker or health professional help a service user or patient to deal with stress? Either of the models of stress previously described could be used to underpin either a stress counselling or stress management programme, either for an individual in one-to-one counselling or a group of individuals attending a stress management workshop or group stress counselling (Ellis *et al.* 1997; Palmer and Dryden 1995). In this section I shall focus on the multimodal-transactional model of stress which I developed specifically to help in these contexts.

Stress counsellors can teach service users how to intervene at the most appropriate stage of the multimodal-transactional model. Typical Stage 1 skills involve helping service users to improve their coping skills/resources, such as assertiveness skills or time management. For effective stress management, their internal demands, such as 'I must give excellent presentations', need to be modified, otherwise innocuous activating events will continue to trigger the stress response. Modifying the internal demands is a proactive strategy, as it helps service users to keep problems or events in perspective.

Stage 2 strategies include showing service users how to moderate their cognitive appraisal of difficult situations and not necessarily 'make mountains out of molehills'. With prior training, if the person has still triggered Stage 3 of the model, he or she may then apply a range of useful techniques and strategies taken from the seven BASIC I.D. modalities and promptly control, or even stop, the stress response.

Service users suffering from prolonged stress will usually be in Stage 5 of the model and will need a thorough assessment and therapeutic programme.

In counselling, the counsellor and service user devise a modality profile. This consists of the problem areas divided into modalities stating the proposed counselling programme:

> John, aged 46, had been referred by his general practitioner to the practice counsellor, suffering from occupational stress. The

counselling programme was negotiated with John, who was keen to manage his stress.

John found the modality profile very useful as it highlighted a number of key problem areas. He decided that his high expectations of himself and of others was a major contributory factor to his occupational stress.

The modality profile helps to keep both the counsellor and service user focused on specific problems, dealing with them in manageable steps. It can also be used to monitor progress over a period of time, and is revised if and when necessary.

Other forms of stress counselling and stress management

There are a number of different approaches to stress management and counselling. These include stress inoculation training (Meichenbaum 1985; Meichenbaum and Cameron 1972); anxiety management training (Suinn 1990; Suinn and Richardson 1971); cognitive approaches to stress (Beck 1993); problem-solving therapy (D'Zurilla 1986); problem-focused stress counselling (Milner and Palmer 1998); rational-emotive behaviour stress counselling and management (Ellis et al. 1997); the self-help/correspondence or trainer/counsellor-led stress management approach (Clarke and Palmer 1994a,b); and cognitive-affective stress management training (Smith 1980).

However, it is worth noting that these approaches are behavioural or cognitive-behavioural and are similar, although not identical, in their application. Essentially, these approaches help service users to examine and modify unhelpful behaviours and cognitions and improve skills. Other therapeutic approaches, such as person-centred counselling (Clarke 1996), have also been successfully applied to the field of stress counselling and management, and do not necessarily focus on cognitive-behavioural techniques.

Counsellor and casework practitioner intrapsychic stress

So often with counsellors and casework practitioners the most difficult service users they experience are themselves! The psychologist Albert Ellis (1983) believes that we put ourselves under extreme pressure at times due to our own internal demands. He has found the key self-defeating demands are:

- I have to be successful with all my clients virtually all of the time.
- I have to be greatly respected and loved by all my clients.
- I must be an outstanding therapist, clearly better than other therapists that I know or hear about.

- Since I am doing my best and working so hard as a therapist, my clients should be equally hard working and responsible, should listen to me carefully and should always push themselves to change.

- Because I'm a person in my own right, I must be able to enjoy myself during therapy sessions and to use these sessions to solve my personal problems as much as to help my clients with their difficulty.

These beliefs can trigger high levels of anxiety and reduce the practitioner's effectiveness. Clare had the self-defeating belief: I have to be greatly respected and loved by all my clients. She challenged the belief by asking herself questions in the following manner (adapted from Palmer and Dryden 1995, p.225):

- *Logical*: Although it may be preferable to be greatly respected and loved by my clients, does it logically follow that I *have to* be thus respected and loved? *Answer*: It does not logically follow.

- *Empirical*: There is evidence for my strong preference to be greatly respected and loved by my clients, but where is the evidence that they *have to* at all times greatly respect and love me? Where is it written that they *have to* greatly respect and love me? *Answer*: There is no evidence anywhere, nor is it written anywhere (apart from inside my own head) that my clients *have to* greatly respect and love me.

- *Pragmatic*: If I carry on holding on to this belief that my clients *have to* greatly respect and love me, where is it going to get me or my clients? *Answer*: Whether my clients greatly respect and love me or in fact do not, either way I will remain anxious. This will reduce my therapeutic effectiveness and I may back off from encouraging my clients to change in case I lose their respect and love. This will be a no-win situation and potentially unprofessional.

Once Clare had examined and disputed her self-defeating thinking she could develop a helpful coping statement:

- *Coping statement*: Although it may be preferable to be greatly respected and loved by my clients, it is by no means essential. In fact, to do the best for my clients it would be better just to concentrate on the therapeutic goals of my clients and not on my own personal desires.

Counsellors and casework practitioners can benefit from regular supervision, which can also help to reduce stress.

Counsellors and casework practitioners do not work in a social or organizational vacuum. When attempting to manage their own occupational stress or help service users to manage theirs, an understanding of the main issues involved can be useful. The next section covers the key issues involved.

Organizational and occupational stress

In the past decade, stress has become one of the major causes of absenteeism in the workplace. The personal cost to employees of prolonged occupational stress is the negative effect it has on their mental and physical health. In extreme cases it can lead to early death due to coronary heart disease.

Cooper, Cooper and Eaker (1988) found that many occupations shared a number of common stress factors: organizational structure and climate, career development, role in the organization, relationships at work, and the home/work interface. Palmer (1993) also found that internal demands exacerbated stress.

To understand occupational stress it is useful to look at the common factors and internal demands.

Factors intrinsic to the job

The common environmental workplace stressors include air pollution, dust/fibres, heat, humidity, lighting, noise, noxious chemicals/nicotine, sick-building syndrome, static electricity, uncomfortable chairs/work stations and visual display unit screen glare. Quality of life can be greatly improved for employees by modifying these environmental stressors. Changes are likely to increase productivity and general morale. Other factors that may need to be considered are boring repetitive tasks, dangerous work, deadlines, excessive travel, isolated working conditions, long hours, shift work, work underload/overload and work too difficult for the employee.

Organizational structure and climate

Organizational structure and climate may restrict the autonomy of employees, who may feel that they do not have much control over their workload. They may find the work boring and unchallenging, and this can contribute to job dissatisfaction, apathy, resentment, reduced self esteem and a loss of identity. Not surprisingly, this can lead to increased absenteeism. Employers can help to overcome these problems by increasing participation in decision making and encouraging team work to overcome an actual or perceived lack of control.

Employees living under the fear of redundancy or forced early retirement often experience increased levels of stress. It is important that the senior management are seen to communicate as quickly as possible on all issues. Some organizations involve trade unions or staff representatives at board level to encourage active participation in important decisions in an attempt to reduce these problems. Sexism, racism and ageism can exist in some organizations. An enforced policy and procedures to deal with these issues are crucial.

Career development

As an employee moves higher up in an organization, promotion prospects can become more limited. Older staff may need to retrain to be able to use new technology. This challenge can be a major stressor. Older employees are generally concerned about demotion, redundancy, obsolescence, job security and forced early retirement. These concerns can reduce employees' self esteem and self worth.

Role in the organization

There are a number of different role demands that can contribute to stress: ambiguity, conflict, definition, expectations, incompatibility, overload and underload.

In my experience, the three main role demands that often trigger high levels of stress are role ambiguity, role conflict and role overload. When staff suffer from role ambiguity, they are unsure about the role expectations that are required of them. They may receive conflicting or inadequate information about their job, and their role objectives may be unclear. Induction training and a specific job description may help to clarify these areas.

Role conflict involves different expectations or sets of expectations made by the following groups on the employee: superiors, superiors' superiors, peers, service users, subordinates and subordinates' subordinates. Conflict can also arise when too many different roles are expected or where the role behaviour is too difficult to perform for a particular employee. Conflict can occur when the employee's own value system conflicts with the expectations of the organization.

In recent years, with organizations 'down-sizing' – in other words, less people doing more work – one of the most commonly reported stressors has been role overload. Often, teaching employees time management skills is insufficient as they have been given too much work. In these cases assertiveness and cognitive thinking skills training is required. However, the employer needs to address the cause of the problem too.

Relationships at work

Difficult relationships with either co-workers or management at work can be major occupational stressors. Staff may have had insufficient training in people management and may exhibit skills deficits such as unhelpful, aggressive behaviour. Key personnel can learn appropriate skills as part of a management training programme. However, hostile employees may need to receive specialist training or counselling to help them modify their behaviour. Co-workers can be a source of support which can be a buffer against stress (Cowen 1982), although sometimes relationships can be negative due to 'office politics', harassment and competition. Relationships and social support can be enhanced by organizations that offer sports and social facilities (Cox *et al.* 1988).

Home/work interface

When employees experience occupational stress, such as work overload and role ambiguity, then this can affect their home life. The converse is also true. Therefore employees with problems in their home life, such as bereavement or relationship difficulties, are likely to under-perform at work. Assuming that these problems are recognized by their supervisor, then the workplace problem could be dealt with or the employee referred to a counsellor for help with personal problems. Many organizations now use an employee assistance programme which offers a telephone stress counselling service or the opportunity to visit a counsellor.

Internal demands

As we noted earlier, people tend to place internal demands upon themselves. In particular, perfectionists often expect to reach deadlines even when they lack the resources to achieve such targets. Palmer (adapted 1993) highlighted a number of internal demands that can exacerbate occupational stress:

- I/others must perform well at all times.
- I/others must always reach deadlines.
- I/others must be perfect.
- The organization must treat me fairly at all times.

- I should get what I want otherwise I can't stand it.
- Significant others must appreciate my work otherwise I am worthless.
- I must be in control of the situation otherwise it would be awful and I couldn't stand it.

Stress management training and stress counselling based on one of the cognitive-behavioural approaches can help staff to appraise situations more realistically and modify their self-defeating beliefs.

Organizational interventions

Although stress management interventions may incur financial costs, effective programmes may increase performance and reduce absenteeism. Interestingly, Jones *et al.* (1988) found that the level of stress in a group of hospitals correlated with the frequency of malpractice claims. Hospitals in the group that implemented a stress management programme significantly reduced the number of claims. Organizations can undertake stress audits to ascertain where stress 'hotspots' exist and where an intervention is necessary. Stress audits may indicate that the organizational structure needs modifying and/or additional training is necessary. In some cases a need for an employee assistance programme or a stress counselling service becomes apparent (Allison, Cooper and Reynolds 1989). However, in my experience some organizations may not be able to fund such programmes or believe that they could not justify 'expensive' interventions.

Referrals

Casework practitioners and health professionals may need to refer service users to suitably qualified counsellors, psychotherapists and psychologists. The British Association for Counselling, British Association for Behavioural and Cognitive Psychotherapies, and the British Psychological Society hold registers of qualified practitioners. In my experience I would recommend that referrals are made to therapists who are qualified to practise cognitive-behavioural forms of therapy and who have specialized in stress and anxiety management. If qualified trainers or health educators are required to run in-house stress management workshops or seminars, then the three main organizations to contact which hold registers are the Institute of Health Education, the International Stress Management Association (UK branch) or the Centre for Stress Management (which I direct).

It may also be clear that people facing additional issues such as disability or serious illness may benefit from being given information about relevant advocacy groups. Similarly, when they present evidence about stress, inter-agency or inter-organizational conflict, there are now mediation services which specialize in providing conciliation. In all cases, people should be free to make their own choices about where they go for help.

Conclusion

In this chapter we have looked at a number of issues related to stress manage-ment and counselling. We have also focused on occupational stress and its possible control. With the recent changes in society in the home and work contexts, it is likely that we will continue to see a rise in people suffering from stress and stress-related disorders.

References

Allison, T., Cooper, C. and Reynolds, P. (1989) 'Stress counselling in the workplace.' *The Psychologist 2,* 384–388.

Beck, A. (1993) (2nd edn) 'Cognitive approaches to stress.' In P. Lehrer and R. Woolfolk (eds) *Principles and Practice of Stress Management.* New York: Guilford Press.

Bowers, K. (1973) 'Situationism in psychology: an analysis and critique.' *Psychological Review 80,* 307–335.

Clarke, D. and Palmer, S. (1994a) *Stress Management.* Cambridge: National Extension College.

Clarke, D. and Palmer, S. (1994b) *Stress Management: Trainer Notes.* Cambridge: National Extension College.

Clarke, P. (1996) 'A person-centred approach to stress management.' In S. Palmer and W. Dryden (eds) *Stress Management and Counselling: Theory, Practice, Research and Methodology.* London: Cassell.

Cooper, C., Cooper, R. and Eaker, L. (1988) *Living with Stress.* Harmondsworth: Penguin Books.

Cowen, E. (1982) 'Help is where you find it.' *American Psychologist 37,* 385–395.

Cox, T. (1978) *Stress.* Basingstoke: Macmillan Education.

Cox, T. (1993) *Stress Research and Stress Management: Putting Theory to Work.* Sudbury: HMSO.

Cox, T., Gotts, G., Boot, N. and Kerr, J. (1988) 'Physical exercise, employee fitness and the management of health at work.' *Work and Stress 2,* 1, 71–76.

Cox, T. and Mackay, C. (1981) 'A transactional approach to occupational stress.' In E. Corlett and J. Richardson (eds) *Stress, Work Design and Productivity.* Chichester: Wiley.

Dewe, P., Cox, T. and Ferguson, E. (1993) 'Individual strategies for coping with stress at work: a review of progress and directions for future research.' *Work and Stress 7*, 5–15.

D'Zurilla, T. (1986) *Problem-Solving Therapy: A Social Competence Approach to Clinical Intervention.* New York: Springer Publishing.

Ellis, A. (1983) 'How to deal with your most difficult client: you.' *Journal of Rational-Emotive Therapy 1*, 1, 3–8.

Ellis, A., Gordon, J., Neenan, M. and Palmer, S. (1997) *Stress Counselling: A Rational Emotive Behaviour Approach.* London: Cassell.

Jones, R., Barge, B., Steffy, B., Fay, L. Kunz, L. and Wuebker, L. (1988) 'Stress and medical malpractice: organizational risk assessment and intervention.' *Journal of Applied Psychology 73*, 727–735.

Lazarus, A. (1989) *The Practice of Multimodal Therapy.* Baltimore, MD: Johns Hopkins University Press.

Lazarus, R. (1966) *Psychological Stress and the Coping Process.* New York: McGraw-Hill.

Lazarus, R. and Folkman, R. (1984) *Stress, Appraisal, and Coping.* New York: Springer.

Meichenbaum, D. (1985) *Stress Inoculation Training.* Elmsford, NY: Pergamon Press.

Meichenbaum, D. and Cameron, R. (1972) *Stress Inoculation Training: A Skills Training Approach to Anxiety Management.* Unpublished manuscript. Waterloo, Ontario: University of Waterloo.

Milner, P. and Palmer, S. (1998) *Integrative Stress Counselling: A Humanistic Problem-Focused Approach.* London: Cassell.

Palmer, S. (1993) 'Organizational stress: symptoms, causes and reduction.' *Newsletter of the Society of Public Health*, November 2–8.

Palmer, S. (1996) 'Developing stress management programmes.' In R. Woolfe and W. Dryden (eds) *Handbook of Counselling Psychology.* London: Sage.

Palmer, S. (1997) 'Stress counselling and management: past, present and future.' In S. Palmer and V. Varma (eds) *Future of Counselling and Psychotherapy.* London: Sage.

Palmer, S. and Dryden, W. (1995) *Counselling for Stress Problems.* London: Sage.

Smith, R. (1980) 'A cognitive-affective approach to stress management training for athletes.' In C. Nadeau, W. Halliwell, K. Newell and G. Roberts (eds) *Psychology of Motor Behavior and Sport-1979.* Champaign, IL: Human Kinetics.

Suinn, R. (1990) *Anxiety Management Training.* New York: Plenum.

Suinn, R. and Richardson, F. (1971) 'Anxiety management training: a non-specific behavior therapy program for anxiety control.' *Behavior Therapy 2*, 498–510.

Useful addresses

British Association for Counselling

1 Regent Place
Rugby CV21 2PJ
Tel: 01788 578328

British Association of Behavioural and Cognitive Psychotherapies

23 Partridge Drive
Baxenden
Accrington RB5 2RL
Tel: 01254 875277

British Psychological Society

St Andrews House
48 Princess Road East
Leicester LE1 7DR
Tel: 0116 2549568

Centre for Stress Management

156 Westcombe Hill
London SE3 7DH
Tel: 0181 293 4114
Fax: 0181 293 1441

Institute of Health Education

Department of Oral Health and Development
University Dental Hospital
Higher Cambridge Street
Manchester M15 6FH
Tel/Fax: 0161 275 6610

United Kingdom Council for Psychotherapy

167 Great Portland Street
London W1
Tel: 0171 436 3002

CHAPTER 17

Cross-Cultural Mediation

Masana De Souza and Yvonne Joan Craig

In *The Politics of Hope* (Sacks 1997), the Chief Rabbi of the United Hebrew Congregations wrote that the dislocations of modern life make us all members of minorities, itinerant members of different kinds of diaspora. Increasing inter-migration with Europe reinforces this trend.

Our chapter endorses the socially inclusive approach of this book, welcoming cultural diversity, but focuses on the adversities people face, recognizing that additionally age, class, gender and other differences affect social contexts (Hopkins 1997).

This chapter also advocates effective empowerment based on a regard for human rights (Rawls 1971), redistribution of decision-making control to lead to an equalization of power relations between competitive groups, and a just society which benefits economically challenged and marginalized people.

In addition we affirm ordinary human abilities and potential skills in managing as well as generating our own conflicts, even though specialized mediation services can empower people in negotiating complex cases. So this chapter is in two main parts, introduced by a rationale for the increasing importance of mediation in contemporary multicultural society.

The first part notes current needs for cross-cultural mediation, its evolution from tribal settlement based on spiritual traditions of peacemaking into modern methods supported by the multicultural national voluntary organization, Mediation UK, with concluding case illustrations. The second part describes the emergence of the Newham Conflict and Change Project (NCCP), pioneering mediation in diverse communities, and its services and typical cases. Comments are made about the use of advocacy and counselling.

Cultural demonization

A 1997 Runnymede Trust Commission on British Muslims referred to the 'Islamophobia' imperilling community relations. Negative social stereotypes, religious prejudices and political dogmas all combine to increase ethnocentrism, polarize people and demonize ethnic groups (Mindell 1993, 1995).

Although groups have factions which favour fighting discrimination forcefully, most members adopt the social realism and moral maxims of Martin Luther King, who preached that 'an eye for an eye and you will be blind', and of Nelson Mandela, who said, 'if you decide to settle problems through negotiation, then you must be prepared to compromise' (*The Times*, 15 February 1990).

Cross-cultural mediation has developed as a rights-based and principled process of negotiation to empower people in non-violent conflict resolution, generally situated in services run by culturally diverse citizens of inner-city areas, as at the NCCP. This development has evolved from early systems of tribal settlement and spiritual traditions of peacemaking, and it has been suggested that the male term, *Homo sapiens*, thinking man, could be more appropriately conceptualized as *conciliator* (Craig 1988) to remind us of our human potential for peacemaking.

The spiritual foundations of mediation

Spiritual traditions still influence us, in conscious and hidden ways. The Buddhist Eightfold Path, the Taoist view of conflict as a means for peaceful change, and the Confucian edict about respect for others preceded the Judaeo-Christian cultural emphasis on good neighbourliness, love, peace and justice, while Gandhi was a modern advocate of these ideas in Hinduism. Jewish concepts of *shalom*, Christian ideas of Jesus as mediator and translations of Islam as *entering into peace* are popularly promoted, if not always practised.

Through tribal dispute settlement, people worked out consensual solutions to local conflicts, as in the palm tree justice of the Indian *panychats* where generally five elders would mediate. Traditionally and currently older people have been valued mediators (Srivastava and Craig 1997). *Panychats* still function in India, but the NCCP also offers this form of mediation to any Asian service users who prefer it.

A West African volunteer mediator there, Bisi Okun, has informally described a similar system in Nigeria, where esteemed elders act as mediators, sometimes switching to the role of arbitrator or judge, in reconciling people. Bisi says there is a stress on encouraging understanding and apologies while helping people not to lose face, and that the mediators have good negotiation and communication skills, which they also use when asked to be go-betweens in arranging marriages, and disputes about these.

Another NCCP volunteer has described long-established similar mediation in Ghana, where people prefer to keep disputes out of the public eye of Western courts. If the elders cannot resolve a conflict, it goes before the tribal chief, who acts as an informal judge. However, a 'linguist', acting as an impartial mediator, presents the cases of all parties, who may not speak to the chief directly. The chief urges everyone to keep the peace and be reconciled, ordering reparation with livestock or food.

The *husay* (to be peaceful) and *barangay* (village dispute settlement) customs of the Philippines are even more interesting examples of how some developing countries are reinstating old traditions which are more acceptable than Western justice models in minor matters where close communities want to repair relationships.

A recent chairman of the Commission for Racial Equality described the centrality of 'healing the hurts' (Day 1989, p.13) in cross-cultural conflict. Even though the law must be used to prosecute discrimination and racism, its processes can ignore people's feelings and silence them (Smart 1989). In Hawaii, *ho'oponopono* (making right) rituals include apologies, forgiveness and reintegration of the disputants into communities.

Despite this cultural lineage of mediation, in *The Politics of Informal Justice* (Abel 1982), a critique shows the limits of mediation and how it has been abused. In China, 10 million 'mediators', on a million 'mediation' committees, belong to political cadres which suppress social conflict by pressure (Utter 1990).

Modern cross-cultural mediation

Americans, with their 'melting-pot culture', pioneered modern developments in mediation, taking different routes. They were conspicuously led by black people such as community activist, Gloria Patterson, training people to be 'street mediators', and by mediators in the San Francisco Community Boards (Shonholtz 1984).

Quakers and Mennonites applied their beliefs in non-violence to practical cross-cultural mediation, developing an impressive literature on their work (Augsburger 1996; Lederach 1995). Jean Paul Lederach pioneered in-depth mediation and reconciliation in Nicaraguan and Latin American political situations, training local people by elicitive rather than prescriptive methods, using indigenous ways of resolving conflict, and empowering people to build on these with contemporary insights.

Cross-cultural aspects of general British mediation are also linked with national traditions of informal and formal global diplomacy, and Mediation UK members have worked in Bosnia, the Middle East, southern Africa and elsewhere, while the Republic of Ireland and Northern Ireland have mediation services contributing greatly to peace initiatives.

Mediation UK is committed to social and racial justice through equal opportunity policies, ethical practices about referrals for legal and police assistance in criminal and discrimination situations, its promotion of cross-cultural training, and networking with advocacy and counselling groups, as well as statutory and voluntary agencies.

Cross-cultural cases

Community conflict can often be between the good guys and the good guys, as in the following case:

> Ali Aziz Khan, a papershop manager, his wife Amina and daughter Alia, were strict Muslims keeping early hours of prayer and work. They lived in a council tenement next to Akosua and her sister Akua, who were both West African shift nurses whose male relatives visited them at asocial hours when loud music was played. Ali felt sure that his neighbours were prostitutes and pimps, banged on their walls at night and reported them to the council. The nurses were furious and wrote a letter to Ali threatening libel action. His lawyers advised mediation. When the neighbours met face to face for the first time, having never spoken before, misunderstandings were erased. They made a mediated agreement to keep music playing within set hours, for a formal apology to be made by Ali, and for future friendly discussions if other problems arose.

It can be speculated that power and gender issues were also at the cutting edge of this conflict, with poorly paid nurses resenting the fact that 65 per cent of all independent shops are now owned by Asians (*Independent,* 4 March 1997), while Muslim male anger at the autonomy of female tenants exacerbated the situation.

In another case, a Gujarati Hindu family were involved in a distressing situation with Irish neighbours:

> Vijay and his wife Leela kept hearing Paddy and Eileen refer to Gerry Adams during all the many noisy visits they had from Irish friends, and IRA terrorism was suspected, so fearsome stories were spread among the other local Indians. At the same time Paddy and Eileen were gossiping to their Irish friends about the continual smells of

curry and incense, so group hostilities became marked. The estate manager suggested mediation, and as both parties had no liking for the police, they agreed to this. Mediation revealed that it was Paddy's dog that was called Gerry Adams, and Eileen's laughter made Leela laugh too, the two women eventually deciding to visit each other to exchange recipes for Indian and Irish cooking.

This amusing story has serious implications for good community relations, as latent simple misunderstandings escalate into conflicts which can become ignited into riotous group activity. It is essential that conflicts are confronted constructively at the earliest stages before individual or group feelings and attitudes harden. Even then, some conflicts are ideologically intransigent, as in intergenerational, intergroup ones such as those occurring between young Asian men forming vigilante groups, and their much older religious leaders who favour traditional peacemaking methods of seeking social justice.

Here mediators have played helpful roles in facilitating community forums where issues can be discussed openly with problem-solving not blaming approaches which the process involves. Community mediation services such as the NCCP can thus offer a range of social interventions, including referrals to advocacy groups and counsellors.

The NCCP

One of the most important aspects of the NCCP's foundation in 1984 was that it was a locally led pioneer project in which the director of the Newham Community Renewal programme and other social activists played key roles in a borough with one of the highest cultural mixes, unemployment rates, poor housing and environmental problems in London.

NCCP now has volunteer mediators representing about 30 different ethnic groups, speaking 20 different languages, with an ongoing commitment to meet service users' needs. Its pioneering cross-cultural work has made it a flagship for Mediation UK, of which the NCCP was one of the first members, while it attracts increasing international interest from American, European, African and Asian countries.

Another major concern of the initiative was to use and develop local talent and not to import social experts. From the first, it was a community empowerment project, so that local citizens could learn skills in helping them manage all the many different kinds of conflicts occurring in their culturally rich community, whether in agencies, groups or between individuals. The NCCP recognizes that various cultures have different ways of resolving conflict: for example, in the African context, elders are valued in direct mediation, whereas in Asia shuttle diplomacy will be more widely used, with the disputants not meeting face to face until a mutually agreed solution is appropriately incorporated into the case.

NCCP's respect for different cultural traditions has been central to its community mission, as can be seen in its existing vision statement: 'Our vision is a global community in which people are nurtured and empowered to value differences and to experience conflict as an opportunity for change.'

Ever since the beginning, its policies and plans have been led by local people, who have developed the diverse services of the NCCP as they felt them to be needed.

NCCP started community empowerment and conflict management education through outreach meetings and activities based on a local resource centre run by volunteers, with a paid co-ordinator who trained them in conciliation and communication skills. However, there were soon local demands for a central mediation service and specialized consultancies.

Local schools and colleges, housing associations, employment agencies, statutory, voluntary and religious organizations, community centres, health services and businesses asked for training in conflict management. This has led to the NCCP developing a consultancy service and a total of four full-time and two part-time staff, as well as having about 50 multicultural mediators. These are volunteers who are given extensive certificated training in general conflict management skills, as well as ongoing courses to increase their knowledge and capacities to work in different cultural and generational contexts. Many volunteers also take additional courses in becoming trainers themselves, and in facilitating workshops at the centre and for outside agencies.

For example, one recent workshop for 17 Asian youths was held at the NCCP, and the role-plays of conflict situations, full of fun as well as drama, helped the participants to develop confidence in dealing with the disputes prevalent in their peer group, without people getting hurt. Many young people who attend such workshops become enthused about taking mediation training, and develop into valued members of the NCCP team. This continual injection of youthful energy and interest is doubly valuable in that it ensures that policy making progresses to meet emerging community concerns of young people, although equal attention is given to the area's ageing, disabled and other vulnerable populations.

The NCCP's school programmes have been particularly valued, as these teach conflict management skills to pupils, teachers and parents, so that the entire educational environment gradually becomes oriented to constructive ways of dealing with children's quarrels and bullying, racial harassment, parent–teacher complaints and parent–child problems, to note just a few of the typical disputes.

However, although outreach work is a vital part of NCCP's community empowerment and educational activities, the conciliation and mediation casework services, which are based at its resource centre, have been of special value to the local citizens who are confronted with complex conflicts for which they ask for help, as illness, stress and socioeconomic pressures can combine to make them feel they can no longer cope themselves.

Here it is necessary to note that, in contrast to those who refer to conciliation and mediation as interchangeable terms, the NCCP distinguishes the processes in its casework. Conciliation is used to describe situations where the volunteers visit and actively listen to the complaining service users, who may then feel sufficiently empowered to deal with the conflicts on their own. In addition, it may include home visits to the respondents, or also telephone enquiries about dealing with disputes by any of those involved.

Conciliation is felt to be an appropriate term, as the visits or contacts always increase service users' insights into their conflicts, and into the interests and needs of each other, even though these may be contested, and how situations and relationships can be improved. Conciliation here is conceptually linked to community educational empowerment by increasing awareness of the dangers of escalating conflict, and how this can be prevented by constructive communication.

However, it is through the fuller process of mediation that written agreements can be reached and printed out at the NCCP, either as a result of face-to-face or shuttle mediation, both of which have been described elsewhere in this book. The former is generally recommended as it can encourage real reconciliation between people who have sadly developed enmities, although never having talked together previously. Here it is significant to note that the founders of the NCCP initially called it a 'reconciliation service', as they hoped that, in addition to helping individuals, it would create the widest cultural and community changes in encouraging the acceptance and valuing of social diversity.

The social value of the Newham model

The uniqueness of the Newham model demonstrates visibly the ability of mediators of various ethnic, religious, gender, age and income groups to build bridges in communication and relationships by being matched culturally and socially with those in conflict. This sensitivity to individual and group differences develops trust in the service users, and provides a model of respect for human diversity which can enable the dynamics of the mediation process to flow more easily and constructively:

> Mr Menon, an elderly, sick Sri Lankan Hindu whose wife had diabetes and depression, angrily complained that noise from their Bengali Muslim neighbours was destroying their sleep and health. The police were called, which upset the Bengalis who felt persecuted in the home they owned. Both neighbours agreed to mediation, and the Menons learned that the Bengalis had a grandmother and seven children, the youngest being ill and crying continuously, while cooking had to be done late at night because of Ramadan. The Menons became sympathetic and agreed to be more tolerant, and the Bengalis invited them to call if there was future trouble.

The mediators helped the neighbours to recognize shared problems of illness and family relations of which they had been unaware, and the underlying issue of differing religious practices. This gave them confidence to talk to each other in the future using the process of listening and problem-solving without blaming, while Mr Menon promised not to call the police again:

> The Browns, a white couple, were furious that after a year's allegations of racial harassment and nuisance made about them by their Asian neighbour, Fatima, the council were threatening to prevent them buying the property. The neighbours agreed to mediation and Fatima learned that Mrs Brown was having post-operative chemotherapy for cancer, said to be worsened by the stress of the dispute.

Mediation helped the neighbours to respect each other and their rights, as well as learning to talk together for the first time. Despite their cultural differences, they discovered a mutual interest in country and western music, and they all said that they wanted to live in peace. They made a written agreement about conversing and helping one another in the future.

An ongoing dispute between an asthmatic West African couple, with two young children and a third on the way, is representative of the many neighbour conflicts involving loud stereo music. In this case, it was being played late at night by a white disc jockey who was later given a council noise abatement order. This made him very cross, and he denied the noise, but alleged that the West Africans complained to get a housing transfer as they found the borough to be racist. Both neighbours agreed to mediation, and as the disc jockey's wife is also in late pregnancy, it might be hoped that at the post-confinement meeting, comparisons about babies and their shared needs for peaceful and happy environments may lead to an improved situation – in comparable mediations, agreements have even included plans for mutual baby-minding.

This brief selection from some of the NCCP's many activities must include mention of its comprehensive volunteer support work, enlivened by an excellent regular member-written newsletter, which also links with its extensive networking with statutory and voluntary agencies in the borough and outside, especially those running varied services for culturally diverse groups with special interests. Many of these are advocacy groups, and volunteers may belong to these as well as to the NCCP. This supports a theme of this book that mediators can work well with citizen advocacy, and that mutual learning can be beneficial to both.

Similarly, NCCP volunteers are trained to recognize when deep emotional issues, or those of addiction, need counselling, and they offer information about referrals so that their service users can make knowledgeable choices about obtaining appropriate help. Two examples illustrate this, although not from the NCCP caseload:

> Karamajit Singh, as the eldest son of a Sikh family, had a duty to care for his mother, Jaswinder, when she became widowed. However, she suffered from dementia, and the stress on his wife led to family conflict with shame and guilt involved. Karamajit's daughter, Amarjit, a volunteer at a local community mediation project, persuaded the family to use its services.

This resulted in Jaswinder's other adult children taking turns caring for her and the social services becoming involved. Karamajit joined a local MIND advocacy group which gave him advice and support in obtaining improved psychogeriatric treatment and counselling for his mother:

> Shaka was an Afro-Caribbean youth caught up in a neighbour conflict with Tom, white, single and disabled, who threatened to report him for suspected drug dealing, and who shouted abuse when loud reggae music was played. Shaka was afraid of the police, so contacted his probation officer who recommended the local community mediation service.

Tom agreed to a meeting and this revealed that both men were orphans and lived lonely lives. Shaka denied drug dealing, but admitted to a crack habit that he could no longer afford, saying he was sorry that the music had upset Tom. Tom was mollified and offered to teach Shaka how to read and write properly if he went to a drug counselling centre. This became a trial mediation agreement, with a further one scheduled after six months to see if the arrangement had held.

The NCCP also gives its local police mediation training. Even if mediation is not a first choice in dealing with some cross-cultural conflicts, it may be the last and only one in situations where police involvement can make the situation worse because of racial prejudice and discriminatory policing practices arising from what has been called 'canteen culture' (Reiner 1985). Although police chiefs have learned a lot since the Brixton and Broadwater Farm riots (Beynon 1984; Gifford 1989) about the necessity for co-operative community policing (Willmott 1987), some street officers are still criticized and hated for being literally on the beat.

Nevertheless, infrastructural power imbalances continue to jeopardize the empowerment and unity of diverse communities for which advocates, counsellors and mediators work, hindered by inadequate funding. Although we strive to make an impact at the micro levels of society, with conspicuous success, as at the NCCP, we have no illusions about the challenging tasks of achieving the multicultural reconciliation for which we all have responsibilities and reparative roles to play.

References

Abel, R. (1982) *The Politics of Informal Justice: Vols. 1/2.* New York: Academic Press.

Augsberger, D. (1996) *Helping People Forgive.* Louisville KY: Westminster John Knox Press.

Beynon, J. (1984) *Scarman and After.* Headington: Pergamon.

Craig, Y. (1988) 'Homo conciliator.' *Mediation 4,* 3, 6–8.

Day, M. (1989) 'Satanic curses and conciliation.' *Mediation 5,* 3, 11–13.

Gifford, L. (1989) *Broadwater Farm Revisited.* London: Karia Press.

Hopkins, W. (1997) *Ethical Dimensions of Diversity.* London: Sage.

Lederach, J. (1995) *Preparing for Peace.* Syracuse, NY: Syracuse University Press.

Mindell, A. (1993) *The Leader as a Martial Artist.* London: HarperCollins.

Mindell, A. (1995) *Sitting in the Fire.* Portland, OR: Lao Tse Press.

Rawls, J. (1971) *A Theory of Justice.* Cambridge, MA: Harvard University Press.

Reiner, R. (1985) *The Politics of the Police.* Hassocks: Harvester.

Sacks, J. (1997) *Faith in the Future.* London: Darton, Longman and Todd.

Shonholtz, R. (1984) 'Neighbourhood justice systems.' *Mediation Quarterly 5,* 3–30.

Smart, C. (1989) *Feminism and the Power of the Law.* London: Routledge.

Srivastava, A. and Craig, Y. (1997) 'Neighbours.' In Y. Craig (ed) *Changes and Challenges in Later Life.* London: Third Age Press.

Utter, R. (1990) 'Dispute resolution in China.' *Family and Conciliation Courts Review 28,* 1, 65–70.

Willmott, P. (1987) *Policing and the Community.* London: Policy Studies Institute.

Useful addresses

Commission for Racial Equality

Elliott House
10–12 Allington Street
London SW1
Tel: 0171 828 7022

Mediation UK

Alexander House
Telephone Avenue
Bristol BS1 4BS
Tel: 0117 904 6661

Newham Conflict and Change Project

Christopher House
Streatfield Avenue
London E6
Tel: 0181 552 2050/470 5505

CHAPTER 18

Advocacy, Empowerment and the Development of User-Led Outcomes

Sue Balloch, Peter Beresford, Clare Evans, Tessa Harding,
Martin Heidensohn and Michael Turner

Introduction

This chapter focuses on the hitherto neglected issue of service users' involvement in the conceptualization and measurement of outcomes in social care. With the increasing interest in the rights and needs of service users in social care and social services, there has been a growing focus on professional and service-led discussions on standard setting and the definition and measurement of 'outcomes'. This reflects a political and professional concern to improve standards of service in accordance with new consumerist approaches to welfare and social care. There is now a growing literature in this field (see Ager 1993; Ludlow and Morris 1995; Nocon and Qureshi 1996; Pollitt 1988; Priestley 1995; Shalock 1995).

So far, however, little work has been done to explore service users' own ideas about what the outcomes in social work and social care should be, or to develop user-led approaches to defining and measuring such outcomes. Exploring user-led outcomes is clearly also of central importance as part of developing comprehensive strategies for self advocacy and user involvement and in the establishment of collective advocacy through the building of links and networks between user organizations.

Most initiatives for user involvement have been concerned with increasing service users' input into the planning and management of services. Yet professional practice plays a major role in shaping the quality of support which service users receive and in determining their opportunities to live independently and according to their own choices and priorities. Because of this, there has been an increasing concern among service users' organizations to increase service users' say and involvement in professional practice and personal assistance. However, there is evidence that as the low expectations of many users can be associated with the disempowering effect of receiving services, there is an important role for collective advocacy in developing the skills and confidence for users to engage in this debate.

This chapter builds on the three-year Shaping Our Lives project, funded by the Department of Health through the Community Care Development programme, which is being undertaken by the authors and which is concerned to explore and develop user-led approaches to outcome definition and measurement. It will explore this approach to involvement and empowerment, as well as relating it to broader issues about user involvement.

Shaping Our Lives

Shaping Our Lives is a user-led project being run under the auspices of the National Institute for Social Work, looking into users' views and definitions of outcomes, and how these views feed into the overall debate on the development of definitions and measures of outcomes.

The project has set out three main objectives for its initial two years:

- to research the way service users and their organizations are defining and working towards the outcomes that they want for themselves

- to research the way outcome determination is being approached in theoretical literature, comparing and contrasting the more traditional approaches with the new thinking that is being developed by users and their organizations

- to bring together an 'expert' group of people in the user movements who are working on these issues; to discuss and consolidate their thinking and develop well-researched and well-founded perspectives on outcomes.

Background to the project

The Shaping Our Lives project developed directly from a report, *The Standards We Expect* (1996), which was compiled by Tessa Harding and Peter Beresford, who are now both members of the Shaping Our Lives management team.

The *Standards We Expect* was part of a study of standards of service commissioned by the Department of Health. A range of service users contributed to the report with their views of the qualities that they felt should be present in the provision of community care services. Emphasizing the importance of empowering relationships between workers and users, and the quality and appropriateness of staff skills and of services as a whole, the service users and carers involved in the report's preparation identified practical proposals for how standards might be set and what those standards might include. The implementation, monitoring, evaluation and long-term maintenance of such proposals would require both public and political commitment to them:

> There needs to be a social conscience, which informs public and political approaches to services and which prioritises the rights, needs and perspectives of service users and carers in practice as the Children Act and National Health Service and Community Care Act do in principle. (Harding and Beresford 1996, p.44)

At the conclusion of this study, discussions with Clare Evans of the Wiltshire and Swindon Users' Network (now also a member of the Shaping Our Lives management team) brought out the fact that, in looking at the ways in which services are provided, the report had not considered standards in terms of the actual outcomes and results of community care provision from the service users' perspective. This issue was identified as being particularly important in view of the developing work of academics and professionals in this area, and the Department of Health's interest in developing measures of outcome for community care. Encouragement from the Department of Health for social services departments to develop measures of service outcomes had previously resulted in summaries of the range and number of services delivered without any assessment of their quality or effectiveness for users.

Unless service users had a strong voice in defining such outcomes at an early stage, there was a real risk that professional and academic perspectives would dominate the definition of outcomes to the very exclusion of other views. The project set out to rectify this situation and to create the opportunity for service users to shape the debate themselves.

Initial research for Shaping Our Lives

The first stage of Shaping Our Lives has involved an assessment of current views about outcomes from both user and professional/academic perspectives. The primary concern has been to put together a picture of users' opinions on the subject and discover what user-controlled organizations are doing in relation to outcomes. Before we could begin this we needed to establish our contacts with user groups around the country. This involved spending some time working through the membership lists of organizations such as the British Council of Organisations of Disabled People and other membership organizations to build a database of local groups. This database now contains over 200 groups, culturally diverse and with a wide range of experience of using services. It continues to expand as more groups are made aware of the project.

The database is clearly an essential tool for the project itself, and should provide a useful resource for user groups themselves when they need to make links with others and gain information about how to engage effectively with service purchasers and providers, local elected members and others.

Having set up the database we arranged discussions with groups of users to seek their views on outcomes. We did not set out to produce anything like a comprehensive study of views on this subject – such a venture would probably be impractical and of limited use anyway – so we limited ourselves to holding discussions using a semi-structured questionnaire with groups of up to 14 people.

As a user-controlled research project, it was paramount that the approach and methods were *participatory* and *emancipatory*: that the research proved to be collaborative, empowering and based on equal and reciprocal relationships between the researchers and the subjects of research (see Beresford and Turner 1997, pp.25–27). Such work has a vital role to play in encouraging self-advocacy through providing comfortable and secure opportunities for individuals and groups to discuss and express their views on outcomes in their lives and on the services they receive. The establishment of networks and information resources also serves to promote collective advocacy by enabling users and user organizations to support and empower themselves and each other in developing effective user participation.

Meetings were held with three generic user groups, two disability organizations, two People First groups and a group at a user-run 'drop in' service for Asians with mental health problems. The interview with the mental health group provided insights into issues surrounding user empowerment as well as demonstrating that people from ethnic communities want services that are more culturally sensitive:

> I think in order for me to live a fulfilled life, be more empowered, every angle, every opportunity [should be] given ... I think I should actually be empowered to appoint my own key worker, for example ... I want a key worker ... who talks my language, from my community, my background. (Service user (1), Manchester 1997)

There seems to be no really good reason why service users should *not* have a say in who their key worker, care manager or personal assistant is, or what they do. The fact that this does not happen would appear to owe more to the inertia of established custom and the convenience of provider agencies than the objective of good practice. If people can 'shop around' and choose their general practitioner, then why not their care manager too?

This concept of consumer choice is an inherent part of the market ideology which has changed the organization of welfare provision in the last two decades. Whether or not users are truly empowered by the model of 'welfare consumer', in relation to traditional and user-run services, having a choice of services managed in a different spirit, with a range of options open to the individual, is seen as imperative:

> If you go to buy a pair of shoes, there's lots of shops there; you've got choices. ...I mean users have to have the choice of using a user-managed service. If you go out in the street, you want to buy a pair of shoes, you can't say that there should only be one shoe shop on such a street. I mean sometimes you like this guy, you just end up buying in that shop, somebody likes the other one. It's about choice. Why not have user-managed services run, you know, in parallel with services? (Service user (2), Manchester 1997)

The professional and service-led discussion on outcomes has focused on measurement as well as definition. In the course of our meetings with user organizations, some people questioned whether user-defined outcomes could, by their nature, be measured:

> These things are not very easy to measure. How do you measure quality of life? ... you probably can't. The only [thing] you can find is whether people ... tell you, 'I feel I have a much better quality of life than I had about five years ago ... you have really helped me'. This is our yardstick. This is how we measure it ... But I don't think there is any formula of measuring everything. (Service user (2), Manchester 1997)

It is not always appropriate to look at outcomes of services as being separable from the way in which services are provided or from the attitude of those providing the service. Delays in a service being provided, poor treatment from staff and other experiences in the process of service provision will have a substantial impact on the user's view of the outcome of the service. The process of providing a service is, after all, a large part of the outcome if it is empowering and makes new aspirations possible. But outcomes, which are about results in the quality of people's lives, go far wider than services, which are, after all, merely the means to such ends.

Also, many users believe that independent living should be defined in terms which go beyond those used by personal care service providers, covering issues such as social activities, transport and mobility, and employment.

Such thinking builds on the concepts of independent living developed by disabled people in the international disability movement.

Being treated as part of a category rather than as an individual can be disempowering – even offensive. The scope for choice and the advocacy of the individual is severely restricted when services view, and provide for, people as groups rather than individuals. The experience of being labelled as disabled or elderly and being treated accordingly as part of a category, rather than a distinct person with particular needs and wants, was described clearly as a negative outcome:

> What occurs to me, I'm not quite sure how to address it, but it's this thing of putting people together in a group all the time. All the disabled people are over here; all the disabled people go on a bus to Scarborough together, and I don't want to do that, you know. I don't want to have to wait for somebody to organize a bus for other people. I want to do what everybody else does. I don't want things to be done specially for me. (Service user (3), York 1997)

Perhaps the most important finding to arise from our initial contacts with users was the realization that the whole concept of looking at outcomes or results of services is a new one for many service users. Their expectations are relatively low and often their concern is focused on obtaining any sort of service at all. They do not consider outcomes, as do purchasers and providers, in terms of obvious results. This confirmed our belief about the large gap between the way service users view their lives and the services they receive, and the way purchasers and providers consider outcomes. One user summed up the situation concisely by stating that the only outcome she could see was the fact that services were just about keeping her out of residential care.

Basic measures to use in relation to community care services have been developed within the professional and academic literature that, as stated earlier, is also being reviewed. Such measures have been developed in similar fashion to those now regularly used in the health services. They can include a simple count of the number of people supported in the community who might otherwise have been placed in residential care, assessment of the mortality rate among older people, and the length of time people with mental health problems are able to live independently without the need for medical support. However, there is growing awareness that such measures provide a very limited assessment of the outcome of services, and say little, if anything, about the process of service delivery.

The amount of literature on the subject of social care outcomes, although growing, is not extensive, and that which addresses user involvement in defining and measuring outcomes is even more limited. It is, perhaps, especially remarkable that the growing body of literature on the subject of user involvement has included so little assessment of the actual results of this involvement (though this is in no way suggesting that user involvement is ever anything less than effective). However, service users themselves are clear that they consider their involvement to be about changing a system which they feel is currently inappropriate to their needs.

How service users judge the services they receive: influencing the quality of practice

For many service users who rely on more traditionally provided services, the priority is greater control in their own lives and a more equal relationship with those who deliver the service.

The Standards We Expect asked a wide range of service users' organizations what it was they valued in their contacts with social services workers. The consistency of what they said was both significant and remarkable: the single most important factor in a good quality service was the relationship between the individual worker and the service user:

> So often it is the style of the way services are delivered rather than the service itself which produces a quality service. This makes it quite difficult to separate out quality of services from quality of relationships; the home carer who gets you up in the morning can do this in an empowering way which enables you to face the effort of the day positively or in a way which means you are dressed and ready but not psychologically ready. Beyond these basic skills, this empowering experience comes from the quality of relationships. (Evans, quoted in Harding and Beresford 1996, p.5)

Service users were quite specific about what made such a relationship:

> These qualities, which are all really commonsensical, are the natural attributes which make most relationships work positively: self-respect, dignity, honesty, confidentiality, trust, reliability, being treated equally, valid and good communication and listening skills, and in particular a sound partnership and an enabling role. (Harding and Beresford 1996, p.7)

Beyond the quality of relationships, service users mention the quality of skills they believe are needed – listening and communicating, counselling and understanding, and enabling and negotiating are all cited, together with good information and good basic skills and a sense of judgement about risks. They are also explicit about the range and nature of services they would like to see.

The organizations that took part in this study wanted to be involved in defining quality, setting and monitoring standards, and evaluating services. They were also clear that they had a role to play in promoting quality through their own involvement in recruiting staff, in designing job specifications and in all aspects of staff training.

As has been observed elsewhere, most efforts to date have been directed at involving service users in planning services, on the macro level. But what matters most immediately to most people is the quality of the service they receive personally and on which they may well depend. There is scope for involving service users to a much greater extent in the day-to-day promotion of quality through direct interaction with staff in a variety of ways, such as participating in reviews of services and carrying out user-controlled research.

Regulation: a General Social Services Council

As has been revealed by the discussions of both Shaping Our Lives and *The Standards We Expect*, the setting of standards, the accountability of staff, the right to have complaints heard and dealt with, and involvement and control in such processes are important issues for many service users. However, the fear of reprisals and of the loss of much needed (even if inadequate, inappropriate or poorly provided) services, means that, on the whole, users do not find complaining very worthwhile. Children and young people can find it very difficult to complain and to get peer support to do so. Older people can be reluctant to make complaints, especially to people who are often of a different generation. Shaping Our Lives is working in partnership with a project funded by the Joseph Rowntree Foundation to involve users in the establishment of a General Social Services Council (GSSC). The task of the Council would be to strengthen safeguards for the public who use social services, by setting and enforcing standards of conduct and practice for all social services staff in the statutory, voluntary and private sectors. It would maintain a register of suitable staff, investigate complaints about serious breaches of its standards, and apply disciplinary and remedial measures where staff were found guilty of such breaches.

A questionnaire circulated to over 240 national and local user organizations and a consultation workshop attended by representatives of over 60 service user organizations in July 1997, revealed that there is a great deal of interest and enthusiasm for such a body, provided those at the centre of its concerns – service users – really would be at the heart of the Council itself. Some see a watchdog, a means of complaining about and preventing bad practice and abuse, as both necessary and potentially empowering. It could encourage and enable both individual and collective advocacy, as an independent voice and as an accessible forum for complaints and the setting of standards by users themselves. However, others have expressed concerns about the establishment of just another body to protect and promote professional, rather than user, interests. The setting of standards by unrepresentative or professionally dominated committees is viewed as potentially detrimental. Other possible disadvantages raised include the use of GSSC information to restrict users employing who they want as carers or assistants, and the danger of such a body over-emphasizing people's vulnerability and need for protection rather than actually empowering them. If users are to have a real say in the development of a GSSC, there is a clear message that consultation is not enough. They need to be fully represented in all stages of the process; to participate in its planning, implementation and, ultimately, its management.

Conclusions

Service users, therefore, are judging the quality of services in two ways: they are concerned that services will help them achieve the outcomes to which they aspire; and they are concerned that services are delivered in ways which empower rather than disempower them and their peers as individuals. The motivation for becoming involved with service agencies is primarily to achieve these two objectives. User involvement is not an end in itself, but a means of effecting change, both in the outcome of services and in the behaviour of workers:

> We are very proactive in seeking opportunities for user involvement … The aim is not participation for the sake of it … it is actually to bring about change. Users in the network say 'What is the point of me going and being involved, what effect will it have?' and they will not go and participate unless they know that they are going to be able to have an effect by giving their perspective as service users. (Evans 1995, p.117)

It is encouraging that in the UK currently there is a new focus on the outcome of services – not on organizational structure or efficient systems alone, but on the basic purpose of services and what they are there for.

As with the debate about quality, there is an ever-present risk that it is service purchasers and providers who will set the parameters by which outcomes are defined and specified. But Shaping Our Lives is setting out to enable service users to develop their own definitions of outcomes: to create the space and the opportunity for people from service user organizations to define desired outcomes from the point of view of their own values, their own priorities and their own form of discourse.

From the initial findings of the project, it seems likely that service users will want to avoid coming up with any predetermined set of quality standards. Rather, they are more likely to see quality as the extent to which services enable individuals to meet their own aspirations, which will vary from person to person; and as the extent to which they enable people to enhance control over their own lives.

In this context, the participation of service users can be seen as both a route to quality and a measure or criterion of it. It offers a route to quality in the sense that service users are fully involved in defining, developing, monitoring and evaluating quality according to their own values. Participation is also a criterion of quality since a key objective is that service users have more say and control over their lives and over decision making about the specific service or arrangements for support.

However, such an approach requires professionals to consider service outcomes in a new way which challenges professional power and authority and definitions of need. It also challenges the concept of outcome measurement itself, since users in user-controlled groups do not see themselves as defining outcomes for *all* users with appropriate measures developed from these definitions. Instead each user's view of her or his own desired service outcomes will be unique and can be developed within the existing legal framework through, for example, the care management process. However, most service users' experience of this process to date is not an empowering one. To enable service users to gain the choice and control they seek in their lives, the interaction between professionals and users in negotiating their care needs requires nothing less than a redefinition of the role of the professional and the competences required for this, to one where users' expertise is recognized and valued alongside professional expertise in defining needs and outcomes. In short, the professional role must change from that of 'defining' and 'doing' to that of 'facilitating users to define their own needs' and enabling them to achieve the outcomes they desire. The implementation of the Direct Payments legislation requires local authorities to re-examine the relationship between the assessment process and the amount of funding available as a result of it for users to directly purchase their own care. Thus this legislation will give disabled people more power to define their own outcomes and have more control over services to meet these outcomes.

All forms of advocacy are a means of enabling users to achieve empowerment. In enabling users to define their own outcomes, individual advocacy, self advocacy and collective advocacy all have a role to play. The project's research has shown how difficult many users find it to use professional jargon and to describe their experience of services in terms of outcomes. This is both a challenge to professionals to learn how to communicate more effectively and an opportunity for short-term individual advocacy partnerships to develop to support users in their care management negotiations. Better still, users can learn to advocate for themselves about their preferred service outcomes based on their aspirations in relation to quality of life, by gaining confidence and skills through self-advocacy groups. Finally, the collective advocacy users gain from joining together in their own user-controlled organizations to achieve effective user participation is the key to enabling social care professionals to learn to work in a more empowering way to enable users to define their own outcomes.

References

Ager, A. (1993) 'Life experiences checklist.' *Mental Handicap 1993, 21,* 7–9.

Beresford, P. and Turner, M. (1997) *It's Our Welfare: Report of the Citizen's Commission on the Future of the Welfare State.* London: National Institute for Social Work.

Evans, C. (1995) 'Disability, discrimination and local authority services 2: users' perspectives.' In G. Zarb (ed) *Removing Disabling Barriers.* London: Policy Studies Institute.

Harding, T. and Beresford, P. (1996) *The Standards We Expect: What Service Users and Carers Want from Social Services Workers.* London: National Institute for Social Work.

Ludlow, V. and Morris, J. (1995) *Service User Involvement: Synthesis of Findings and Experience in the Field of Community Care.* London: King's Fund.

Nocon, A. and Qureshi, H. (1996) *Outcomes of Community Care for Users and Carers.* Milton Keynes: Open University Press.

Pollitt, C. (1988) 'Bringing consumers into performance measurement: concepts, consequences and constraints.' *Policy and Politics 16, 2,* 77–87.

Priestley, M. (1995) 'Dropping "E's": the missing link in quality assurance for disabled people.' *Critical Social Policy 44/45,* 7–21.

Shalock, R.L. (1995) *Outcome Based Evaluation.* London: Plenum Press.

Further reading

Beresford, P., Croft, S., Evans, C. and Harding, T. (1997) 'Quality in personal social services: the developing role of user involvement in the UK.' In A. Evers and R. Haverinen (eds) *Developing Quality in Personal Social Services.* Aldershot: Ashgate.

Conclusion

Yvonne Joan Craig

Yet we are more than rights-bearing creatures, and there is more to respect in a person than his rights. It is because fraternity, love, belonging, dignity and respect cannot be specified as rights that we ought to specify them as needs and seek ... *to make their satisfaction a routine human practice.* (Ignatieff 1984, pp.13–14)

All ye that kindle a fire, that carry yourselves about with firebrands, walk ye in the flame of your fire and along the brand which ye have kindled. (Tillers 1994)

If, out of the four corners of a subject, I have dealt thoroughly with one corner, and people cannot find out the other three for themselves, then I do not explain any more. (Confucius (attribution))

This conclusion acknowledges the valuable contributions which authors have made to our book without further comment, but briefly evaluates how far advocacy, counselling and mediation have the potential to fulfil useful roles in the work of social pioneering, social transformation and social reconstruction. It concludes with a reference to Paolo Friere's *Pedagogy of Hope* in which he writes that 'without a minimum of hope, we cannot so much as start the struggle' for what he later calls 'humanization' (1996, p.9).

Advocacy, counselling and mediation in partnership

Our contributors, in general, have principally demonstrated the value of specialization in their work, and their professional observation of differing roles and boundaries has clearly fulfilled a main aim of the book to illustrate these through case studies. They also indicate where service users may benefit from referrals elsewhere, either alternatively, concurrently or subsequently. This in no way contradicts the experience of general caseworkers, and in personal or professional daily activities, when we may use the processes of advocacy, counselling and mediation at various times in real life situations. It is not a question of either/or, but both/and, as is often the case in comparing the general and specific.

Nevertheless, it is the quality of our services which is crucial, and the skilled work of our authors can be seen as related to the extensive experience, knowledge, training and ongoing learning which they have in their special areas, which they have shared with readers.

It is also recognized that health and social workers are at the cutting edge of helping increasing numbers of people in need, and will reciprocally have much to teach advocates, counsellors and mediators about where the most critical problems of human suffering are emerging in community life.

All our authors have made important affirmations about social values and the ethical bases on which advocacy, counselling and mediation in casework should develop (Biestek 1976; Hancock 1997; Hugman 1995; Timms 1983; Watson 1985), and there is a clear case for suggesting that collaboration in producing consensual, if not identical, codes of good practice could be an advantage.

This will assist interdisciplinary co-operation, and professional mobility between agencies and service users, who should be able to rely on consistency in confidentiality, integrity and fair dealing from what Charles Husband calls, in the context of anti-racial casework, 'the morally active practitioner' (1995, p.84).

In *Radical Social Work Today* (Langan and Lee 1989), it was argued that the empowerment of services users *and* workers is the key to moral and social justice. Barbara Simon (1997) suggests that this has been a traditional aim of much casework since Victorian times, but challenges of current community care (Stevenson and Parsloe 1993) have suspiciously sharpened the focus on encouraging people in self help, which also suits cost-cutting market ideology (Glennerster 1983).

However, although the Introduction charted the dangers of advocacy, counselling and mediation being seen mistakenly, and misused, as social adjustment technologies dealing with the casualties of change and promoting self-management to offset reduced resources, the work of our authors is a strong witness to how these processes have empowered people in utilizing change for positive personal and social development, and advancing their self determination, self direction and self realization. The self critique of our contributors monitors their work as rigorously as any general or academic critique.

A recently published poll denied the value of counselling, but the public freely and increasingly chooses this service, especially in bereavement, illness and other life crises. In Northern Ireland, paramilitaries have called for mediation regarding Maze prison protests, while advocacy groups multiply daily. An essential attribute of advocacy, counselling and mediation is that they are all voluntary processes which service users can enter or leave at any time.

One of the most important social indicators of their worth is that often service users then wish to share the knowledge, skills and values they learn by volunteering or making empowering career changes. In this way self interest can be linked to the common good, as Bill Jordan (1989) suggests, although this raises issues about who controls the power to define this in a multiracial society where cultural views are different (Thompson and Hoggett 1996), even respecting basic human rights.

Empowerment is thus linked to social justice. This is not only a declared objective of central government, but is best determined by local knowledge (Geertz 1983), especially that evidenced by experienced workers in different fields, as demonstrated in this book. *Local Routes to Social Justice* (McCormick and Harvey 1997) links this to what Mike Geddes calls 'the partnership model of social justice', and his stress on 'pluralist and participatory local democracy' (1997, pp.4, 11) is echoed by many writers (Croft and Beresford 1992; Rees 1993; Twine 1994; Wann 1995). Suzy Croft and Peter Beresford, in *From Paternalism to Participation* (1990) are especially concerned that relationships between service users and providers should be more democratic and egalitarian.

Interdisciplinary collaborative relationships among agencies and individual caseworkers will be crucial in the coming years in order to fulfil service users' different needs, and in order to develop professional and social coalition building which makes our united struggle against poverty, discrimination, inequalities and oppressions more effective.

Social pioneering in advocacy, counselling and mediation

However, we all have duties as responsible members of a democracy (Selbourne 1995) to support and strengthen central and local government's work for civil society, and to contribute our own specialized services to the state's constructive health and welfare provisions. Thus although social construction theory points to the danger of state manipulation of voluntary organizations, our authors have clearly shown that their work creatively serves individual and community interests, often in pioneering ways.

This pioneering role is just one among many others for which the British voluntary organizations have been historically noted and socially valued (Handy 1988; Powell 1994). Their independence, commitment to care in special areas, and freedom to choose how to combine criticism and cooperation with other agencies, including government ones, may be currently challenged by the decreasing availability of charitable and public funding, but their pioneering work nevertheless continues.

It is to this powerful tradition of social pioneering that the voluntary organizations associated with advocacy, counselling and mediation belong. The majority are concerned that their ideas, processes and skills are adopted by, and integrated into, mainstream and establishment bodies, as well as being continuously developed, refined and extended within their own specialized areas.

Another aspect of this pioneering work is the role of social prophecy. Although this has been currently most conspicuously promoted by 'green organizations', social or deep ecology (Bookchin 1980; Button 1995) considers pollution in the wider context of distressed and deteriorating social relationships, disadvantaged groups and decaying urban areas. Advocates, counsellors and mediators have been among those social prophets protesting about the serious effects of such 'social pollution' on the individuals and groups with whom they work, pointing out that macro infrastructural changes are needed if social justice, personal fulfilment and interpersonal reconciliation are to be realized at micro levels.

Social transformation in advocacy, counselling and mediation

Here, another aspect of voluntary organizations is relevant to this conclusion, concerning the yardstick of personal experiential involvement in their operational areas which many workers possess, and which can provide a useful commonsense measure of how networking with other agencies is in the best interests of service users. Advocates may be members of a minority group; counsellors may be having continual supervision and/or analysis; and mediators will be receiving ongoing training and evaluation.

All are continuously acquiring social knowledge and experience, and often in painful, personal ways. Their views, whether voiced individually, as by the contributors to this book, or collectively in their organizations, have the hallmarks of genuine, authentic real life experience, and are realist as well as idealist.

In suggesting that advocacy, counselling and mediation are processes of social transformation, this is based not on rhetoric but on the personal transformation which can be experienced in casework by service users, and also by service providers. The challenge of campaigning in advocacy, healing through counselling and interpersonal reconciliation through mediation is met by transformative processes which empower service users in self direction and self fulfilment, thus enriching society.

In *The Consequences of Modernity* (1990), Giddens writes of the recasting of disembedded social relations being dependent on 'trust ... a form of faith' and 'mechanisms of trust' (pp.27, 83) which provide people with security and confidence in their own and institutional change. He later adds that 'as modes of radical engagement having a persuasive importance in modern social life, social movements provide significant guidelines to potential future transformations' (Giddens 1990, p.158).

As has already been indicated, no claim is being advanced here that advocacy, counselling and mediation organizations are formally involved in any new social movement, but they are all 'carriers' (Castells 1983) of socially progressive ideas, values and norms for enriching community life and transforming society.

Social reconstruction in advocacy, counselling and mediation

Trust in the transformative potential of these processes is not based on messianic idealism but on the practical and pragmatic experience of casework with a great variety of people in widely different situations, as this book has shown.

This trust is allied to hope of beneficial social change and progress, instead of the popular doomsday cant about increasing social decadence and moral regress. Mulgan's recent book, *Connexity* (1990), reintroduces this old English word as a symbol for the partnership between progressive people which he believes to be essential for the social reconstruction of society so as to remedy injustice and inequity. This partnership is perhaps most essential in relationships between service users and providers, which is why the work of the Shaping Our Lives was chosen as the concluding chapter in this book.

Partnership philosophy involves community education, that raising of social awareness which has been the life work of Paulo Friere at grass roots levels of Latin America, yet with world-wide influence. He says that there is 'a need for a kind of education in hope … one of the tasks of the progressive educator, through a serious, correct political analysis, is to unveil opportunities for hope, no matter what the obstacles may be' (1996, p.9).

This book has been an attempt to unveil opportunities for hope through raising awareness about the work of advocacy, counselling and mediation, and its potential to contribute to personal and social fulfilment.

References

Biestek, F. (1976) *The Casework Relationship*. London: Allen and Unwin.

Bookchin, M. (1980) *Towards an Ecological Society*. Montreal: Black Rose Books.

Button, J. (1995) *The Radicalism Handbook*. London: Cassell.

Castells, M. (1983) *City and the Grassroots*. London: Arnold.

Croft, S. and Beresford, P. (1990) *From Paternalism to Participation*. London: Open Services Project.

Croft, S. and Beresford, P. (1992) 'The politics of participation.' *Critical Social Policy 35*, 20–44.

Friere, P. (1996) *Pedagogy of Hope.* New York: Continuum.

Geddes, M. (1997) 'A partnership model of local justice.' In J. McCormick and A. Harvey (eds) *Local Routes to Social Justice.* London: Institute of Public Policy Research.

Geertz, C. (1983) *Local Knowledge.* New York: Basic Books.

Giddens, A. (1990) *The Consequences of Modernity.* London: Polity Press.

Glennerster, H. (1983) *The Future of the Welfare State.* London: Heinemann.

Hancock, M. (1997) *Principles of Social Work Practice.* New York: Haworth.

Handy, C. (1988) *Understanding Voluntary Organisations.* Harmondsworth: Penguin.

Hughes, G. (1996) 'Communitarianism, law and order'. *Critical Social Policy 49*, 4, 17–41.

Hugman, R. (ed) (1995) *Ethical Issues in Social Work.* London: Routledge.

Husband, C. (1995) 'The morally active practitioner and the ethics of anti-racial social work.' In R. Hugman (ed) *Ethical Issues in Social Work.* London: Routledge.

Jordan, B. (1989) *The Common Good.* Oxford: Blackwell.

Langan, M. and Lee, P. (eds) (1989) *Radical Social Work Today.* London: Unwin Hyman.

McCormick, J. and Harvey, A. (1997) (eds) *Local Routes to Social Justice.* London: Institute of Public Policy Research.

Mulgan, G. (1990) *Connexity.* London: Chatto and Windus.

Powell, T. (1994) (ed) *Understanding the Self-Help Organization.* London: Sage.

Rees, A. (1993) 'The promise of social citizenship'. *Policy and Politics 3*, 4, 313–325.

Selbourne, D. (1995) *The Principle of Duty.* New York: Sinclair Stevenson.

Simon, B. (1997) *The Empowerment Tradition in American Social Work.* New York: Columbia University Press.

Stevenson, O. and Parsloe, P. (1996) *Community Care and Empowerment.* York: Joseph Rowntree Foundation.

Thompson, S. and Hoggett, P. (1996) 'Universality, selectivism and particularism.' *Critical Social Policy 16*, 1, 21–43.

Tillers, I. (1994) *Izkliede.* Graffiti on painting at Australian art exhibition: In Place (Out of Time), Oxford, July–November 1997.

Timms, N. (1983) *Social Work Values.* London: Routledge and Kegan Paul.

Twine, F. (1994) *Citizenship and Social Rights.* London: Sage.

Wann, M. (1995) *Building Social Capital.* London: Institute of Public Policy Research.

Watson, D. (ed) (1985) *A Code of Ethics for Social Work.* Birmingham: British Association of Social Workers.

The Contributors

Sue Balloch is Director of Policy at the National Institute for Social Work, where the Shaping Our Lives project is based. She was formerly lecturer in social policy at Goldsmiths' College, and was also involved in developing an anti-poverty strategy at the Association of Metropolitan Authorities.

Colin Barnes is a disabled writer, researcher and activist, with an international reputation in disability studies, which he teaches as founder/Director of the Leeds University Disability Research Unit. He is Research Director for the British Council of Organisations of Disabled People, Britain's national umbrella for organizations controlled and run by disabled people.

Peter Beresford works at the Open Services Project, teaches at Brunel University and is a member of Survivors Speak Out. He has a long-standing involvement in issues of participation and empowerment as a service user, writer and researcher and has written widely on the subject.

Tim Bond teaches and researches counselling at the University of Durham, is a former Chairperson of the British Association of Counselling (BAC) (1994–96) and a Fellow of BAC. His publications include *Standards and Ethics for Counselling in Action* (1993), and other books and articles on professional issues, counselling and multidisciplinary work.

David Brandon is Professor in Community Care, Anglia Polytechnic University, Cambridge; a former Chair of the British Association of Social Workers; a Zen Buddhist monk; a long-term advocacy worker and user of mental health services; and author of *Advocacy – Power to People with Disabilities* (1995).

Val Carpenter pioneered the National Coalition Building Institute (England), developing its unique leadership training to end prejudice and discrimination in the UK, America, Switzerland and Northern Ireland. She is published widely, co-authoring with Kerry Young *Coming in from the Margins: Youth Work with Girls and Young Women* (1996).

Yvonne Joan Craig, MA, JP is a retired social worker, counsellor and magistrate; current community activist; mediator and founder of the Elder Mediation Project; author of *Elder Abuse and Mediation* (1997) and editor of *Changes and Challenges in Later Life* (1997), as well as this book.

Masana De Souza, MA, SRN is a British Jamaican who manages the Newham Conflict and Change Project, following extensive experience as a health and social care practitioner and policy maker. She pioneered the first Jamaican mediation service.

Stephanie Ellis is Chair of an inner city Community Health Council, Secretary of the Patients' Association and currently studying for a degree in medical ethics at Middlesex and Beijing Universities. She is especially interested in advocacy to help those who feel unheard.

Clare Evans is a disabled person with a background in social work and training. She was the founder and former Director of Wiltshire and Swindon Users' Network, a national example of good practice in user-controlled organizations. She now works as co-ordinator of the Leonard Cheshire Foundation User Empowerment Project.

Tessa Harding is head of planning and development at Help the Aged. Previously she was a consultant at NISW on projects about user involvement and user-led services. She is the author/editor of a number of publications, and in 1993/94 obtained a Harkness Fellowship to study in America.

Martin Heidensohn is a Policy Assistant in the Policy Unit at the National Institute for Social Work. He is studying social policy at the Open University and has practical experience of working with people who have learning difficulties.

Ann Heyno is head of the Counselling and Advisory Service, University of Westminster, and senior tutor on the Master's degree course in psychodynamic counselling (student specialism) at Birkbeck College. Formerly a teacher and journalist, she has contributed to many conferences and publications in Britain and Europe.

Vera Ivers, MA, author of *Citizen Advocacy in Action* (1993), a Beth Johnson Foundation publication associated with the European Commission, has wide experience as a practitioner, policy maker and consultant in the statutory and voluntary sector of the health and social services. She has recently specialized in working with older people.

Bill Kirkpatrick, B.Th, RN, RMN, SEN, CPN, is an Anglican priest/counsellor, known as Fr. Bill, who founded the Reaching Out Centre in west London, and has co-founded centres for people suffering from HIV/AIDS, homelessness, addiction and psychiatric problems, about which he has become a leading international consultant and author.

Graz Kowszun, MSc is a United Kingdom Council for Psychotherapy (UKCP) registered psychotherapist, BAC accredited counsellor and trainer, and team leader of the Humanistic Integrative Counselling Diploma course at Morley College, where she trains and supervises substance abuse counsellors. She has been BAC's representative to Alcohol Concern and contributed to *Pink Therapy* (1996).

Marian Liebmann, Director of Mediation UK from 1991–95, is currently its part-time special projects adviser. She is a qualified teacher who has trained schoolchildren as mediators, and, as a former senior probation officer, has developed victim offender mediation. She is a practising art therapist, editing three volumes on art and conflict.

Stephen Palmer is Director of the Centre for Stress Management, London, honorary visiting lecturer in psychology at Goldsmiths' College, a chartered psychotherapist, a UKCP-registered psychotherapist and Fellow of the Royal Society of Health. He has authored/co-authored 11 books and training manuals, and edits/co-edits counselling and health journals.

Christine Piper is senior lecturer in the Law Department of Brunel University. Formerly a teacher and foster mother, she has researched in the areas of child law, mediation and divorce. Her publications include *The Responsible Parent* (1993) and (with Michael King) *How the Law Thinks about Children* (1991/1995).

Michael Turner is a freelance writer and researcher, and is currently the Shaping Our Lives project worker. His previous work includes research for the Citizen's Commission on the Future of the Welfare State, published in *It's Our Welfare* (NISW 1997), and many publications on disability issues in the specialist and mainstream press.

Gillian Walton is Director of Training and Clinical Services at London Marriage Guidance, the largest couples counselling agency in the country. She is involved in psychosexual and psychodynamic work, having practised as a marital therapist, supervisor and consultant for nearly 20 years. She also co-directs experienced counsellors working conjointly with couples.

Jean Wynne, co-ordinator of the West Yorkshire Probation Service Victim Offender Unit since 1987, provides training and consultancy for related new services across the United Kingdom. She has carried out research on mediation and reconviction rates, and studied differences in practice between the UK and America.

Subject Index

Author Index